Pentium™ Processor System Architecture

Second Edition

MINDSHARE, INC.

DON ANDERSON
AND
TOM SHANLEY

Addison-Wesley Publishing Company
Reading, Massachusetts • Menlo Park, California • New York
Don Mills, Ontario • Wokingham, England • Amsterdam
Bonn • Sydney • Singapore • Tokyo • Madrid • San Juan
Paris • Seoul • Milan • Mexico City • Taipei

Chapter 4: Multiple Processors and the MESI Model

Chapter 5: Pentium Signal Interface

Contents

Chapter 6: The Code Cache and Instruction Pipeline

Contents

Chapter 7: The Data Cache and Burst Bus Cycles

Contents

Chapter 8: Summary of Pentium Bus Cycles

Chapter 9: System Management Mode (SMM)

Chapter 10: Summary of Software Changes

Contents

Chapter 11: Test and Debug

Part II: The Pentium 90/100MHz Processors

Chapter 12: P54C Processor Overview

Chapter 13: P54C Signals

Chapter 14: Dual Processors

Contents

Chapter 15: The APIC

Contents

Chapter 16: P54C SMM Enhancements

Part III: Other Pentium Processors

Chapter 17: The Pentium 610/75MHz Processor

Chapter 18: OverDrive Processors/Sockets

Appendices

Figures

Figures

Tables

Pentium Processor System Architecture

Acknowledgments

The authors would like to thank Addison-Wesley and the publishing staff who guided us through the publishing process. Without their patience and professional assistance, the process of publishing MindShare's PC Architecture series with our ambitious schedule would have been unbearably painful.

We would also like to thank the many students who have provided valuable feedback during Pentium training classes. Many of their suggestions have been incorporated into this edition of the book, while others have helped fine-tune our classroom delivery.

We especially thank those at Intel who provided information, insight, and many helpful suggestions.

The MindShare Architecture Series

The series of books by MindShare on system architecture includes; *ISA System Architecture, EISA System Architecture, 80486 System Architecture, PCI System Architecture, Pentium™ Processor System Architecture, PCMCIA System Architecture, PowerPC™ System Architecture, Plug and Play System Architecture*, and *K5 System Architecture*, all published by Addison-Wesley.

Rather than duplicating common information in each book, the series uses a building-block approach. *ISA System Architecture* is the core book upon which the others build. The figure below illustrates the relationship of the books to each other.

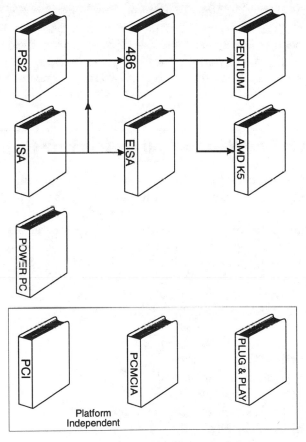

Architecture Series Organization

Pentium Processor System Architecture

Organization of This Book

Pentium™ System Architecture is divided into three parts preceded by an introductory chapter entitled the Pentium Processor Overview. These three parts include:

- Part I: The Pentium 510/60MHz and 567/66MHz Processors
- Part II: The Pentium 735/90MHz and 815/100MHz Processors
- Part III: Other Pentium Processors

The Pentium Overview

The overview chapter reviews the problems that limited performance with earlier x86 processors. The chapter further discusses the enhancements that have been made by each successive processor in the x86 processor family to continually boost performance. This evolutionary discussion traces the x86 processor family starting with the 8088 microprocessor and leads to the latest features and techniques incorporated into the latest Pentium processors.

Part I: The Pentium 60 and 66MHz Processors

Part I introduces the primary functional units within the original Pentium processors and provides an in-depth look at each unit. Focus is placed on the performance and compatibility issues related to these units. The processor's internal cache organization and MESI protocol is discussed along with the signals implemented to provide internal and external cache coherency. The processor's signal interface is also discussed, along with a detailed look at bus cycles run by the Pentium processor. Part I also includes a summary of software changes introduced by Pentium, and a review of its test and debug features. Part I consist of the following chapters:

- The Functional Units
- Pentium Cache Overview
- Multiple Processors and the MESI Protocol
- Pentium Signal Interface
- The Code Cache and Instruction Pipeline
- The Data Cache and Burst Line Fills
- Summary of Pentium Processor Bus Cycles

- System Management Mode Features
- Summary of Software Changes
- Test and Debug

Part II: The Pentium 90/100MHz Processors

Part II details the changes introduced to the Pentium family of products by the Pentium 90 and 100MHz processors, commonly known by their Intel code name of P54C. Signals that have been added to or removed from the P54C processors with relation to the original Pentium processors are detailed. Part II also discusses the dual-processor capability included with these processors, and covers the related bus arbitration and cache coherency issues. An overview of the Advanced Programmable Interrupt Controller (APIC) subsystem (consisting of the I/O APIC, APIC bus and local APIC modules) is provided, along with an in-depth discussion of the local APIC module that is integrated into the P54C processors. Enhancements to the System Management Mode (SMM) features are also detailed. The chapters include:

- P54C Overview
- P54C Signal Interface
- Dual Processor Operation
- APIC
- SMM Enhancements

Part III: Other Pentium Processors

Part III introduces other processors in the Pentium family. This includes the 75MHz Pentium and future Pentium OverDrive processors. The chapters include:

- Pentium 610\75MHz Processor
- OverDrive Processors/Sockets

Appendices

The appendices is segmented into four sections and is intended for quick reference. The appendices include the following:

- Glossary of Terms
- Signal Glossary
- Pairable Instructions
- References

Who Should Read This Book

This book is intended for use by hardware and software design and support personnel. Due to the clear, concise explanatory methods used to describe each subject, personnel outside of the design field may also find the text useful.

Prerequisite Knowledge

We highly recommend that you have a good knowledge of the PC and 486 architecture prior to reading this book. The publications entitled *ISA System Architecture* and *80486 System Architecture* provide all of the background necessary for a complete understanding of the subject matter covered in this book. Also the chapter entitled "Summary of Software Changes," assumes knowledge of the i486 registers and software environment. See the publication entitled *80486 System Architecture* for background information on the software environment.

Documentation Conventions

This section defines the typographical conventions used throughout this book.

Hex Notation

All hex numbers are followed by an "h." Examples:
    9A4Eh
    0100h

Binary Notation

All binary numbers are followed by a "b." Examples:

    0001 0101b
    01b

Decimal Notation

When required for clarity, decimal numbers are followed by a "d." Examples:

    256d
    128d

Signal Name Representation

Each signal that assumes the logic low state when asserted is followed by a pound sign (#). As an example, the BRDY# signal is asserted low when a target device is ready to complete a data transfer.

Signals that are not followed by a pound sign are asserted when they assume the logic high state. As an example, BREQ is asserted high to indicate that the Pentium processor needs control of the buses to perform a bus operation.

Identification of Bit Fields

All bit fields are designated as follows:

[X:Y],

where "X" is the most-significant bit and "Y" is the least-significant bit of the field. As an example, the Pentium address bus consists of A[31:3], where A31 is the most-significant and A3 the least-significant bit of the field.

We Want Your Feedback

MindShare values your comments and suggestions. You can contact us via mail, phone, fax, BBS or internet email.

E-Mail/Phone/FAX

Email: mindshar@interserv.com
Phone: (214) 231-2216
Fax: (214) 783-4715

Bulletin Board

BBS: (214) 705-9604

Because we are constantly on the road teaching, we can be difficult to contact. To help alleviate problems associated with our migratory habits, we have initiated a bulletin board to supply the following services:

- Download course abstracts.
- Automatic registration for public seminars.
- Message area to make inquiries about public seminars.
- Message area to log technical questions.
- Message area to log comments on MindShare books and seminars.

Mailing Address

Our mailing address is:

MindShare, Inc.
2202 Buttercup Drive
Richardson, Texas 75082

Chapter 1

This Chapter

This chapter takes a look at the problems that limited performance with earlier x86 processors, and discusses the enhancements that have been made within the x86 processor family to continually boost performance. This evolutionary discussion traces the x86 processor family starting with the 8088 microprocessor and leads to the latest features and techniques incorporated into the latest Pentium processors.

The Next Chapter

The next chapter describes the function units within the Pentium processor.

X86 Processor Evolution

Slow Processor, Slow Memory

When the IBM PC was introduced, it was based on the Intel 8088 microprocessor running at 4.77MHz. The 8088 took four ticks of its 4.77MHz clock to run a zero wait state bus cycle, a duration of 838ns (4 x 209ns = 838ns). Virtually any DRAM or ROM on the market at that time could respond well within this period of time, so memory did not throttle processor performance.

Faster Processor, Slow Memory

As the x86 processors have increased in speed, the access time of economically priced DRAMs has not decreased dramatically. This results in a performance bottleneck — one or more wait states are inserted in every access to memory. Since the processor accesses memory far more than any other device, the slow access memory has a severe throttling effect on the processor.

Several new instructions have been added to the publicly documented instruction set in the Pentium processor. See the chapter entitled "Summary of Software Changes" for details.

Prefetcher: A Small Look-Ahead Cache

In an effort to decouple the processor's execution unit from the slowness of memory, Intel incorporated a prefetcher and a prefetch queue into each processor. The prefetcher works on the assumption that the execution unit will want the next instruction from the next sequential memory location. While the execution unit is executing an instruction, the prefetcher takes advantage of the idle bus time to issue a memory read request to the processor's bus unit in order to prefetch the next instruction from memory before the execution unit requests it. In this way, the memory access is hidden behind the execution of the current instruction. The prefetched instruction is placed into the processor's prefetch queue. If the execution unit still has not completed execution of the current instruction, the prefetcher issues another read request to prefetch the next sequential instruction. When the execution unit completes execution of the current instruction, it issues a read request to the prefetcher. If the instruction is found in the queue, the request is fulfilled immediately and the execution unit doesn't have to stall while the instruction is fetched from memory. Since most program execution is sequential in nature, the hit rate on the prefetch queue will be fairly high. Whenever a jump instruction is executed, however, the prefetcher gambled and lost. The queue is flushed and the execution unit is stalled while awaiting the completion of the memory read bus cycle that must be initiated to fetch the instruction from memory.

Table 1-1 defines the depth of the prefetch queues on the various processors in the x86 family.

Table 1-1. Prefetch Queue Depth

Processor	Prefetch Queue Depth (bytes)
8088	4
8086	6
80286	6
80386	16
80486	32
Pentium	two 64-byte queues

Chapter 1: Introduction to the Pentium Processors

The Memory Bottleneck

When processor speeds reached the 20 to 25MHz vicinity, reasonably-priced DRAM memory could no longer be accessed with zero wait state bus cycles. One or more wait states would be inserted into every bus cycle that accessed memory. Memory access time, therefore, became a serious impediment to good processor performance. There were two possible solutions:

- Populate the entire memory with SRAMs
- Implement a cache subsystem

The Static Ram, or SRAM, Solution

In order to gain the maximum performance benefit of the faster and more powerful processors, faster and more expensive static RAM, or SRAM, devices must be used. SRAM is easily capable of providing zero wait state performance at higher processor speeds; however, for several reasons, this solution is not economically viable:

- SRAM is typically ten times more expensive than DRAM memory.
- SRAM chips are physically larger than DRAMs, requiring more real-estate for the same amount of memory.
- SRAMs consume more power than DRAMs and may require a more powerful, and therefore more expensive, power supply.
- SRAMs generate more heat than DRAMs and may therefore require a larger cooling fan.

External Cache

Advantage: Reduces Many Memory Accesses To Zero Wait States

System designers achieved a performance/cost trade off by implementing an external cache consisting of a relatively small amount of SRAM coupled with a cache controller, and populating the bulk of system memory with inexpensive DRAM memory. The cache controller attempts to keep copies of frequently requested information in SRAM so that it can be accessed quickly if requested again. If the controller experiences a high percentage of hits on the cache, the number of memory accesses requiring the insertion of wait states is substantially reduced.

Disadvantage: Memory Accesses Still Bound By Bus Speed

A drawback associated with the external cache approach (when the processor does not incorporate an internal cache) is that every memory request requires a bus cycle and even zero wait state bus cycles take time. The bus speed presents a bottleneck to processor performance.

Unified Internal Code/Data Cache

General

As pointed out in the previous section, the external cache will only provide a limited performance improvement. The processor must still run memory read bus cycles to fetch data and code from memory.

Faster Memory Accesses

One way to alleviate this problem would be to move the cache on board the processor chip itself. When the requested code or data is found in the internal cache, memory read requests initiated by the processor core can then be fulfilled from the cache without running bus cycles. The only delay incurred is that necessary to perform the internal cache lookup and to deliver the target data or code to the internal requester. Due to the exceedingly short length of the data paths involved and the fast access time of the on-board SRAM these accesses will complete appreciably faster than would zero wait state bus cycles.

Frees Up the Bus

Every time a memory read request is fulfilled from the on-chip cache, that is one less bus cycle that needs to be run on the external buses. This frees up the buses for use by other bus masters in the system. The processor core can be feeding out of its internal cache at the same time that another bus master is using the external buses to perform a data transfer. The bus concurrency thus achieved improves the overall performance of the system.

Internal Data/Code Contention For Cache

The i486 processor incorporates a unified code/data cache. Although this yields performance improvements (as discussed in the previous section), the fact that the internal cache is used to store both data and code can lead to internal contention for access to the cache. At any given instant in time, the execution unit may be executing a move instruction to read data from memory into a register. The memory read request will be submitted to the unified code/data cache for a lookup. If, at this same instant, the code prefetcher issues a memory read request to the cache for code, the cache will service the execution unit first (so that it may complete the currently-executing instruction) and then service the prefetcher's request. This can lead to instruction pipeline starvation, resulting in performance degradation.

Separate Code and Data Caches: Eliminates Internal Contention

The Pentium processor incorporates separate code and data caches, thereby solving the internal cache contention problem described in the previous section. The dual execution units can submit requests to the data cache at the same time that the code prefetcher submits requests to the code cache.

Pipeline Becomes the Bottleneck

By including separate on-chip code and data caches and also incorporating an external cache to handle misses on the internal caches, the Pentium processor-based system minimizes the throttling affect of slow external memory on the processor's performance. Instructions are now fed to the instruction pipelines at a very high rate.

The x86 processors prior to Pentium only had a single instruction pipeline. If the methods discussed in the previous sections are utilized to deliver the requested instruction stream and data to the processor as fast as possible, the processor's internal instruction pipeline becomes the new performance bottleneck, or chokepoint. The instructions must be fed to the instruction pipeline one-at-a-time and must be executed in sequential order.

Answer: Go Superscalar

To address this problem, the Pentium processor incorporates dual-instruction pipelines. A check is performed on each pair of instructions to determine their pairability. If deemed pairable, the two instructions are fed to the dual-instruction pipelines simultaneously, move through the pipelines in unison, and complete execution at the same time. This obviously results in increased processor performance. The inclusion of multiple instruction pipelines is referred to as superscalar architecture.

Prefetcher Handles Branches Inefficiently

Prior to the advent of the Pentium processor, the instruction prefetchers incorporated in the x86 processors were simple in nature. The prefetcher always worked on the assumption that the execution unit would want the next instruction from the next sequential memory location. While the execution unit was executing an instruction, the prefetcher would issue a request for the next instruction from the next sequential memory location. It would blindly fetch instructions ahead of the execution unit, attempting to keep the prefetch queue full. When the execution unit completed the execution of a non-branch instruction, the instruction immediately behind the non-branch instruction in the pipeline would therefore be the correct instruction.

When the execution unit executed a branch instruction, however, program flow would be altered. The instruction to be executed next was not the one fetched from the next sequential memory location. As a result, the instruction(s) behind the branch in the instruction pipeline were incorrect. In addition, the instructions resident in the prefetch queue were wrong as well. The pipeline and the queue would both be flushed and the prefetcher would be forced to fetch the next instruction from the branch target address specified by the branch instruction. While the memory read is being fulfilled, the execution unit would be stalled until the requested instruction was fetched and delivered to the instruction pipeline for decode and execution. While the instruction was being executed, the prefetcher would then initiate a series of memory read requests to refill the queue again. The instructions would be prefetched from the sequential series of memory locations immediately following the branch target address.

The prefetchers incorporated into processors prior to Pentium were so simple that they couldn't detect a jump to an instruction that was already resident in the pipeline or queue. The branch target address was not taken into consideration. The queue and pipeline were unequivocally flushed.

Answer: Add Branch Prediction

The Pentium processor has added branch prediction logic to permit the prefetcher to make more intelligent decisions regarding what information to prefetch from memory. The processor incorporates two independent prefetch queues, but only one of them is used at a given instant in time. Whenever a branch instruction enters the pipeline, the prediction logic predicts whether the branch will be taken (by examining the execution history of the instruction). If it predicts that the branch will not be taken, the prefetcher continues to prefetch instructions into the current queue from the next sequential memory locations. If the branch is predicted to be taken, the prefetcher will switch to the other prefetch queue and begin to prefetch instructions from memory starting at the branch target address.

When the branch actually arrives at the execution stage and is executed, the branch will either be taken or not. If the prediction mechanism predicted correctly, the instruction stream immediately behind the branch in the pipeline is correct and the execution unit is not stalled. If, on the other hand, the prediction was incorrect, the instructions behind the branch in the pipeline and those in the active prefetch queue are incorrect. The pipeline and queue are flushed. The prefetcher switches back to the original queue. The instructions still in that queue are the correct ones and can be routed directly into the instruction pipeline for execution. The prefetcher resumes prefetching into this queue starting at the next instruction after the last one currently in the queue. A performance hit of three or four clocks is incurred on an incorrect prediction.

Uni-Processing Systems Become Bottleneck

As is apparent in the previous discussions, uni-processor systems have increased performance dramatically since the first 8088-based IBM-PC. This performance increase has been obtained primarily by increasing processor clock speed, implementing faster memory and support chips and enhancing the instruction pipeline inside the processors. Despite these dramatic increases in performance, uni processor systems can become a major bottleneck to increased performance in many sophisticated networking environments. For example, client-server applications running programs such as data bases and on-line transaction processing (OLTP) place heavy demands on the PCs processor.

Solution: Implement Multi-processor Systems

Multi-processor solutions add additional processor's to obtain incremental gains in overall processor performance. Two primary categories of multi-processor implementation exist:

- Asymmetrical
- Symmetrical

Asymmetrical multi-processing dedicates specific tasks to the various processors. As an example, one processor might be dedicated to handling the file system and disk access, while another manages network activity, etc. The shortcoming of this type of multi-processing is that the operating system's ability to balance the execution load evenly among processors is restricted to the mix of tasks required by the application.

Symmetrical multi-processing allows all processor to perform the same tasks. This permits the operating system to implement load-balancing, so that the processors can be utilized more efficiently. In other words, the operating system can assign any task to any free processor. Such implementation however, complicate hardware and software design.

Features of the Pentium Processors

Intel's Pentium microprocessors introduce several new features that address many of the performance bottlenecks experienced by earlier x86-based systems. This section describe the primary features of the following Pentium processors.

- Pentium 510\60MHz and Pentium 567\66MHz Processors
- Pentium 735\90MHz and Pentium 815\100MHz Processors

Intel's naming convention identifies Pentium processors by performance and core operating frequency. For example the Pentium 735\90MHz processor has an iCOMP index of 735 and a core clock frequency of 90MHz. The iCOMP index was developed by Intel to provide a relative measure of performance between their processors. In this book for the sake of brevity, the Pentium 510\60MHz and Pentium 567\66MHz Processors are referred to as the "Pentium" processors and the Pentium 735/90 and Pentium 815/100 processors are jointly referred to by their Intel code name of "P54C."

Chapter 1: Introduction to the Pentium Processors

The Pentium 60MHz and 66MHz Processors

Figure 1-1 depicts the primary changes to the Pentium microprocessor over the i486 microprocessor. These changes fall into six major areas:

- Wider Data Bus
- Dedicated Instruction Cache
- Dedicated Data Cache
- Two Separate Execution Units (integer math)
- Enhanced Floating-Point Execution Unit
- New Instructions

These features improve most of the performance bottlenecks associated with the earlier x86 processors as discussed below.

The 64-bit Data Path

The Pentium processor has a 64-bit data bus that permits eight bytes (a quadword) of information to be transferred to and from system memory in a single bus cycle. This wider data path permits faster cache line fills from its two internal caches. This wider data path is supported by a new 64-bit addressing scheme that uses eight byte enable lines.

Instruction Cache

The Pentium microprocessor incorporates a dedicated 8KB instruction cache that feeds its two integer execution units and a floating-point unit via a dual instruction pipeline. The instruction cache is a read-only cache and is organized as a 2-way set associative cache with 32-byte lines.

Data Cache

The data cache is an 8KB cache that serves all three execution units. The data cache is a write-back cache, and, like the code cache, is organized as a 2-way set associative cache with 32-byte lines. External pins are implemented to control the write-back feature, thus, ensuring cache coherency with other caches and main memory.

Pentium Processor System Architecture

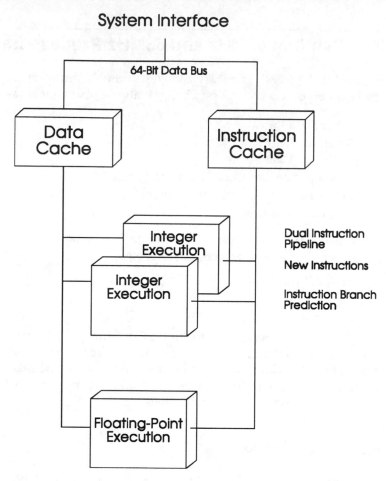

Figure 1-1. The Pentium Microprocessor Enhancements

The Parallel Integer Execution Units

The instruction pipeline includes two parallel paths called the U pipeline and the V pipeline. The dual instruction pipeline and execution unit allows two instructions to be decoded and executed simultaneously, permitting two instructions to complete execution in a single processor clock; hence, its superscalar performance.

Another feature of the Pentium microprocessor is its branch target buffer and branch predication algorithm. The branch target buffer keeps track of execution history to determine when an instruction branch is likely to occur again. When a branch operation is predicted, the branch target buffer in conjunction with the prefetcher fetches the next instruction that is predicted, rather than continuing in a sequential fashion. This means that the execution pipelines do not always stall when a branch operation executes, as with earlier processors.

Floating-Point Unit

The floating-point unit employs a new design that provides substantial performance increases over the i486 design. The floating-point performance gains result mainly from pipelined execution of floating-point instructions.

The Pentium 90MHz and 100MHz Processors

These P54C processors include the same features as the original Pentium processors, but add dual-processing support. These processors greatly simply to system manufacturers job of designing a multi-processor system. The features added include:

- Faster processor core (90 or 100MHz) yielding higher performance.
- Fractional bus speed (60 or 66MHz).
- Dual processing support.
- Local Advanced Programmable Interrupt Controller (APIC).
- Enhanced power management features.
- 3.3vdc logic levels.

Faster Processor Core/Slower Bus Clock

The P54C processors operate at an internal frequency that is a multiple of the processors clock input. This permits the processor to operate at internal clock frequencies that are significantly higher that the input clock frequency. Bus cycles run at the lower input clock frequency making system implementations less costly and much easier to design.

Dual Processing Support

The P54C processors provide dual-processing capability without the need for external "glue logic". This dual processor configuration permits two P54C processors to communicate directly with one another over a private bus to provide arbitration and cache coherency.

Advanced Programmable Interrupt Controller (APIC)

An advanced programmable interrupt controller (APIC) is also integrated into each P54C processor. This adds to the dual processor support by providing a mechanism to deliver interrupts to either of the dual processors, thus providing symmetrical processing support.

3.3 vdc Logic Levels

The P54C processors use 3.3 vdc logic levels. This significantly reduces the power requirements and simplifies heat dissipation issues.

Part I:

The Pentium 60 and 66MHz Processors

Chapter 2

The Previous Chapter

This chapter discussed the issues that limited performance with earlier x86 processors, and discussed the enhancements that have been made within the x86 processor family to continually boost performance. This evolutionary discussion traced the x86 processor family starting with the 8088 microprocessor and lead to the latest features and techniques incorporated into the latest Pentium processors.

This Chapter

This chapter describes the relationships between the processor's functional units and provides a more detailed description of each unit.

The Next Chapter

The next chapter gives a general overview of memory caching and introduces the Pentium processor's caching mechanisms.

The Pentium Processor's Functional Units

The Pentium processor's functional units are illustrated in figure 2-1. A description of each functional unit can be found under the section entitled, "Functional Unit Description." First, an overview of each functional unit is included to facilitate understanding of the relationship between them.

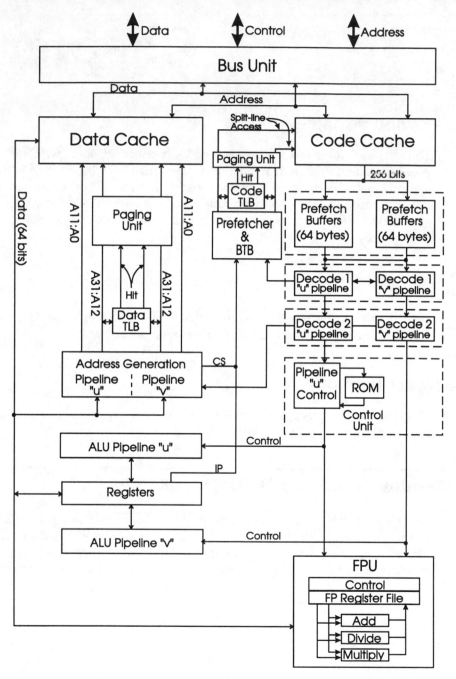

Figure 2-1. The Pentium Processor's Functional Units

Chapter 2: The Functional Units

Functional Unit Overview

Assume for the purposes of this discussion that the prefetcher is requesting instructions from the Code (Instruction) Cache, and the address from which the prefetcher is fetching instructions is contained in the Code Cache. As a result, a cache hit would occur.

The Instruction Pipeline

The prefetcher sends an address to the code cache which performs a look-up to determine if the requested address is present. If present, a line of information (32 bytes) is sent to one of the prefetch buffers.

The prefetch buffer transfers the instructions to the decode unit where they are decoded. Note that the prefetch buffer may contain more than one instruction. Initially, the instructions are partially decoded to determine if they can be paired. If paired, one instruction goes into the instruction pipeline known as the "U" pipeline, and the other goes into the "V" pipeline. Instructions are paired as long as no dependencies exist between them, such that one instruction must complete execution before the other begins.

Note that the branch prediction buffer also checks to see if a branch is likely to follow a given instruction based on execution history. When a branch is predicted to be taken, the address of the predicted branch is requested from the code cache. If found in the cache, a line of code is sent to the other prefetch buffer so that no delay is incurred when an instruction branch is taken. If the predicted branch is not taken, both instructions pipelines are flushed and prefetching continues in a linear fashion.

Pairs of instructions enter and exit each stage of the pipeline in unison. Instruction pairing allows each execution unit to complete the execution of an instruction at the same time. Figure 2-2 illustrates a sequence of ten instructions that have been paired in the dual execution pipelines, and shows the super scalar performance obtained with the dual pipeline and execution units.

Figure 2-2 also illustrates that the Pentium processor uses a five stage execution pipeline, as does the 486. During the first clock cycle a pair of instructions are prefetched from the processor's code cache. During clock two, this first pair of instructions is issued in parallel to the U- and V-pipes, while another pair of instructions is being prefetched. The first pair of instructions moves to the decode 2 stage during clock three. Also, during clock three, the second instruction pair is issued to the decode 1 stage in both pipelines. At this point, a third pair of instructions can be prefetched. Each pair of instructions can proceed to the next stage in the pipeline with each PCLK cycle, as another instruction pair enters the pipeline. During clock five the first two instructions complete execution. During each succeeding clock cycle another instruction pair can complete execution. This represents the fastest integer execution that the Pentium processor is capable of performing, whereby, two instructions can be executed during each clock cycle.

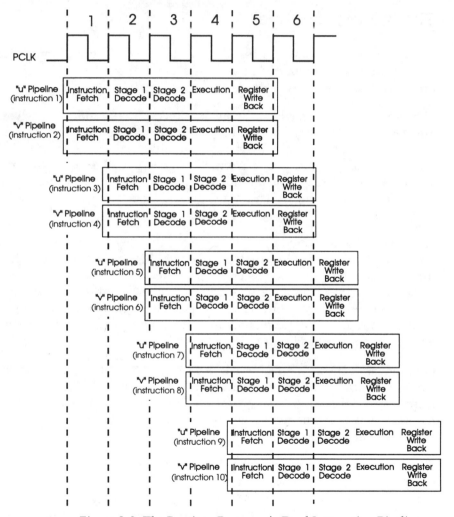

Figure 2-2. The Pentium Processor's Dual Instruction Pipeline

Chapter 2: The Functional Units

Executing Integer Instructions

Two separate execution units are dedicated to their respective pipelines. The execution units share access to a single set of registers. When the result of a computation is completed, the information is written back to the appropriate register. No additional instructions can begin execution until both execution units complete their operation.

Associated with each unit is an address generator that forms addresses specified by instructions when required. As an example, assume that the current instructions being executed are two MOVE operations from sequential memory locations. Each execution unit requests data from the address specified in its instruction. These memory read requests go to the internal data cache, which determines if the information is present in cache memory.

The data cache can simultaneously perform cache look-ups for each execution unit. In this way, two separate requests for data can be satisfied at once. The cache lines in the data cache are 32 bytes wide as they are in the code cache. If the access to memory is not contained in cache, the processor will perform a cache line fill operation to get the required data from external memory. Since 32 bytes of data are needed to fill the cache, only 4 transfers are needed using the 64-bit data bus. Cache line fills are always accomplished in a single burst bus cycle.

Floating-Point Unit

The floating point unit uses an eight stage instruction pipeline. It shares the first five pipeline stages with the integer pipeline. When floating-point instructions are fetched they are passed on to the floating-point unit where the final stages of the execution pipeline are completed. Note that three floating-point operations can occur simultaneously.

Pentium Processor System Architecture

Functional Unit Description

The following sections describe the functions performed by each unit inside the Pentium processor.

Bus Unit

The bus unit provides the physical interface between the Pentium processor and the rest of the system. As shown in figure 2-3, the Bus Unit is comprised of the following functional entities:

- **Address Drivers and Receivers**. During bus cycles the address drivers push the address onto the processor's local address bus (A31:A3 and BE7:BE0). The address bus transfers addresses back to the Pentium address receivers during cache snoop cycles. Only address lines A31:A5 are input during cache snoop cycles.
- **Write Buffers**. The Pentium processor employs two write buffers, one for each of the two internal execution pipelines, increasing performance when back-to-back writes occur. These two buffers each hold 64 bits (a quadword). Each write buffer can hold a single memory write operation that misses the internal data cache. If the bus unit is busy running a bus cycle, the write is placed in the buffer and the execution unit is allowed to continue.
- **Data Bus Transceivers**. The transceivers gate data onto the Pentium processor's local data bus during write bus cycles, and gate data into the processor during read bus cycles.
- **Bus Control Logic**. The Bus Control Logic controls whether a standard or burst bus cycle is to be run. Standard bus cycles are run to access I/O locations and non-cacheable memory locations, as well as cacheable memory write operations. During these bus cycles the transfer size will be either 8, 16 or 32 bits as dictated by the instruction. Burst cycles are run by the Pentium processor during cache line fills and during cache write-back bus cycles from the data cache. Four quadwords are transferred during each burst bus cycle.
- **Bus Master Control**. Bus Master signals are included to allow the processor to request the use of the buses from the arbiter and to be preempted by other bus masters in the system.

- **Level Two (L2) Cache Control.** The Pentium processor includes the ability to control whether a L2 (secondary) external cache should treat a given request sent by the processor as cacheable, and whether a L2 cache that employs a write-back policy should instead transfer a write operation on through to main memory.
- **Internal Cache Control.** During cache line fill operations, external logic can specify the cache state that a line is to be stored at, to ensure proper cache coherency. Internal Cache Control logic also monitors input signals to determine when to snoop the address bus and outputs signals to notify external logic the results of a snoop operation.
- **Parity Generation and Control.** Generates even data parity for each of the eight data paths during write bus cycles and checks parity on read bus cycles. Also generates a parity bit for the address during write bus cycles and checks address parity during external cache snoop operations.

Data Cache

The internal Data Cache keeps copies of the most frequently used data requested by the two integer pipelines and the Floating Point Unit. The internal data cache is an 8KB write-back cache, organized as two-way set associative with 32-byte lines. The Data Cache directory is triple ported to allow simultaneous access from each of the pipelines and to support snooping. For a detailed discussion of the data cache organization and operation, see the chapter entitled, "The Data Cache".

Code Cache

The internal code cache (instruction cache) keeps copies of the most frequently used instructions. The internal code cache is an 8KB cache dedicated to supplying instructions to each of the processor's execution pipelines. The cache is organized as a two-way set associative cache with a line size of 32 bytes. The cache directory is triple ported to allow two simultaneous accesses from the prefetcher and to support snooping. For a detailed discussion of the code cache organization and operation see the chapter entitled "The Code Cache and Instruction Pipeline."

Prefetcher

Instructions are requested from the code cache by the prefetcher. If the requested line is not in the cache, a burst bus cycle is run to external memory to perform a cache line fill. Prefetches are made sequentially until a branch instruction is fetched. The prefetcher also accesses two lines simultaneously when the starting prefetch address falls in the middle of a cache line. In this way, a split-line access can be made to fetch an instruction that resides partially in two separate lines within the cache.

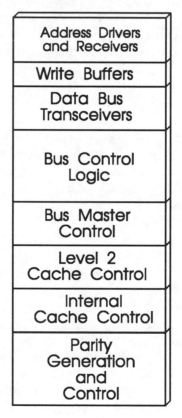

Figure 2-3. The Elements Comprising the Pentium Processor Bus Unit

Prefetch Buffers

Four prefetch buffers within the processor work as two independent pairs. When instructions are prefetched from the cache, they are placed into one set of prefetch buffers, while the other pair remains idle. When a branch operation is predicted in the Branch Target Buffer (BTB), it requests the predicted branch's target address from cache, which is placed in the second pair of buffers that was previously idle. The second pair of buffers continue to be used until another branch is predicted by the BTB, at which time a switch occurs back to the first buffer pair.

During linear fetch and execute, the prefetch buffer sends a pair of instructions to the instruction decoder. The first instruction is sent to the "U" pipeline and the second instruction goes to the "V" pipeline where they are analyzed for instruction pairing.

Instruction Decode Unit

Instruction decode occurs in two stages known as Decode 1 (D1) and Decode 2 (D2). These decode stages are similar to the decode process of the 486 processor, except for instruction pairing issues. During D1, the opcode is decoded in both pipelines to determine whether the two instructions can be paired according to the Pentium processor's pairing rules. If pairing is possible, the two instructions are sent in unison to the stage two decode. During D2 the address of memory resident operands are calculated.

Control Unit

Also referred to as the Microcode Unit, the Control Unit consists of the following sub-units:

* the Microcode Sequencer
* the Microcode Control ROM

This unit interprets the instruction word and microcode entry points fed to it by the Instruction Decode Unit. It handles exceptions, breakpoints and interrupts. In addition, it controls the integer pipelines and floating-point sequences.

Arithmetic/Logic Units (ALUs)

The two ALUs perform the arithmetic and logical operations specified by the instructions in their respective pipeline. The ALU for the "U" pipeline can complete an operation prior to the ALU in the "V" pipeline, but the opposite is not true.

Registers

For a detailed description of the registers, see "Summary Software Changes."

Address Generators

Two Address Generators (one for each pipeline) form the address specified by the instructions in their respective pipeline. The address generators are equivalent to the segmentation unit of the 486 microprocessor.

Paging Unit

If enabled by setting the PG bit in CR0, the Paging Unit translates the linear address (from the address generator) to a physical address. It performs the same functions as the 486 microprocessor's paging mechanism, but can handle two linear addresses at the same time to support both pipelines. Unlike the 486, two Translation Lookaside Buffers(TLB) are implemented. One TLB is associated with each cache.

Floating-Point Unit

The floating point unit can accept up to two floating point operations per clock when one of the instructions is an exchange instruction. Normally, the Pentium processor accepts only one instruction per clock. The floating point unit uses an 8 stage pipeline, the first five of which are shared with integer instructions. Note that floating point instructions do not get paired with integer instructions, but limited pairing of two floating point instructions can be done when the floating point exchange instruction is the second instruction issued. Furthermore, only F set instructions can pair with the exchange instruction.

These instructions include: FLD single/double, FLD ST(i), all forms of FADD, FSUB, FMUL, FDIV, FCOM, FUCOM, FTST, FABS, and FCHS. All other combinations of floating point instruction are issued singly to the FPU.

Three types of floating point operations can operate simultaneously within the FPU as shown in figure 2-1. In other words, the FPU can simultaneously perform floating point addition, division, and multiplication.

Chapter 3

The Previous Chapter

The previous chapter introduced the Pentium processor's functional units.

This Chapter

This chapter provides a general overview of caching and introduces the Pentium processor's caching mechanism.

The Next Chapter

The next chapter details the Pentium processor's implementation of the MESI model that is used to maintain cache coherency in both single processor and multiprocessor systems.

Introduction

This chapter provides background information necessary to understand the rationale and operation of the Pentium processor's internal caches. Readers who are familiar with cache concepts, including level 1 (L1) and level 2 (L2) cache coherency issues related to 486 implementations may want to go directly to the section entitled "Pentium Processor Cache Overview" on page 53.

Overview of Cache Operation and Cache Types

Many manufacturers of fast 80386-based PCs (25MHz and faster) included an external cache. Implementation of a cache memory subsystem is an attempt to achieve a high percentage of zero wait state bus cycles when accessing memory, but at an acceptable system cost.

Pentium Processor System Architecture

A cache memory subsystem is implemented by populating system board memory with relatively slow access, inexpensive DRAM, while also incorporating a relatively small amount of high cost, fast access SRAM into the system. The SRAM memory is referred to as cache memory and a cache memory controller maintains copies of frequently accessed information (previously read from DRAM memory) within the cache.

Refer to Figure 3-1. The cache controller keeps track of the information it has copied into the cache memory. When the processor initiates a memory read bus cycle, the cache controller determines if it has a copy of the requested information in cache memory. If a copy is present, it immediately reads the information from the cache, sends it back to the processor over the processor's data bus, and asserts the processor's ready signal. This is referred to as a read hit. The access can be completed in zero wait states because the information is fetched from the fast access cache SRAM.

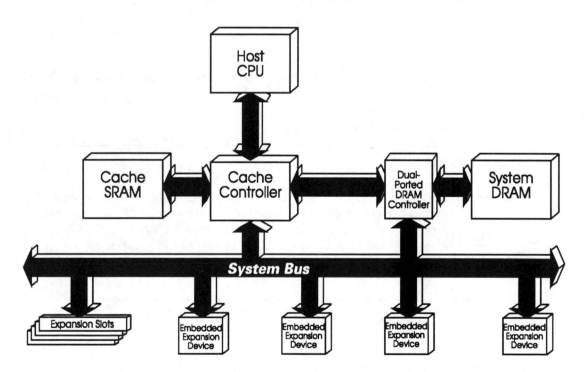

Figure 3-1. The Cache Memory Concept

If, on the other hand, the cache controller determines that it does not have a copy of the requested information in its cache, the information must be read from DRAM memory. This is known as a read miss and results in wait states (due to the slow access time of the DRAM memory). The requested information is sent from DRAM back to the processor to fulfill the request. In addition, the information is also copied into the cache memory by the cache controller. The cache controller updates its directory to track the information stored in cache memory.

On the surface, it may not be evident how this can speed up the processor's memory accesses. However, most programs contain code loops that are executed many times and data structures that are accessed repetitively. A loop is a series of instructions that must be executed a number of times in succession to produce the desired results.

As an example, spreadsheet applications typically use a program loop to recalculate multiple spreadsheet cells. Depending on the number of calculations to be made during a recalc, this program loop may have to be executed hundreds or even thousands of times.

Assume that the cache memory is empty: it contains no copies of information from DRAM memory. The first time the program loop is executed, the following series of events takes place:

1. The processor initiates a memory read bus cycle to fetch the first instruction from memory.
2. The cache memory controller uses the memory address to determine if a copy of the requested information is already in the cache memory. Since the cache is initially empty, a copy doesn't exist and a read miss occurs.
3. The cache memory controller initiates a memory read bus cycle to fetch the requested information (the instruction) from DRAM memory. This will incur one or more wait states, depending on the access time of the DRAM.
4. The information from DRAM memory (the instruction) is sent back to the processor. The cache controller also copies it into the cache memory and updates its directory to reflect the presence of the new information. No performance advantage was realized during this memory read because the information had to be read from slow DRAM memory.
5. Upon completion of the first instruction, the processor's prefetcher initiates a series of memory read bus cycles to fetch the remaining instructions in the program loop. If the cache is sufficiently large, all instructions in the program loop can become resident in cache memory.
6. The last instruction in the program loop is an instruction to jump to the beginning of the loop and start over again. The processor starts fetching

and executing instructions at the memory address of the first instruction in the program loop again.

7. When the processor initiates the memory read bus cycle to fetch the first instruction again, the cache controller checks its cache directory and detects the presence of the requested information in cache memory. It reads the information from SRAM and sends it back to the processor with zero wait states incurred.

The processor is thus able to fetch and begin executing the instruction faster than it was able to the first time through the loop. This proves true for the remaining instructions in the program loop as well. The second and subsequent times through the program loop, the processor incurs no wait states in fetching the instructions, so the program runs substantially faster.

Principles of Locality

The term used to explain the characteristics of programs that run in relatively small loops in consecutive memory locations is locality of reference. As described in the previous example, cache subsystems work because most programs that run on PCs require the same information from consecutive memory locations over and over again. The locality of reference principle is comprised of two components: temporal locality and spatial locality.

Temporal Locality

Since programs run in loops, the same instructions must be fetched from memory on a frequent and continuing basis, meaning that programs tend to use the most recently used information again. The longer its been since information in the cache has been used, the less likely it is to be used again. This is known as the principle of temporal locality. How well a cache subsystem performs is tied directly to how often the software requests the same information from memory. If a program were intentionally designed to never access information more than one time, the cache subsystem would provide absolutely no performance increase.

Spatial Locality

Programs and the data they access tend to reside in consecutive memory locations. This means that programs are likely to need code or data that are close to locations already accessed. This characteristic is called the principle of spatial locality.

The performance gains realized from cache memory subsystems are the result of the high frequency of memory reads that occur at zero wait states due to the principles of locality.

Cache Performance

Performance of cache subsystems depends primarily on the frequency of cache hits. Performance is usually stated in terms of the percentage of cache hits, or the hit rate. The hit rate can be expressed as:

$$\text{Hit Rate \%} = \frac{\text{Cache Hits}}{\text{Total Memory Requests}} \times 100\%$$

Since cache hits only occur on subsequent accesses to the same location, performance of cache systems can be linked directly to the manner in which a program utilizes memory (how well it satisfies the principle of locality of reference). If the program runs in a fairly small area of memory and repeats (or loops), a high percentage of accesses to memory will be cache hits. If, on the other hand, the program runs long sequences of non-looping code, many accesses will result in cache misses. Fortunately, most programs run in a looping fashion and cache hits therefore occur a high percentage of the time (approximately 85-95%).

Several factors in addition to the principle of locality of reference contribute to the cache hit rate. These include the cache's architecture, size of the cache memory and the cache memory organization. These factors are discussed later in this chapter.

Overall System Performance

In addition to providing fast access to memory, cache subsystems can also provide performance advantages by improving bus utilization. Bus utilization is of particular concern when multiple processors and bus masters are incorporated in a system. The percentage of time that any bus master uses the system bus is referred to as bus utilization. If the percentage of bus time required by all bus master devices adds up to over 100%, performance would decrease since the bus bandwidth is exceeded. Well designed cache subsystems reduce the amount of time processors spend on the system bus by reducing the number of accesses that must be passed to the system bus. When a processor is experiencing a high hit rate on its cache, its requirement for the system or memory bus is substantially reduced.

An additional benefit related to a reduction in bus utilization, bus concurrency, is possible when look-through architectures are used. Bus concurrency means that a processor can access its cache memory while another bus master accesses memory or I/O over the system or memory bus at the same time. Look-through cache designs permit concurrency because they decouple the processor's local bus from the system and memory buses. Refer to the section on look-through cache designs for additional information.

Cache Architectures

Two basic architectures are found in today's systems:

- Look-through cache designs
- Look-aside cache designs

Each type of cache architecture exhibits advantages and disadvantages. The following sections detail both types of architectures and analyzes their benefits and liabilities.

Look-Through Cache

Overall, the performance of systems incorporating look-through cache designs is typically higher than that of systems incorporating look-aside designs. Figure 3-2 illustrates the look-through cache design. The look-through cache

performs a look up in its cache directory to determine if a copy of the requested information is in the cache. If found, the requested information is sent
back to the processor with zero wait states. The memory request from the
processor is not automatically transferred to the memory or system bus. This
keeps the buses available for use by other bus masters. Only on cache misses
must a request be passed to the memory or system bus. Look-through cache
designs isolate the processor's local bus from the system and memory buses,
thereby reducing the utilization of the system and memory buses and permitting concurrent operations to take place.

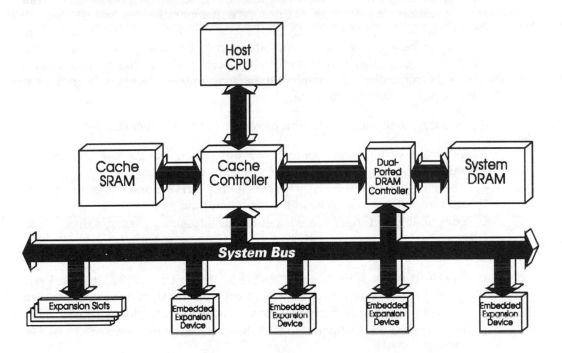

Figure 3-2. Look-Through Cache Architecture

A major advantage of look-through designs is that they permit two bus masters to operate simultaneously in the same system. The processor can be
performing zero wait state operations in its local, look-through cache, while a
bus master (such as the DMA controller or an intelligent bus master subsystem) can utilize the system or memory bus to access memory. These two
operations can occur at the same time without affecting each other. These are
referred to as concurrent bus operations.

To expansion devices, a look-through cache controller appears to be the system processor. In single-processor systems, when a bus master needs access to the system bus, it requests use of the system bus directly from a bus arbiter. If the bus arbiter determines that it is the requesting bus master's turn to use the bus, it removes control of the system bus from the host processor's look-through cache controller and grants control to the bus master. The host processor can continue to access its cache while the bus master performs transfers over the system bus.

During memory writes, look-through cache designs can provide zero wait state operation for write misses. During a write operation, many look-through designs trick the processor into thinking the information was written into memory in zero wait states. The look-through cache subsystem memorizes the entire write operation and immediately asserts ready to the host processor. The cache controller can complete the actual write to memory later. This is called a posted or buffered write.

In summary, look-through designs provide performance benefits by:

- reducing system and memory bus utilization, leaving the system and memory buses available for use by other bus masters.
- allowing bus concurrency, where both the processor and another bus master can perform bus cycles at the same time, and
- completing write operations in zero wait states using posted writes.

The primary disadvantages of look-through designs are:

- The host processor's memory requests are first submitted to the look-through cache to determine if it has a copy of the target line in its cache. In the event that the memory request is a cache miss, the lookup process delays the request to memory. This delay is commonly referred to as the lookup penalty.
- Look-through caches are more complex and difficult to design and implement.
- Look-through designs are costly.

Look-Aside Cache

Refer to figure 3-3. Look-aside caches do not isolate the processor bus from the system and memory buses as do look-through caches. When the processor initiates a bus cycle, all devices in the system immediately detect the bus cycle address (as they would in non-cache systems). The cache controller sits off to the side and monitors each processor memory request to determine if the cache contains a copy of the requested information. The cache controller terminates the bus cycle in zero wait states if the operation is a hit, and instructs the memory subsystem to ignore the request. If the operation is a miss, the bus cycle completes in normal fashion from memory (and wait states are incurred).

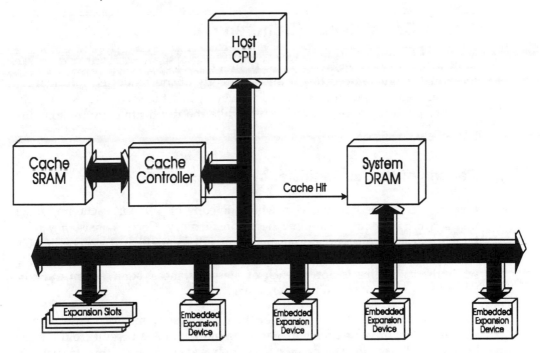

Figure 3-3. Look-Aside Cache Architecture

The major advantages of look-aside cache designs are:

- Improved response time on cache miss cycles. Cache miss cycles complete faster in look-aside caches because the bus cycle is already in progress to memory and no lookup penalty is incurred.
- Simplicity of design. Look-aside designs need only monitor one address bus, whereas, look-through designs must interface with both the processor bus and system bus.
- Lower cost of implementation due to their simplicity.

The disadvantages of look-aside cache designs are:

- System bus utilization is not reduced. Each access to memory goes to both the cache subsystem and memory.
- Concurrent operations are not possible because all masters reside on the same bus.

Cache Consistency (Coherency)

In order for cache subsystems to work properly, the CPU and other bus masters must be guaranteed to get the latest copy of the requested information. There are several possible instances, however, in which data stored in cache memory or in memory can be altered while the duplicate copy remains unchanged.

Causes of Cache Consistency Problems

Loss of cache consistency occurs when the copy of a line in cache no longer matches the contents of the line stored in memory. Cache consistency (also known as cache coherency) problems can result from either the cache line being updated while the memory line is not, or the memory line being updated while the cache line is not. In each of these instances, some action must be taken to ensure that the conflict is resolved.

In both situations cited above either the cache line or memory line contains stale data and must be updated. Stale data in memory can result from a write hit within the cache. The cache's write policy dictates how this consistency problem is handled. In the second case, the coherency problem occurs when another bus master writes to memory. The cache controller must monitor, or snoop, the system bus in order to detect memory write operations to lines currently resident in the cache.

Write Policy

When a write hit occurs, the cache memory is updated. Cache memory then contains the latest information and memory contains stale, outdated information. The cache line is referred to as dirty or modified because it no longer mirrors its corresponding line in memory. To correct this cache consistency problem, the corresponding memory line must be updated to reflect the change made in cache. If memory is not updated, another bus master could

receive stale data if it reads from a memory location that has not been updated. Three write policies are commonly used to prevent this type of
consistency problem:

- Write-through
- Buffered, or posted, write-through
- Write-back

These three write policies are covered in the following sections.

Write-Through Cache Designs

Many look-through cache controllers immediately pass each write operation
initiated by the processor through to memory. This ensures that memory always contains valid data. This is called a write-through policy. Even on a
write hit operation, the cache controller updates the line in the cache and the
corresponding line in memory, thereby ensuring that consistency is maintained between the cache and memory. This implementation is very simple
and effective, but results in poor performance because each write operation
must access slow main memory.

Buffered Write-Through Designs

A variation of the is the buffered or posted write-through. The buffered
write-through cache has the advantage of providing zero wait state write operations for both hits and misses. When a write occurs, buffered write-through
caches trick the processor into thinking that the information was written to
memory in zero wait states, when, in fact, the write has not been performed
yet. The look-through cache controller stores the entire write operation in a
buffer, enabling it to complete the memory write later without impacting the
processor's performance.

Assume that the posted write buffer is only one transaction deep. If there are
two back-to-back memory write bus cycles, the cache controller will insert
wait states into the second bus cycle until the first write to memory has actually been completed. The second bus cycle is then posted and the processor's
ready line is asserted. Since memory writes typically occur as single occur-
rences, a large percentage of memory writes can be completed in zero wait
states.

With a buffered write-through cache, another bus master is not permitted use
of the buses until the write-through is completed, thereby ensuring that the
bus master will received the latest information from memory.

The write-through operations described above require use of the system or memory bus. As a result, when the write-through to memory is in progress, bus masters are prevented from accessing memory. Note however, that the actual cache consistency problem only occurs when a bus master reads from a location in memory that has not yet been updated by the cache controller. The frequency of this type of occurrence is very small. In fact, the memory line will likely be updated numerous times by the processor before another bus master reads from that particular line. As a result, write-through designs, as well as buffered-write-through designs, update memory each time a memory write is performed, though the need for such action may not be required immediately.

In summary, cache coherency problems can occur when the cache is updated on a write hit, but the corresponding line in memory is not updated. Problems would occur if another bus master were permitted to read this stale data from memory. The write-through policy prevents this potential consistency problem by automatically passing each write operation on to memory, thereby ensuring that memory always has the latest data.

Write-Back Cache Designs

Write-back designs improve overall system performance by updating memory only when necessary, thereby keeping the system bus free for use by other processors and bus masters. Memory is updated (written to) only when:

- Another bus master initiates a read access to a memory line that contains stale data.
- Another bus master initiates a write access to a memory line that contains stale data.
- A cache line that contains modified information is about to be overwritten in order to store a line newly acquired from memory.

Cache lines are marked as modified in the cache directory when they are updated by the processor. When another master is reading from or writing to memory, the cache subsystem must monitor, or snoop, the system bus to check for memory accesses to lines marked as modified in the cache.

Write-back cache designs are more complicated to implement than write-through designs because they must make decisions on when to write modified lines back to memory to ensure consistency.

Chapter 3: Pentium Cache Overview

Bus Master/Cache Interaction

When another device in the system requires the use of the buses, it must become bus master. In a system that doesn't incorporate a cache controller, the device requesting bus mastership asserts HOLD to seize the buses from the processor. In a system incorporating a look-through cache, however, the requesting device must force the cache controller, rather than the processor, to relinquish control of the system buses. To do this, the requester will take one of the following actions:

- In a system that does not incorporate a bus arbitration scheme, the bus master activates the cache controller's HOLD input to request control of the buses. In response, the controller disconnects from the buses and asserts HLDA (Hold Acknowledge) to grant the buses to the requester. The new bus master can then use the buses to run one or more bus cycles to transfer data.
- In a system that incorporates a bus arbitrator, the bus master issues a bus request to the arbitrator. When the arbitrator determines that the previous bus master has disconnected from the bus and that it is the requesting bus master's turn to use the bus, it grants the buses to the bus master.

Since bus masters can read from and write to memory, cache consistency problems can occur under three circumstances:

- **Writes to memory (with write-through cache).** When bus masters write to memory, they update locations that may also be cached by the cache controller. In these instances, memory is updated and the line in the cache becomes stale. The cache controller must therefore monitor writes to memory to detect potential coherency problems. When the write is detected, the cache line is invalidated because it will contain stale data after the write to memory completes. Alternatively, a cache can be designed to snarf the data (update the cache contents with the data being written to memory), thereby avoiding the cache incoherency.
- **Reads from memory (with write-back cache).** When bus masters read from memory in a system incorporating a write-back cache, they may read from a line containing stale data. That is, the location has been updated in cache but not in memory. To detect this potential coherency problem, write-back caches must also snoop reads from memory. The system can be designed to back the bus master off (cause the read transaction to be temporarily suspended) and write the cache line to memory, before releasing

47

back-off and allowing the read to continue. Alternatively, the cache can be designed to provide the latest data directly to the bus master.

- **Writes to main memory (with write-back cache).** Assume that another bus master is performing a memory write to a line containing stale data (the corresponding line in the cache has been modified). The bus master is updating one or more locations in memory that are also contained within the cache line. Assuming that the cache is not capable of data snarfing (capturing the data being written in order to keep the line updated), it could invalidate the cache line. This, however, would be a mistake. The fact that the line has been marked modified indicates that some or all of the information in the line is more current than the corresponding data in memory. The memory write being performed by the current bus master will update some item within the memory line. Invalidating the line in cache would quite probably discard some data that is more current than that within the memory line.

If the cache permits the bus master to complete the write, and then flushes (writes) the cache line to memory, the data just written by the bus master may be over-written by stale data in the cache line. The correct action would be to force the bus master off the bus (bus master back off) before it is able to complete the write to memory. The cache controller then seizes the bus and performs a memory write to transfer (write-back) the entire cache line to memory. In the cache directory, the cache line is invalidated because the bus master will update the memory cache line immediately after the line is flushed. The cache then removes backoff, permitting the bus master to reinitiate the memory write operation. When the bus master completes the write to memory, the memory line will contain the most current data. Alternatively, the cache could implement snarfing.

The following section discusses the process of monitoring the buses to detect potential cache consistency problems and reviews the possible remedies.

Bus Snooping/Snarfing

Bus snooping is the method used by cache subsystems to monitor memory accesses performed by other bus masters. The cache controller monitors, or snoops, the system bus when another bus master is performing an access to memory. If the line that is accessed in memory is also resident in the cache, this is referred to as a snoop hit. In such cases, the cache or memory line may contain stale data. Two conditions arise that create the need to snoop the bus:

1. **Memory write by another bus master**. Assume that the cache controller has relinquished control of the system bus to the DMA controller so that it may transfer a block of data from a disk controller into memory. It is quite possible that the DMA controller will alter the contents of memory lines that have already been copied into the cache. This means that the cache and memory would no longer be coherent. In other words, the information in the cache will not accurately reflect the actual information in memory. This is a potentially dangerous situation because the processor may now fetch stale information from the cache and make bad decisions based on it.

   Cache subsystems handle this situation differently depending on how they are designed.

   a. **Invalidate the line** in cache that contains stale data. The next time that particular line is accessed by the processor, it will result in a cache miss, forcing the cache subsystem to read the line from memory.

   b. **Snarf the data**. The cache subsystem snoops the bus during another bus master's write operation and detects a snoop hit. It will capture the data from the system bus while it's being written to memory by the bus master. In this way, both the memory and cache lines are updated at the same time. This would eliminate the potential consistency problem.

2. **Memory read by another bus master**. Only cache subsystems that use a write-back policy must snoop the system bus during memory reads initiated by other bus masters. The cache controller snoops memory reads by another bus master to determine if the line being read from has been updated in cache, but not in memory (i.e., the cached location is marked modified). If so, this would result in a snoop read hit to a modified line. The cache subsystem must force the bus master attempting the memory read to suspend its bus cycle (backoff) until the cache subsystem has updated memory. Once the memory line has been updated by the cache subsystem, the bus master is allowed to complete its memory read operation.

   Alternatively, when a snoop read hit is detected, the cache controller could instruct system memory not to supply the requested data and could supply the requested data directly to the bus master performing the read operation.

The 486 Caching Solution

The 486 Internal Cache

The internal cache introduced by Intel in the 486 processor provides the additional benefit of limiting the number of memory accesses that the processor must submit to external memory. The 486's internal cache keeps a copy of the most recently used instructions and data (typically referred to as a unified cache). The processor only has to access slow external memory when it experiences an internal (L1) cache read miss or a memory write.

The 486 employs a burst transfer mechanism to speed up transfers from external memory. Each internal cache miss forces the processor to access slow external memory. Because the internal cache's line size is 16 bytes, four complete bus cycles would be required to transfer the whole cache line (because the 486 only has a 32-bit data path). The burst transfer capability permits the processor to complete the four transfers faster than it could with zero wait state bus cycles. If the DRAM subsystem utilizes an interleaved memory architecture, the transfers can complete faster than would be possible otherwise.

The Advantage of the L2 Cache

Some 486 systems use two levels of cache to improve overall system performance. Figure 3-4 illustrates the relationship between first, or L1, and second level, or L2, caches in typical 386 and 486 systems.

An L1 cache provides the processor with the most often used code and data. The 486 employs an 8KB four-way, set-associative internal L1 cache.

Since all information destined for the internal L1 cache must pass through the external L2 cache, the advantage of the L2 cache may not be immediately apparent. If the L2 cache were the same size as the L1 cache, there would be no advantage. If, however, the L2 cache is substantially larger than the L1 cache, the advantage becomes clear. L2 caches are usually much larger (64KB-512KB) than L1 caches.

L2 caches improve overall performance because the L1 cache can get information from the L2 cache quickly on most internal read misses. Furthermore, to take full advantage of the 486 burst cycles, the typical L2 cache can accommodate the fastest possible burst transfer.

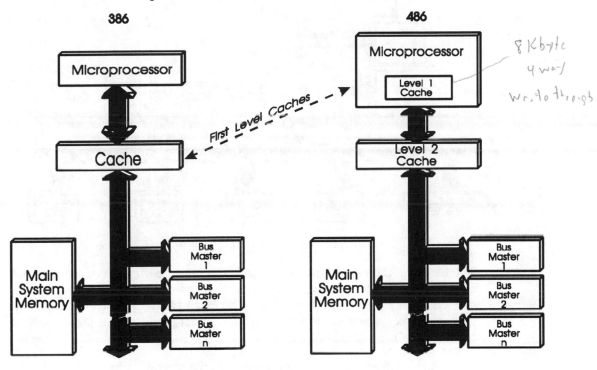

Figure 3-4. First and Second Level Caches

Cache Coherency with an L1 and L2 Cache

Refer to figure 3-5. When an L2 cache is used in conjunction with the 486, care must be taken to ensure that cache consistency is maintained between the L1 and L2 caches and memory. To help maintain cache consistency, the 486 L1 cache implements a write-through policy to ensure that the external cache is notified of all write operations to the 486 L1 cache.

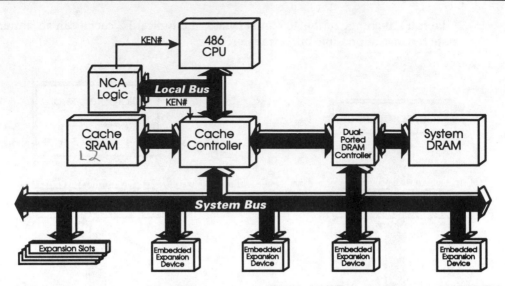

Figure 3-5. A 486 System Incorporating an L2 Cache

The L2 cache can be designed to utilize either a write-through or a write-back policy. These cache types maintain cache coherency with memory as described earlier. However, if both the L2 cache and L1 cache have copies of the line that is being written to by another bus master, additional steps must be taken by both the L2 and L1 caches.

1. When another bus master performs a write operation to memory, the L2 cache snoops the line address that is being written to in memory. If the L2 cache detects a snoop hit, then the information in the L2 cache will be stale when the write operation completes. To ensure that the processor does not subsequently receive stale data from the L2 cache, it will invalidate the directory entry. The next access to the line will then result in a cache miss and an access to memory.

2. Since the data that is being updated was found in the L2 cache during the snoop, it is also possible that the L1 cache has a copy of the same line. If no further action is taken, the L1 cache will contain stale data. To prevent this type of cache inconsistency, the L2 cache must pass the snoop address back to the 486. It can then determine if a copy of the target line is also contained in its L1 cache. If a cache hit occurs, the 486 will invalidate the directory entry to ensure that stale data isn't contained in the L1 cache.

Non-Cacheable Address (NCA) logic monitors each address that the 486 outputs to determine whether the location should be cached. If the location is cacheable, the NCA logic asserted KEN# to notify the 486 that the location should be cached. Some memory locations such as memory-mapped I/O and dual-ported memories should not be kept in cache memory.

Pentium Processor Cache Overview

The Pentium processor improves performance over the 486 in a variety of ways, including the implementation of separate data and code caches. The line size for each of these caches is 32 bytes and the data bus is eight bytes, or 64 bits in width. A burst of four consecutive transfers is therefore required to fill the cache line. As with the 486, implementing the Pentium processor with an L2 cache provides the highest performance.

Due to its write-back policy, the Pentium processor's L1 data cache introduces additional complexity into the cache consistency logic . The data cache can also use a write-through or a write-back policy on a line-by-line basis. The instruction, or code, cache is read-only, so it doesn't require a write policy .

Figure 3-6 illustrates the relationship between the Pentium processor, the L2 cache, the Non-Cacheable Access (NCA) logic, system memory and devices connected to an expansion bus (ISA, EISA, or Micro Channel). Six major signal groups comprise the processor's interface to the external environment. These signal groups are:

- Address Bus
- Data Bus
- Bus Cycle Control Signals
- Snoop Control Signals
- L2 Cache Control Signals
- Bus Master Control Signals

A detailed description of these signals can be found in the chapter entitled, "Pentium Signal Interface."

When the Pentium processor's data cache utilizes a write-through policy, its operation with an L2 cache is conceptually identical to that of a 486. The following descriptions assume that both the Pentium processor and its L2 cache are using write-back policies.

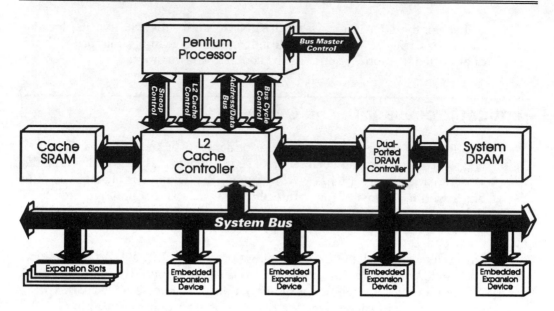

Figure 3-6. The Pentium Processor's Relationship To Its External Environment

Handling of Memory Reads Initiated by the Pentium Processor

When either the prefetcher or one of the execution units requests information from an internal cache, the request is immediately fulfilled if a cache hit occurs. If the information is not in the internal cache, the Pentium processor must perform a cache line fill to read the target line from external memory.

The L2 cache detects the memory read bus cycle and interrogates its directory to determine if it has a copy of the requested information. If it's a hit on the L2 cache, the L2 cache notifies the Pentium processor that the address is cacheable (KEN# is asserted). Note that if the target line is found in the L2 cache, the line must be cacheable. The L2 cache then accesses its cache SRAM memory, satisfying the cache line fill in a burst of four consecutive 64-bit transfers.

If the memory read results in a miss on the L2 cache, the L2 cache passes the bus cycle to the system or memory bus. The non-cacheable access, or NCA, logic evaluates the address to determine if the address is cacheable. If the address is determined to be non-cacheable, the NCA logic notifies the L2 cache and the processor that the addressed location cannot safely be cached (KEN# is sampled deasserted). As a result, the bus cycle is not converted into a cache line fill and a single-transfer bus cycle is run to fetch the requested information directly from memory.

Addresses identified as cacheable (CACHE# asserted by the processor and KEN# asserted by the NCA logic) cause the read cycle to be converted into a cache line fill for both the L2 and L1 caches. Since the access is to slow external memory, wait states will be inserted in the transfer (due to the memory's slow access time). The L2 cache copies the first 64 bits, or quadword, of data into its cache line-fill buffer, while simultaneously forwarding it to the processor and indicating that valid data is present on the processor's local data bus (BRDY# sampled asserted). The processor reads the first quadword and stores it in its cache line-fill buffer while awaiting the other three transfers in the burst. The data or code that was originally requested and caused the internal L1 cache miss is contained in the first quadword. The originally requested information is therefore immediately forwarded to the internal requester, (e.g., an execution unit or the prefetcher). Three additional transfers must occur to complete the cache line fill. Once the entire line has been received, both the L1 and L2 caches copy the lines in their respective line-fill buffers into their respective caches. Refer to the chapter entitled "The Data Cache and Burst Line Fills" for more information.

Handling of Memory Writes Initiated by the Pentium Processor

Memory writes result from the execution of a floating-point or integer instruction, a cache write-back, a page table entry update, or a segment descriptor update. . The data cache can utilize either a write-through or write-back policy. As a result, writes that hit the Pentium processor's internal data cache may update the internal data cache and be written on through to external memory, or may simply update the internal data cache without updating memory. When using a write-back policy with an L2 cache, special interaction between the Pentium processor and the external cache must occur to ensure cache coherency.

Write Misses

The internal data cache checks the target address of the memory write to determine if a copy of the target memory line exists in the cache. In the event of a write miss, the Pentium processor initiates a single transfer bus cycle to the target location(s). The address is received by the L2 cache which interrogates its directory to determine if a copy of the target line is resident in its cache. If the access results in a miss in the L2 cache, the action taken by the L2 cache depends on whether or not it supports allocate-on-write.

If the L2 cache does not have allocate-on-write capability, the L2 cache will pass the memory write bus cycle to the memory subsystem to complete the write operation. When the memory subsystem completes the write, it activates ready to the L2 cache and the processor to notify them that the cycle has completed.

If the L2 cache supports allocate-on-write, it will pass the bus cycle on to the memory subsystem as described above, but will then perform a cache line fill from the same line and store the line in the L2 cache.

Write Hits and the Write-Once Policy

The Pentium processor's write-once policy ensures cache consistency is maintained between the L1 and L2 level caches. Consider the following example.

The Problem

Assume that a new line has just been read from memory and the line of data is marked valid in the L1 cache directory. Because the line passed through the L2 cache, a copy of the line also exists in the L2 write-back cache and in memory. Assume next that one of the execution units writes to the same line. The L1 data cache will interrogate its directory and find that the target line is resident in the data cache. The L1 data cache will modify the cache line. The L1 data cache line then contains modified data and the respective directory entry is updated to reflect the modified state of the cache line.

Some time later, another bus master reads from the same line in memory. The L2 cache, unaware that the L1 data cache has modified this line, snoops the address being driven by the other bus master. The L2 cache interrogates its directory and has a cache hit on a clean (unmodified) line. It takes no action because it believes that the other bus master is about to receive valid data from memory. Since the L2 cache was not notified by the L1 data cache that the line had been modified, it could not properly snoop the bus and, as a result, the other bus master receives stale data from memory.

The Write-Once Solution

The write-once policy ensures that when a line is initially placed in the L1 data cache, it is marked as shared to force a write-through to the L2 cache upon the first internal write hit to that cache line. This means that the first time one of the execution units writes to the line, the line will be updated and the write operation written-through to the L2 cache. The L2 cache will also interrogate its directory and find a copy of the target line. The line in L2 also will be updated and its directory entry updated to indicate that the line has been modified. Now that the L2 cache state indicates that the target line has been modified, it can snoop correctly and will not permit any bus master to read stale data from the line in memory. Upon completion of the write-through, the L2 cache instructs the L1 data cache to transition the state of the line from the shared to the exclusive state.

Subsequently, when an execution unit again writes to this line, the L1 data cache interrogates its directory and again finds the target line in the data cache. All subsequent writes to this line are now treated according to the write-back policy. The L1 line is modified and its directory entry is updated from the exclusive to the modified state, reflecting that the line has been modified since the write-through was performed. The write is not propagated through to the L2 cache, however. Of the two lines, the line in the L1 data cache is now more current than the one in the L2 cache.

Some time later when another bus master reads from the same line in memory, the L2 cache snoops the address being driven by the other bus master. The L2 cache interrogates its directory and finds a cache hit to a modified line. As a result, the L2 cache causes the other bus master to backoff so that the fresh line can be deposited in memory before allowing the bus master to complete the read. First, however, the L2 cache must pass the snoop address to the L1 data cache. The L1 cache must also snoop the address to determine if the line is in the internal cache and if it has been modified more recently than the line in the L2 cache. In this example, the L1 data cache determines that the line contains modified data. As a result, the L1 data cache must perform a write-back to deposit the fresh line in memory to be read by the bus master. When the write-back is completed, the L2 cache releases backoff, allowing the bus master to read the fresh line from memory.

When the L1 cache has written the fresh line to memory, the line in the L1 and L2 caches and memory contain identical information. The L2 cache transitions the line's state from modified to shared (because another bus master just read the line and may have a copy in its cache). In addition, the L2 cache instructs the L1 cache to transition the line from the modified to the shared state (so that it will be informed of any subsequent internal updates made to the line).

Handling of Memory Reads Initiated by Another Bus Master

Since the L1 data cache is a write-back cache, the L2 cache must ensure that the Pentium processor adheres to the write-once policy. This is necessary because the Pentium processor cannot snoop the system bus directly. It therefore cannot prevent another bus master from reading from a memory location that has been modified in the processor's L1 data cache, but that has not been updated in memory.

The write-once policy ensures that the first time a write hit occurs in the L1 data cache it is written through to the L2 cache. This write-through notifies the L2 cache that the line in the processor's L1 data cache has been modified and that subsequent internal updates to the line will not result in a bus cycle to inform the L2 cache. The L2 cache must mark the cache line as modified. This allows the L2 cache to recognize when another bus master is about to read a stale line from memory by snooping memory reads initiated by other bus masters. If a snoop read hit occurs to a line that has been modified, the L2 cache must cause the bus master to back-off (suspend its access until the fresh line has been deposited in memory) and simultaneously pass the address to the Pentium processor so that it can also snoop the address. If the processor detects a snoop read hit to a line that has been modified, it performs a burst write-back cycle to update memory. After the write-back has finished, the bus master is allowed to complete the memory read.

Handling of Memory Writes Initiated by Another Bus Master

When another bus master writes to memory , the L2 cache and, in some cases, the L1 cache must snoop the address to ensure that consistency is maintained between the L1 and L2 caches and memory.

When the L2 Cache Uses a Write-Through Policy

When a bus master initiates the memory write, the L2 cache snoops the bus. If it determines that the bus master is writing new data into a line that is cached in L2, the L2 cache marks its copy of the information as invalid (because the bus master is altering the line). In addition, the L2 cache forces the Pentium processor to snoop the memory address generated by the bus master in order to determine if it has a copy of the target line. If the L1 data cache line is in the shared or exclusive state, it will invalidate its line. If the line is in the modified state, it must tell the L2 cache to backoff the bus master. The L1 cache then writes the line into memory to be updated by the bus master and marks its line as invalid. The L2 cache then removes the backoff, permitting the bus master to update the line in memory.

When the L2 Cache Uses a Write-Back Policy

Assume that another bus master is performing a memory write and a write-back L2 cache is snooping the bus. It experiences a snoop hit on a modified line. This means that the bus master is about to update a portion of a stale line in memory. Assuming that the cache is not capable of data snarfing (to keep the line updated), it could invalidate the cache line. This, however, would be a mistake. The fact that the line is marked modified indicates that some or all of the information in the line is more current than the corresponding line in memory. The memory write being performed by the current bus master is updating some item in the memory line. Trashing the line from the cache would quite probably trash some data that is more current than that in the memory line.

If the cache permits the bus master to complete the write and then flushes its line to memory, the data just written by the bus master is over-written by the stale data in the cache line. The correct action would be to force the bus master off the bus (bus master back off) without letting it complete the write to memory. The L2 cache must also force the Pentium processor's to snoops its L1 cache, since it might have a copy of the line being written to. The L1 reports the results of its snoop to the L2 cache. The action taken by the L2 cache depends on the results of the L1 snoop.

- If the L1 cache does not have a copy of the target, then the L2 cache initiates a memory write to transfer (write-back) the entire cache line to memory.

Pentium Processor System Architecture

- If the L1 cache has a copy of the target line stored in the shared or exclusive state it will invalidate the line. The L2 cache then performs the write-back.
- If it has a copy of the line stored in the modified state, L1 contains the latest information and it must be written-back to memory. The L2 cache waits for the Pentium to start the write-back.

In the cache directories of both the L1 and L2, the cache line is invalidated because the bus master will update the memory line immediately after the line is written to memory, or flushed. The cache then removes back off, letting the bus master reinitiate the memory write operation. Upon completion of the bus master's write operation, the memory line contains the most current data.

Chapter 4

The Previous Chapter

The previous chapter introduced the Pentium's internal caches and the challenge of designing PC systems that can take full advantage of the Pentium processor's performance.

This Chapter

This chapter discusses the Pentium processor's implementation of the MESI cache consistency model. Both single and multiple-processor implementations are discussed.

The Next Chapter

The next chapter details the hardware interface that the Pentium processor uses to communicate with external devices.

Introduction to the MESI Model

In multi-processing environments where several cache subsystems exist, maintaining cache consistency becomes more challenging. More than one cache may contain a copy of information from a given memory location. In such systems, there must be a method to ensure that an access to a given memory location interacts with the latest information. The MESI cache consistency model provides a method of tracking the various states that a cache line can be stored in to ensure consistency across all possible sources of a given line without needlessly invalidating data stored in the caches. The four states are listed in table 4-1.

Table 4-1. The MESI States

State	Description
Modified	The line in cache has been updated (contains modified data) due to a write hit in the cache. This alerts the cache subsystem to snoop the system bus and write the modified line back to memory when a snoop hit to the line is detected.
Exclusive	Indicates that this cache is unaware of any other cache possessing a copy of this line.
Shared	Indicates that the line may be present in several caches and if so, that an exact duplicate of the information (clean data) exists in each source (caches and memory).
Invalid	The initial state after reset, indicating that the line is not present in the cache.

Every line in cache is assigned one of these state indicators to identify the status of the information stored in cache. Transitions from one state to another may be caused by a local processor read or write, or a bus snoop when another bus master initiates bus activity. Ensuring consistency among multiple caches requires that additional signals be implemented for inter-cache communication. Figure 4-1 illustrates the MESI state transitions that take place within the Pentium's data cache.

The MESI model was created primarily to support multiprocessing systems, but is also used by the Pentium processor in single-processor systems. The MESI protocol is therefore discussed under two major headings:

- Single Processor MESI Implementation
- Multiprocessor MESI implementation.

Single Processor MESI Implementation — The Life and Times of a Cache Line

A cache line may go through a number of MESI state transitions after it is first read into the L2 cache and the processor's L1 data cache. The MESI transitions depend on the nature of accesses initiated by the processor and other bus masters. The following description follows the various states that a cache line

Chapter 4: Multiple Processors and the MESI Model

might go through and the actions that the L2 cache and the Pentium processor must take to maintain cache coherency using the MESI model.

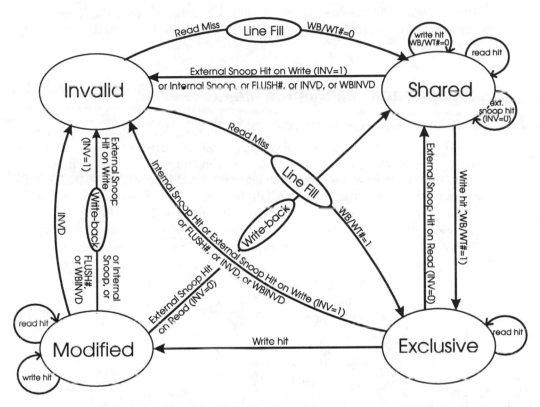

Figure 4-1. State Diagram of MESI Transitions that Occur within the Pentium's Data Cache

The Pentium processor includes signals that allow external logic to tell it when to snoop the buses, as well as signals to tell the processor which MESI state a line should be placed in after each bus cycle or snoop. These signals permit the Pentium processor's data cache to function as a write-back cache and still maintain cache coherency.

During reset, the MESI state bits for the Pentium processor's internal caches and the L2 cache are forced to the invalid (I) state. This causes all initial accesses to the L1 data cache and the L2 cache to be cache misses, forcing accesses to system memory.

Pentium Processor System Architecture

The code cache only uses a subset of the MESI model because it is a read-only cache. The following discussion only covers the L1 data cache because its operation is a superset of the code cache's operation.

The following discussions assume that the L2 cache is a write-back cache that implements back-off when detecting a snoop hit to a modified line. The L2 cache also supports the write-once policy.

Initial Read from System Memory

Refer to figure 4-2. When one of the execution units initially requests information from the processor's internal cache, all state bits are set to the invalid, or I, state and information must therefore be retrieved from external memory. The L2 cache will also have all state bits set to the I state, forcing the transfer to be made from system memory. The data will be placed into both the L2 cache and the L1 data cache. The L2 cache updates its state bits to the exclusive, or E, state. No other processor and L2 cache combination exists in the system that might also have a copy of the line, so the data is exclusive to the L2 cache and its associated processor.

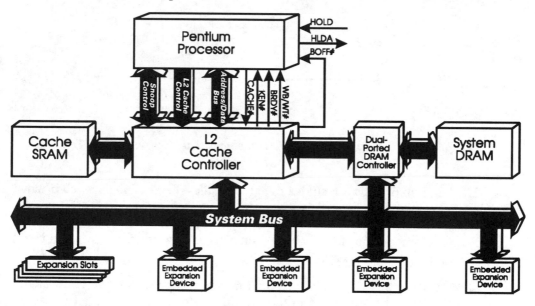

Figure 4-2. The Pentium Processor and L2 Cache: MESI Control Signals Used During Cache Line-Fills

When a line is first placed in the internal cache, its MESI state is determined by the L2 cache. If a look-through L2 cache is used, then it must force the cache line to be initially stored in the shared, or S, state to support the write-once policy. Because the L2 cache line is initially stored in the E state, the L2 cache drives the WB/WT# signal low to indicate that the line should be stored in the internal cache in the shared, or S, state. This action enforces the write-once policy described in the previous chapter.

First Write to the Internal Cache Line

When the first write hit (after the line is initially read from memory) occurs in the L1 data cache, the data cache checks the state bits, now indicating that the line is shared. The cache line is updated by the internal write and the data is written on through to the L2 cache, notifying the L2 cache that the line is being modified. The L2 cache interrogates its directory and finds a copy of the information stored in the E state. Since the cache line is exclusive, it can be updated. After updating the cache line, the L2 cache transitions the state bits to indicate that the line has been modified (M). Since the line is now modified, the L2 cache drives the WB/WT# line high, indicating to the Pentium processor that the L1 data cache can transition the line's state from S to E. This permits subsequent writes to be handled using a write-back policy.

Bus Master Access to Memory Location Stored in the Internal Cache Line (in E State)

The first write operation in the previous example left the MESI state of the L1 data cache line in the E state and the L2 cache line in the M state. When another bus master accesses system memory, it will either perform a read or a write operation. The action taken by the L2 cache and the Pentium processor differs depending on whether the bus master's memory access is a read or write. Both situations are described.

Bus Master Read from Line Stored in the M State in the L2 Cache

Refer to figure 4-3. When another bus master reads from a line in system memory that is also contained within an L2 cache line, the L2 cache snoops the address driven by the bus master. Since the state bits indicate that the line is currently stored in the M state in L2, the bus master would receive stale data if it were allowed to read the data from system memory. To prevent this from occurring, the bus master is backed off by the L2 cache, preventing it from completing the bus cycle. The L2 cache must also transfer the address driven by the bus master to the Pentium processor so that it may snoop the address. This is necessary because the L2 cache cannot be certain whether the internal cache has updated its copy of the line since it last performed a write-through to the L2 cache.

L2 Cache Performs Write-Back

The L1 data cache might be in the process of performing a cache line-fill or of accessing a device on its local bus when the snoop needs to take place. The L2 cache first asserts the AHOLD (Address Hold) signal to force the Pentium processor to float its address bus, and then passes the read address driven by the bus master onto the processor's local address bus. Next, the EADS# (External Address Strobe) signal is asserted by the L2 cache, causing the processor to access its cache directories with the snoop address. The target line is found in the L1 data cache with its state bits in the E state. This indicates that the line has not been updated since it was last written through to the L2 cache. The HIT# signal is asserted by the processor to tell the L2 cache the result of the snoop (snoop hit on a clean line).

The L2 cache also deasserts the INV (invalidate) signal during the snoop cycle to tell the L1 data cache not to invalidate the cache line in the event of a snoop hit. The INV signal is deasserted because the snoop resulted from a bus master's read from memory, indicating that the cache line will still contain valid data after the other bus master completes its bus cycle. The L1 data cache transitions the line's state bits from E to S because the L1 data cache now knows that another bus master is reading the line and may place it in a cache.

After sampling the HITM# signal deasserted, the L2 cache now knows that it has the latest information. It then performs a write-back to system memory, updating the memory line prior to releasing the bus master to read the target line (or a portion thereof) from memory. Backoff is released after the write-back and the bus master can then complete the memory read.

The L2 cache can be designed to transition its state from M to E when the write-back occurs (if it is certain that no other memory caches exist in the system). Otherwise, the state transitions from M to S.

Chapter 4: Multiple Processors and the MESI Model

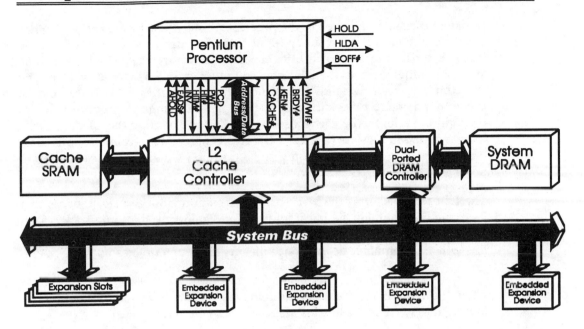

Figure 4-3. The Pentium Processor and L2 Cache: Signals Used to Define the MESI State After a Snoop Hit

Bus Master Write to a Line Stored In the M State in the L2 Cache

When another bus master writes to a location in system memory that is also stored in the Pentium processor's L1 data cache, the L2 cache snoops the address driven by the bus master. In this example, a snoop hit is detected to a modified line in the L2 cache.

The L2 cache cannot permit the write operation to complete until it first writes the modified line back to system memory. If the bus master were permitted to update the line in system memory, it would be updating a stale line. Since the L2 cache line is currently in the modified state, some portion of the line has been previously updated but not written back to memory. To prevent this from happening, the modified line must first be written to system memory before the bus master is allowed to complete its write operation.

Since the L2 cache detected a snoop hit to a modified line, it is possible that the Pentium processor's data cache has even later information. The L2 cache transfers the snoop address to the processor. Since the L1 data cache also has a copy of the target line, a snoop hit occurs. The current state of the L1 cache line is E, indicating that no additional write has occurred to the data cache line since the initial write to the L2 cache, so the L2 cache has the latest data. The Pentium processor responds to the snoop hit by asserting HIT# to tell the L2 cache that a snoop hit occurred on a clean line. During the processor snoop, or inquire, cycle, the L2 cache also asserts INV, instructing the L1 data cache to change the line's state to invalid (I). This is necessary because the bus master will write to memory, causing some portion of the internal cache line to become stale.

The L2 cache performs the write-back to system memory when it learns that its cache line contains the latest information. Following the write-back operation, the L2 cache line's state bits will transition to the I state (because its cache line will also contain stale data once the bus master completes its write operation).

After the write-back, the L2 cache removes backoff from the bus master, allowing it to write to the line just deposited in memory.

Second and Subsequent Writes to the Internal Cache

Assume that the state of the L1 data cache line and the L2 cache line are the same as they were following the first write to memory. The internal cache line is in the E state and the L2 cache line is in the M state. A second internal memory write to the line results in the line being modified in the L1 cache and (since the state bits reflect an exclusive state) no write-through occurs to the L2 cache. The state bits transition to the M state, indicating that the line now contains modified data. Each subsequent internal memory write results in the internal cache line being updated with no write-through bus cycle being generated and no transition of the state bits (because they already indicate that the line contains modified data).

Bus Master Access to Line Stored in the L1 Cache in M State

Another bus master accesses a line in memory that is also resident in the L1 data cache in the M state. The L1 data cache must perform a write-back to system memory so that the latest information will be in memory when the bus master is permitted to complete its transfer. The specific actions that occur during read and write operations by another bus master are covered in the following two sections.

Bus Master Read from a Modified Line in the L1 Data Cache

When a bus master addresses memory during a read , the L2 cache snoops the bus master's address. In this example, a snoop hit occurs to a modified line in the L2 cache. The L2 cache backs off the bus master to prevent it from reading stale data from memory and passes the bus master address to the Pentium processor for snooping. The L2 cache asserts AHOLD and passes the address to the processor. Next, the L2 cache asserts the EADS# signal, causing the processor to snoop the address. The L1 data cache finds a copy of the information in the modified state. The Pentium processor asserts the HIT# and HITM# signals to notify the L2 cache that a snoop hit to a modified line has occurred and that it will run a write-back bus cycle to deposit the latest information into memory. After the write-back completes, the L1 data cache line contains the same information as the L2 cache and memory lines. The L2 cache deasserts INV, telling the L1 data cache to transition the line's state bits from M to S (to force any update to be written through to the L2 cache).

When the Pentium processor performs the write-back, the entire line is written back to memory. Simultaneously, the L2 cache line is updated so that it also has the latest information in its cache line. If it knows that no other processor and cache exists in the system, the L2 cache state bits then transition to the E state (otherwise, they transition to the S state). Once the write-back completes, the bus master is allowed to finish its read from memory.

Bus Master Write to a Modified Line in the L1 Cache

When a bus master attempts to write to a memory line that contains stale data, the bus master must be backed-off. As before, the L2 cache snoops the address driven by the bus master and finds a hit to a modified line. Backoff is asserted and an inquire cycle is run to the processor's L1 data cache to determine if it also has a copy of the line, and if so, whether is has been updated more recently than the line in the L2 cache. AHOLD, EADS# and INV are asserted, and the L1 cache snoops the line address. INV is asserted to indicate that the L2 cache has detected a bus master writing to memory. A snoop hit with INV asserted causes the L1 line's state bits to transition from the M to the

I state after the processor has completed the write-back of the modified line to memory.

When the processor detects the snoop hit on the modified line, it asserts HIT# and HITM#, notifying the L2 cache that a snoop hit has been detected on a modified line and that the L1 data cache line therefore has fresher data than that contained in the L2 cache line. The processor then performs a cache line write-back to update system memory. Following completion of the write-back operation, the L2 cache state bits will also transition to the I state. In addition, the L2 cache removes the backoff from the bus master, permitting it to restart the memory write transaction. The L2 cache once again snoops the transaction, but it now experiences a miss (because the line was invalidated after being written back to memory). The bus master is therefore permitted to complete the update of the line in memory.

Multiprocessor MESI Implementation — The Life and Times of Twin Cache Lines.

Tightly-Coupled Processors

Refer to figure 4-4. In a system incorporating *tightly-coupled* processors, all processors share the same memory subsystem. This is typically the case in PC systems that incorporate multiprocessing. Virtually all multiprocessor systems combine local write-back cache subsystems with each processor to reduce system bus utilization. In this way, each processor accesses its local cache a majority of the time, rather than making frequent accesses to slow DRAM or ROM memory. Multimaster systems not employing write-back look-through caches run the risk of overloading the bus with the numerous accesses made by each bus master. The following discussion uses the term *processor complex* to identify a processor and its local L2 cache subsystem.

In multiprocessor systems, more than one processor complex might have a copy of the same line in its cache(s). If so, the MESI model ensures consistency is maintained between multiple caches, and prevents needless invalidation of cache lines.

Chapter 4: Multiple Processors and the MESI Model

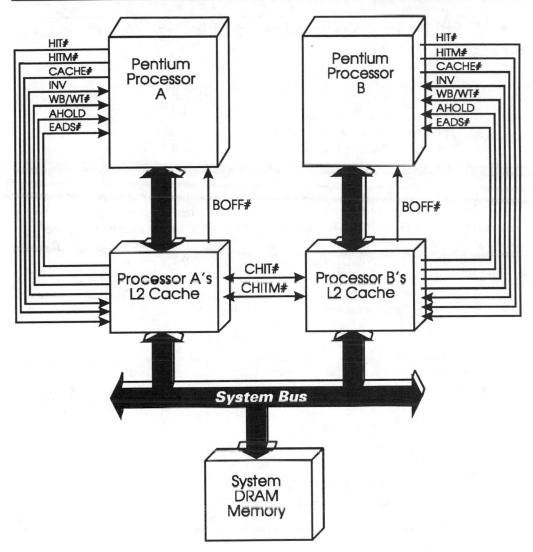

Figure 4-4. Two Processors With Write-back Caches Using the MESI Model

Figure 4-4 illustrates two processor complexes each employing L2 write-back cache subsystems. Notice that communication exists between the L2 cache controllers in order to indicate the result of snoop operations. The following examples illustrate the operation of the MESI model when more than one processor complex is installed.

Read by Processor B from a Line Present in Processor A's Cache

The action taken by each processor complex depends on:

- The current state of its cache line.
- The type of transfer that is in progress.
- The state of the snoop-related signals generated by the other processor complex.

The following scenarios detail the actions that would be taken when one processor complex reads from a line that the another processor complex has a copy of in its cache. The following three scenarios assume that processor complex A currently has a copy of the line that processor complex B is attempting to read from system memory. Each of the three scenarios represent one of the three possible states in which the target cache line within complex A can be stored when processor B initiates a memory read. The initial states of the lines in the four caches are listed in table 4-2.

Table 4-2. Initial State of Cache Lines

Scenario	Process Complex A Status	A's L2 Cache Line State	A's L1 Cache Line State
1	Cache state after reading target line from system memory.	E	S
2	Cache state after 1st internal write to target line.	M	E
3	Cache state after 2nd and subsequent internal writes to target.	M	M

In all these scenarios, the processor's internal data cache is referred to as its L1 cache, while its external cache is referred to its L2 cache.

Scenario One

Figure 4-5 illustrates the first scenario.

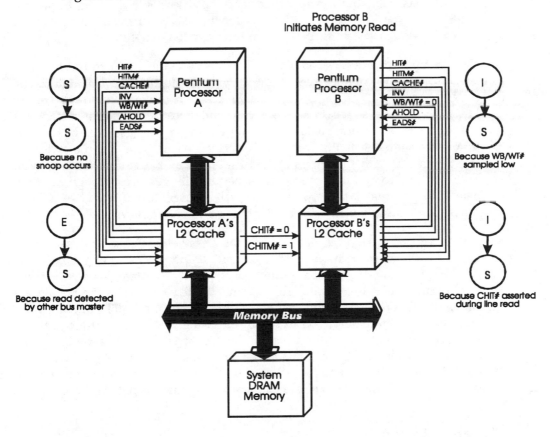

Figure 4-5. Read Scenario One

The Initial Cache State. Assume first that processor A has just completed a read from a memory location for the first time. The actions taken by the Pentium processor and its L2 cache would have been the same as the single-processor examples discussed earlier. Following the initial cache line-fill operation, processor A's L1 cache will have a copy of the target line. The state bits associated with the cache line will be set to S (consistent with the write-once policy). The copy of the line contained in the L2 cache will have its state bits set to E, indicating that processor complex A has the only copy of the target line. Assume that processor B then initiates a read from the line.

The Read Miss In the B Complex. When processor B initiates the read, the target line is not found in its L1 cache and the access is transferred to processor B's L2 cache. The L2 cache directory lookup also results in a miss, followed by a bus cycle to system memory to perform a cache Line-fill.

The Snoop By Processor Complex A. The bus cycle initiated by processor B is passed to the system bus to access memory. Processor A's L2 cache detects the read bus cycle and snoops the address. Processor complex A has a copy of the line in the E state, so it experiences a snoop hit. Because another bus master is reading from a location contained within the cache line, the state bits transition to the shared state (S). This is done because it's possible that the other bus master will store the line in its cache (if it has one). No inquire (snoop) cycle need be sent to Pentium processor A because its L2 cache recognizes that, even if the internal data cache has a copy of the target line, it will already be in the S state. This knowledge is based on the write-once policy.

The Read Bus Cycle Completes. When the hit is detected, the processor A L2 cache asserts its cache hit (CHIT#) signal, notifying processor complex B that it is about to read data shared by another cache in the system. When processor B's L2 cache completes its line-fill, it stores the line of data in the S state because the CHIT# signal was sampled asserted. Had the CHIT# line not been asserted, the line would have been stored in the E state, indicating that the cache line was exclusive to complex B. The L2 cache also drives the WB/WT# signal low, causing the cache line to be stored in the S state within the processor B L1 cache. The L1 and L2 caches in both processor complexes now have a copy of the same line, all with state bits reflecting that the data is shared.

Scenario Two

Figure 4-6 illustrates the second scenario.

The Initial Cache State. Assume that after having read a line from memory, processor A writes to the line. Processor A updates the cache line in the L1 cache and passes the write operation through to external memory (write-through occurs because the target line was stored in S state). Processor A's L2 cache interrogates its cache directory, finding a copy of the target line in the E state. The L2 cache writes the target data into the cache line and transitions its state bits to the M state. The L2 cache also sets the WB/WT# line high, causing the processor's L1 cache to transition its state bits to the E state. Assume that some time later processor B initiates a read from the same line.

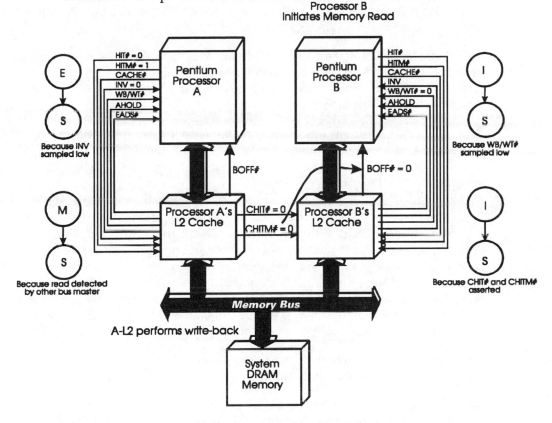

Figure 4-6. Read Scenario Two

The Cache Read Miss In Processor Complex B. When processor B performs a read from a line that processor complex A also has a copy of, the following actions will be taken. Processor B interrogates its L1 cache directory and experiences a read miss. The cache miss causes the processor to initiate a cache Line-fill request on its external buses. The memory read also causes a miss in the L2 cache and the bus cycle is transferred to the system bus for access to system memory.

The Snoop By Processor Complex A. When it detects the memory read bus cycle on the system bus, the L2 cache in processor complex A snoops the address driven by processor B. When the L2 cache interrogates its directory and finds a copy of the target line in the M state, the L2 cache determines that it must back off the other L2 cache or it will receive stale data from memory. Consequently, the processor A L2 cache asserts CHIT# and CHITM#, indicating a snoop hit to a modified line.

The BackOff. The CHIT# and CHITM# are inputs to complex B's L2 cache and direct it to backoff until the memory line has been updated by processor complex A. In turn, the processor B L2 cache asserts backoff (BOFF#) to force processor B to suspend the current bus cycle.

Processor A's L1 Snoop. Processor complex A's L2 cache must determine if processor A's L1 cache has more recent data than L2 does. The L1 cache line is currently in the E state, indicating that it was not updated after the L2 line was updated. An inquire cycle is run to Pentium processor A by its L2 cache to determine if the L1 cache has more recent data than the L2 cache. AHOLD is asserted by the L2 cache and it then passes the address to processor A. EADS# is asserted, telling the processor to snoop the address. INV is deasserted, indicating that the other bus master is performing a read, so there is no need to invalidate the L1 line in the event of a snoop hit. The snoop results in a hit on a line in the E state, indicating that it has not been modified since it was written through to the L2 cache. Processor A then asserts HIT#, informing the L2 cache that the inquire cycle resulted in a hit to a non-modified line. The L2 cache therefore has a copy of the most recent data.

The state of the L1 cache line transitions from E to S (because another bus master is reading from the line and may place a copy in its own local cache).

The Write-Back. When complex A's L2 cache detects HIT# asserted, it determines that it has the most recent data. The processor A L2 cache then performs a write-back cycle to deposit the fresh line in memory. The processor A L2 cache line's state bits are updated from M to S (because the other bus master may then have a copy of the line). Memory now contains the valid line.

BackOff Removed and the Read Completes. Following its write-back to memory, processor A's L2 cache deasserts CHIT# and CHITM#, releasing processor complex B to complete the read from memory. This causes processor B's L2 cache to deasserts BOFF# to processor B. Processor B then restarts the cache line-fill and obtains the target line from system memory. When the bus cycle is reinitiated on the system bus, the L2 cache within processor complex A snoops the address and detects a snoop hit to a shared line. In response to the snoop hit, CHIT# is asserted, telling complex B's L2 cache that another cache has a copy of the line it is reading from memory. As a result, the data is stored in the processor B L2 cache in the S state. Also, when processor B's L2 cache detects CHIT#.asserted, it drives the WB/WT# signal low, forcing processor B to store the cache line in the S state in its L1 cache. Both the L1 and L2 caches within each processor complex now have a copy of the same line, each with its state bits indicating that the data is shared. Any write by processor complex A or B to a location within the cache line will therefore result in a write-through, ensuring that the write can be detected by other processor complexes when the write is transferred to memory.

Scenario Three

Figure 4-7 illustrates the third scenario.

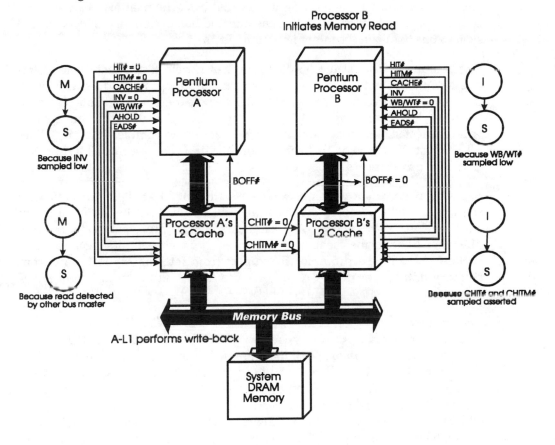

Figure 4-7. Read Scenario Three

The Initial Cache State. Assume that after having read a line from memory (the line is in the shared state in the L1 cache and the exclusive state in the L2 cache) and having written to the cache line one time (the line moves from the shared to the exclusive state in L1 and from the exclusive to the modified state in L2), processor A initiates a second write to the line. Processor A updates the L1 cache line and transitions the line to the modified state and no external bus cycle is generated. Note that the L2 cache state bits for the cache line already indicate that the line has been modified. When processor B performs a read from a line that processor complex A has a copy of, the following actions will be taken.

The Processor B Cache Miss. Processor B experiences a miss on its L1 cache and initiates an cache line-fill on its external bus. The memory read also encounters a read miss on the L2 cache and the bus cycle is transferred to the system bus to obtain the target line from memory.

The Snoop By Processor Complex A. When it detects the cache line-fill request on the system bus, processor A's L2 cache snoops the address driven by processor B's L2 cache. Processor A's L2 cache experiences a snoop hit on a modified line. Processor A's L2 cache determines that the other bus master will read a stale line from memory if it is permitted to complete the cache line-fill request. To prevent this, processor A's L2 cache asserts CHITM# and CHIT# to processor B's L2 cache.

BackOff of Processor B Complex. The assertion of CHITM# instructs processor B's L2 cache to abort the cache line-fill request on the system bus. In addition, processor B's L2 cache asserts BOFF# to processor B, forcing the processor to abort the cache line-fill request in progress on its local bus. The backoff prevents the processor B complex from fetching the stale line from memory until the processor A complex has deposited the fresh line in memory.

The Inquire Cycle to Processor A. Processor complex A's L2 cache must determine if processor A's L1 cache has more recent data than it does. An inquire cycle to processor A is initiated to determine if processor A's L1 cache has the most recently updated copy of the line. AHOLD is asserted and the memory read address generated by processor B's L2 cache is passed to processor A for snooping. EADS# is asserted, instructing processor A to snoop the address. INV is deasserted, indicating that the cache line should remain valid in the event of a snoop hit (because processor B's L2 cache is only going to read the line from memory, not modify it). The snoop on processor A's L1 cache results in a snoop hit on a modified line. To indicate this, processor A asserts HIT# and HITM# to inform the L2 cache that the inquire cycle resulted in a hit to a modified line and that the processor will perform a write-back operation to deposit the fresh line in memory. Upon completion of the write-back, the processor transitions the state of the L1 line from M to S (because another bus master will read the line and may place it in its own local cache).

Processor A Performs the Write-Back. When Processor A detects a hit to the modified cache line, it knows that it has the most recent data. As a result, the processor performs a write-back cycle to update memory. The L2 cache updates its cache line so that it no longer contains stale data and transitions the line from the M to the S state. The burst write-back operation is passed on to the system bus to update memory.

BackOff Removed From Processor B Complex and Its Cache-Fill Completes. Following completion of the write-back, processor A's L2 cache deasserts CHIT# and CHITM#, releasing processor complex B to restart the cache line-fill operation and fetch the fresh line from memory. Processor B's L2 cache deasserts BOFF# to processor B. In response, processor B restarts the cache line-fill operation and obtains the line from memory. When the cache line-fill request is reinitiated on the system bus by processor B's L2 cache, the L2 cache within processor complex A snoops the address and experiences a snoop hit to a shared line. In response, processor A's L2 cache asserts CHIT# but not CHITM#. This informs processor B's L2 cache that another cache in the system has a copy of the target line currently being read from memory by processor B's L2 cache. When the line is stored in processor B's L2 cache, it is therefore stored in the S state. In addition, processor B's L2 cache drives the WB/WT# signal low, forcing processor B to store the cache line in the S state in its L1 cache. The L1 and L2 caches within both processor complexes now have a copy of the same line, all marked as shared.

Write by Processor B to a Line Present in Processor A's Cache

The action taken by each processor complex depends on:

- The current state of its copy of the target cache line.
- The type of transfer in progress.
- The state of the snoop-related signals asserted by processor complex A.

The following four scenarios assume that processor complex A currently has a copy of the line that processor complex B is writing to in system memory.

Each scenario represents one of the four possible states in which the target cache line within complex A can be stored when processor B initiates a memory write. These states are listed in table 4-3.

Table 4-3. Initial State of Cache Lines

Scenario	Process Complex A Status	A's L2 Cache Line State	A's L1 Cache Line State
1	Initial cache line state after reading target line from system memory.	E	S
2	Cache line state upon completion of 1st internal write to target line after it's placed in the L1 cache.	M	E
3	Cache line state after 2nd and subsequent internal writes to target line by the processor.	M	M
4	Cache line state after another bus master reads from target line.	S	S

Scenario One

Figure 4-8 illustrates the state of the four caches before and after a write-miss is experienced by processor complex B.

The Initial Cache State. Assume that processor A has just completed a read from a cacheable memory location for the first time. Following completion of the cache line-fill request, the processor A L1 cache will have a copy of the target line. The state bits associated with the cache line will be set to the S state, consistent with the Pentium processor's write-once policy. The copy of the line in processor A's L2 cache will have its state bits set to the E state, indicating that processor complex A is not aware of any other caches with a copy of the line.

Processor B Experiences a Double Write Miss. Processor B initiates an internal memory write, experiences a miss in its L1 cache, and initiates a write bus cycle to external memory. Processor B's L2 also experiences a cache miss and initiates a memory write bus cycle on the system bus to update memory.

Chapter 4: Multiple Processors and the MESI Model

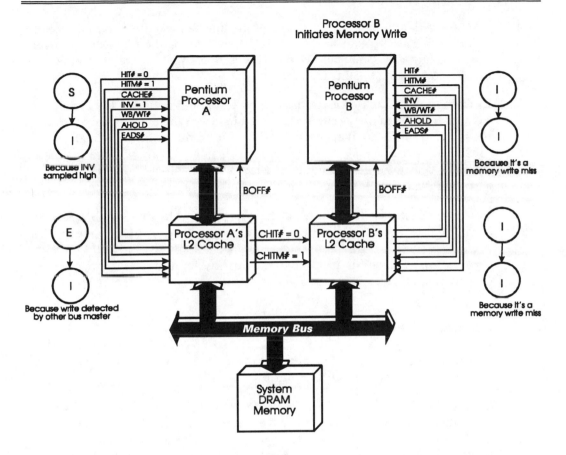

Figure 4-8. Write Scenario One

Processor A's L2 Cache Snoops the Memory Write In Progress. Processor complex A's L2 cache detects the memory write bus cycle and snoops the target line address. The snoop operation results in a hit to an exclusive cache line. This tells processor A's L2 cache that processor B's L2 cache is about to update a line in memory that it has a copy of. Processor A's L2 cache will then contain a stale line. Therefore, processor A's L2 cache transitions its cache line state from E to I, causing the entry to be invalidated.

The Inquire Cycle to Processor A. Processor A's L2 cache assumes that processor A's L1 cache may also have a copy of the target line, so it directs Pentium processor A to snoop the address. It asserts AHOLD and passes the address to the processor's local address bus. Once the address is stable, processor A's L2 cache asserts EADS#, instructing the processor to snoop the address to determine if it has a copy of the line being written to by processor complex B. The L2 cache also asserts INV, instructing the processor to invalidate the line if a snoop hit occurs. This is necessary because the other bus master is changing the line in memory.

In this example, the processor has a copy of the target line in the S state and invalidates the entry by setting the state bits to I. When the processor detects the internal snoop hit, it also asserts HIT#, informing the L2 cache that a snoop hit has occurred to a clean (non-modified) line. No action is taken by the L2 cache as a result of the snoop hit. The L2 cache has already directed the processor to invalidate the cache line in the event of a snoop hit.

Processor Complex B Completes the Memory Write Bus Cycle. Processor complex B completes the write operation to memory and terminates its bus cycle. If processor B's L2 cache supports allocate-on-write, it would then perform a cache Line-fill from the line just written into system memory, otherwise no further action is required.

Scenario Two

Figure 4-9 illustrates the state of the four caches before and after a write-miss is experienced by processor complex B.

The Initial Cache State. Assume that after having read a line into its L1 cache from memory processor A performs a write to the line. When the write operation occurs, the processor updates the L1 cache line and also initiates a write bus cycle (write-through is forced because the line was stored in L1 in the S state). Processor A's L2 cache interrogates its cache directory and experiences a hit on the line in the E state. The L2 cache updates the cache line and transitions the state bits to the M state. The L2 cache also sets the WB/WT# line high, causing processor A's L1 cache to transition the line's state bits to the E state. Assume that processor B then initiates a write to a location within the same line.

Processor Complex B's Double Write Miss. Processor B interrogates its L1 cache directory and fails to find a copy of the target line. As a result, processor B initiates a memory write bus cycle. This bus cycle is detected by processor B's L2 cache which also experiences a write miss. Processor B's L2 cache initiates a memory write bus cycle to update system memory.

Chapter 4: Multiple Processors and the MESI Model

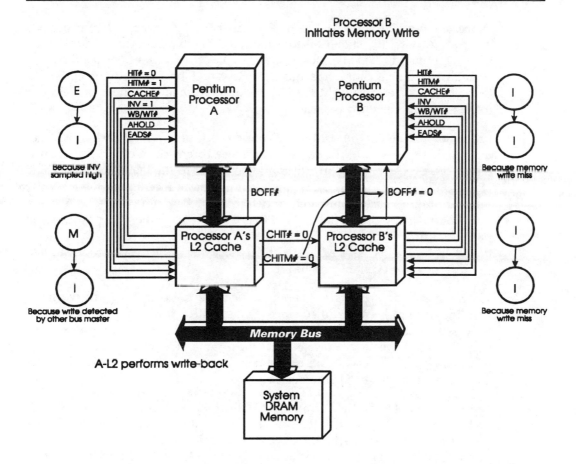

Figure 4-9. Write Scenario Two

Processor Complex A Snoops the Memory Write. When processor complex A detects the memory write bus cycle on the system bus, its L2 cache snoops the line address and experiences a write hit on a modified line. If it permits processor B's L2 cache to complete the memory write, a stale line in memory will be updated.

Consequently, processor complex A must back off processor complex B and deposit the fresh line in memory before allowing complex B to finish the write transaction.

Processor A's L2 Cache Backs Off Processor B's L2 Cache. When processor complex A detects a snoop hit to a modified line, its L2 cache controller asserts CHIT# and CHITM#. This causes complex B to backoff (suspend its bus cycle) until the memory line has been updated by processor complex A. Complex B's L2 cache activates its BOFF# output, forcing Pentium processor B to suspend the current bus cycle.

Processor A Snoops the Address. Processor complex A's L2 cache must determine if processor A's L1 cache has a more recent copy of the line than it has. If the processor has performed another write to the line since the L2 line was modified, then the L1 cache line would be more recent than the L2 cache line. An inquire cycle is initiated to determine if Pentium processor A has a more recent copy of the line. AHOLD is asserted and the snoop address is passed to processor A. EADS# is asserted, instructing processor A to snoop the address. INV is asserted, instructing processor A's L1 cache to invalidate the L1 line in the event of a cache hit.

The internal snoop results in a snoop hit on a clean line in the exclusive state. The line has not been modified since it was written through to the L2 cache. Processor A asserts HIT#, informing its L2 cache that it was a hit on a clean line. The L2 cache now knows it has a copy of the most recent data. The state of the internal data cache line transitions from E to I (because the other bus master will alter the line in memory, rendering the L1 cache line stale).

Processor A's L2 Cache Performs the Write-Back. When Complex A's L2 cache detects HIT# asserted, it knows that it has the most recent data. The L2 cache then performs a write-back cycle to deposit the fresh line in memory so that it may be updated by the other bus master when the backoff is removed. Processor A's L2 cache line's state bits are updated from M to I (because its cache line will also contain stale data after processor complex B finishes its write). Upon completion of the write-back, memory contains the fresh line and the memory write update by the processor B L2 cache can be permitted.

BackOff Is Removed By Processor A's L2 Cache and Processor Complex B Completes the Memory Update. Following completion of the write-back, processor A's L2 cache deasserts CHITM#, releasing processor complex B to reinitiate the write operation to update the line in memory. In response to the deassertion of CHITM#, processor B's L2 cache deasserts BOFF# to processor B. Processor B then restarts the memory write bus cycle. When the bus cycle reappears on the system bus, the L2 cache within processor complex A snoops the address and detects a snoop miss (because the line was marked invalid after completion of the write-back). The write bus cycle completes normally to system memory.

If the processor B L2 cache supports allocate-on-write, it would then perform a cache line-fill to fetch the line just updated in memory and would deposit it in its L2 cache.

Scenario Three

Figure 4-10 illustrates the state of the four caches before and after a write-miss is experienced by processor complex B.

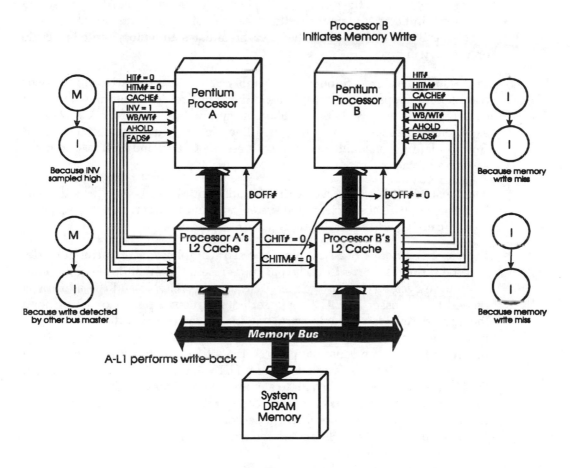

Figure 4-10. Write Scenario Three

The Initial Cache State. Assume that processor A reads a line into its L1 and L2 caches. Initially, the line is stored in the S state in L1 and the E state in L2. The processor then performs a write to a location within the line. The L1 line is updated and the data written through to the L2 cache. The L2 cache updates its copy of the line and changes it from the E to the M state. In addition, the L2 cache gives the L1 cache permission to change it copy of the line from the S to the E state (by setting WB/WT# high). When processor A then performs another write to the line, the L1 line is updated and changed from the E to the M state. The line is not written through to the L2 cache. The line is now in the M state in processor A's L1 and L2 caches.

Processor B Experiences a Double Write Miss. Processor B initiates an internal memory write to the same line. The line isn't present in its L1 cache, so the processor initiates a memory write bus cycle. Since the line isn't present in processor B's L2 cache, either, the L2 cache initiates a memory write bus cycle on the system bus.

Processor Complex A Snoops the Memory Write. The L2 cache in processor complex A snoops the memory write initiated by processor complex B when it detects the memory write bus cycle on the system bus. Processor A's L2 cache experiences a snoop hit on a modified line. To prevent processor complex B from updating a stale line in memory, it asserts CHIT# and CHITM# to processor B's L2 cache.

The BackOff. The assertion of CHITM# causes processor B's L2 cache to abort its memory write bus cycle on the system bus and to assert BOFF# to processor B# (causing it to abort its bus cycle as well).

Processor A Snoops the Address. Processor complex A's L2 cache must determine if processor A's L1 cache has more recent data than it has. It initiates an inquire cycle back to processor A. It asserts AHOLD and the address is passed to processor A. EADS# is asserted, instructing processor A to snoop the address. INV is asserted, instructing the processor to invalidate its L1 line in the event of a snoop hit. The internal snoop results in a snoop hit on a modified line. This means that processor A's L1 cache has the latest copy of the line. The processor asserts HIT# and HITM#, informing the L2 cache that the inquire cycle resulted in a hit to a modified line. This tells the L2 cache that processor A's L1 cache has the latest copy of the line and will therefore perform a write-back to memory. The assertion of INV to the processor tells the L1 cache to invalidate the line when the write-back has been completed.

Processor A's L1 Cache Performs the Write-Back. Processor A performs a write-back cycle to deposit the fresh line in memory to be updated by processor complex B when the backoff is removed. Processor A's L2 cache invalidates its copy of the line as well.

Processor A's L2 Cache Removes Backoff and the Processor B Write Is Reinitiated. Following completion of the write-back, processor A's L2 cache deasserts CHITM#, releasing processor complex B to reinitiate the memory write operation to update the line in system memory. When complex B's L2 cache detects the deassertion of CHITM#, it in turn deasserts the BOFF# signal to processor B. Processor B then reinitiates the memory write bus cycle. When the bus cycle reappears on the system bus, the L2 cache within processor complex A snoops the address again and experiences a snoop miss this time (because the line was invalidated at the completion of the write-back operation). The memory write is allowed to complete normally.

Scenario Four

Figure 4-11 illustrates the state of the four caches before and after a write-hit is experienced by processor complex B.

The Initial Cache State. In this example, assume that both processor complexes contain identical copies of the same line of information. This means that all instances of the target line are stored in the S state. Processor complex B then performs a write to the target line.

The Write Hit and Write-through. Processor B experiences a write hit in its L1 cache. It updates the line and initiates a memory write bus cycle on its bus (because the line is marked shared). Processor B's L2 cache also experiences a write hit. It updates the line and initiates a memory write bus cycle on the system bus (because the line is marked shared). It marks the L2 line as exclusive (because it knows that any other cache that snoops the memory write will invalidate its copy of the line). The processor B L2 cache instructs the L1 cache to keeps its copy of the line in the S state (because the L1 and L2 lines are identical and the L2 cache wants to be informed when the processor makes any modifications to the L1 line).

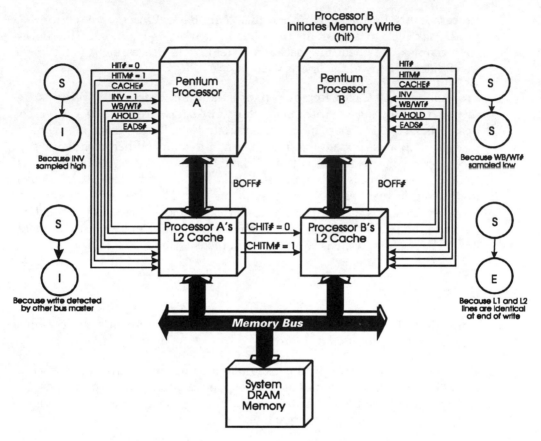

Figure 4-11. Write Scenario Four

Processor A's L2 Cache Snoops the Memory Write. When processor complex A detects the write transaction on the system bus, it experiences a snoop hit to a shared line. Because the other bus master is about to update the line in memory, the processor A L2 cache invalidates the line. In addition, it generates a snoop to processor A (AHOLD and EADS# asserted and the snoop address driven back to processor A) and instructs it to invalidate the line (INV asserted) in L1 in the event of a snoop hit.

The L1 cache experiences a snoop hit on a shared line and invalidates the line. It also asserts HIT# to inform the L2 cache that the snoop resulted in a snoop hit to a clean line.

Processor B's L2 cache completes the update of the memory line. The line is now resident in processor B's caches, but has been cast out of processor A's caches. It is in the S state in processor B's L1 cache and in the E state in its L2 cache.

Summary of L1 MESI State Changes

Table 4-4 describes the L1 cache line state transitions that can occur when an internal memory read request is issued to the L1 cache.

Table 4-4. L1 Cache State Changes During Memory Reads

Present State	Pin Activity	Next State	Description
M	n/a	M	**Read Hit.** Data is provided to processor core by L1 cache. No bus cycle is generated.
E	n/a	E	**Read Hit.** Data is provided to processor core by L1 cache. No bus cycle is generated.
S	n/a	S	**Read Hit.** Data is provided to processor core by L1 cache. No bus cycle is generated.
I	CACHE#, KEN#, PWT low and WB/WT# high	E	**Read Miss.** Data item does not exist in L1 cache. A cache line-fill request is initiated by the Pentium processor. This state transition will happen if WB/WT# is sampled high with first BRDY# or NA#. The L2 cache is either write-through or not present.
I	CACHE#, KEN# low, (WB/WT# low or PWT high)	S	**Read Miss.** Same as previous read miss case except that WB/WT# is sampled low with first BRDY# or NA#. The L2 cache is present and is a write-back cache.
I	CACHE# or KEN# high	I	**Read Miss.** If cache is not asserted by the processor, internal caching is disabled or the target memory location is considered non-cacheable by the paging unit. If CACHE# is asserted by the processor, but KEN# is sampled deasserted by the processor, external logic considers the target address to be non-cacheable. In either case, external logic will only return the byte or bytes requested by the processor, not the entire line.

Table 4-5 describes the L1 cache line state transitions that can occur when an internal memory write is issued to the L1 cache.

Table 4-5. L1 Cache State Changes During Memory writes

Present State	Pin Activity	Next State	Description
M	n/a	M	**Write Hit.** Update L1 cache line. No bus cycle generated to update the L2 cache or memory.
E	n/a	M	**Write Hit.** Update L1 cache line. No bus cycle generated and line is now marked modified.
S	PWT low and WB/WT# high	E	**Write Hit.** L1 cache updated with write data item. A write-through cycle is generated on bus (due to S state) to update memory and/or invalidate contents of other caches. The L2 cache gives L1 permission (high on WB/WT#) to change the L1 state to exclusive. The state transition occurs after the write-through cycle completes on the bus (with the last BRDY#). The processor has deasserted PWT, instructing the L2 cache to use a write-back policy.
S	PWT, WB/WT# low	S	**Write Hit.** Same as above case of write to S-state line except that WB/WT# is sampled low, telling the L1 cache to keep line in the shared state.
S	PWT high	S	**Write Hit.** Same as above cases of writes to S-state lines except that this is a write hit to a line in a write-through page. The state of the WB/WT# pin is ignored.
I	n/a	I	**Write Miss.** A write-through cycle is generated on the bus to update external memory. No cache line-fill performed.

Table 4-6 describes the L1 cache line state changes when the processor is snooping a memory read (INV = 0) or write (INV = 1) initiated by another bus master.

Chapter 4: Multiple Processors and the MESI Model

Table 4-6. L1 Cache State Changes During Read or Write Snoop

Present MESI State	Next State (When INV=1)	Next State (When INV=0)	Description
M	I	S	Snoop results in a **snoop hit to a modified line**. The processor asserts HIT# and HITM#. Processor initiates a write-back to deposit the line in memory for the other bus master to read or update. If the bus master is performing a read, INV is deasserted and the line is changed from the M state to the S state after the write-back. If the bus master is performing a write, INV is asserted and the line is changed from the M state to the I state after the write-back.
E	I	S	Snoop results in a **snoop hit to clean line** in exclusive state. The processor asserts HIT#. If the bus master is performing a read, INV is deasserted and the line is changed from the E state to the S state. If the bus master is performing a write, INV is asserted and the line is changed from the E state to the I state. No bus cycle is initiated.
S	I	S	Snoop results in a **snoop hit to a clean line** in the shared state. If the bus master is performing a read, INV is deasserted and the line remains in the S state. If the bus master is performing a write, INV is asserted and the line is changed from the S state to the I state. No bus cycle is initiated.
I	I	I	Line isn't present in the L1 cache. The snoop results in a **snoop miss**. Neither HIT# nor HITM# is asserted by the processor.

Chapter 5

The Previous Chapter

The previous chapter discussed the Pentium processor's implementation of the MESI protocol, including both single and multiple processor implementations.

This Chapter

This chapter details the input and output signals used by the Pentium processor to communicate with external devices.

The Next Chapter

The next chapter explores the instruction cache and the Pentium processor's instruction pipeline.

Introduction to the Pentium Processor Signals

This chapter discusses the functional signal groups defined by the Pentium processor. Several new signals have been added to the Pentium processor when compared with the 486 microprocessor. However, the Pentium processor has many of the same signals used in the 486 and earlier x86 microprocessors. Some of the signals however, have slightly different functionality. Additionally, some signals that existed in the 486 have been eliminated. Figure 5-1 shows all of the Pentium processor's input and output signals.

Table 5-2 lists the signals that are functionally the same in both the 486 and Pentium processor, while table 5-3 shows signals that exist in both the 486 and Pentium processor but whose functionality differs in some manner.

Pentium Processor System Architecture

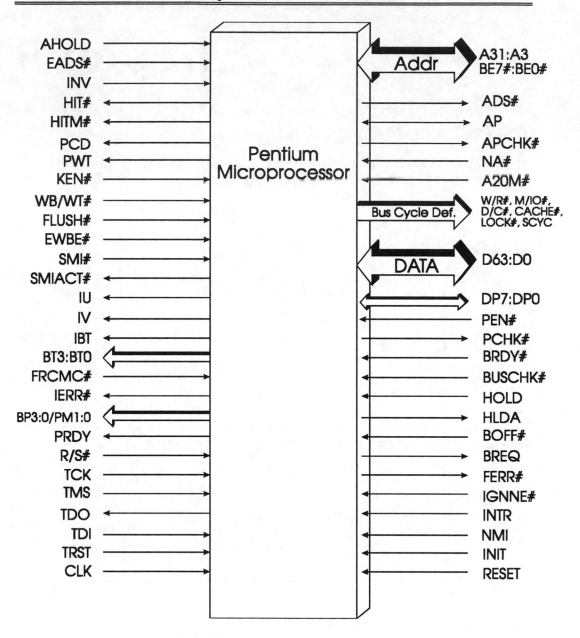

Figure 5-1. The Pentium Processor Pinouts

Table 5-4 lists the signals that are new to the Pentium processor. Note also that several signals used by the 486 no longer exist on the Pentium processor. These signals are listed in table 5-1.

Table 5-1. 486 Signals Not Used by the Pentium Processor

Signals Removed	The Result in Pentium Processor Systems
A2	The Pentium processor outputs only A31:A3. Address line A2 must be decoded from BE7#:BE0#.
BS8# and BS16#	Device size lines (BS8# and BS16#) are not implemented with the Pentium processor. All additional cycles and data bus steering required when communicating with devices smaller than 64-bits must be handled by external logic.
BLAST#	The Burst Last (BLAST#) output has been replaced by the CACHE# output to specify that a burst bus cycle is running. The 486 indicates that a burst cycle is in progress by deasserting BLAST#. The only burst transfers supported by the Pentium processor are those involving cache line transfers (32-bytes), which are indicated by CACHE# being asserted.
PLOCK#	PLOCK# is no longer needed with the Pentium processor because the data bus width is 64-bits. Sixty-four bit operations requiring two PLOCK# cycles to perform on the 486 require can complete is a single Pentium cycle.
RDY#	The Pentium processor uses only the BRDY# signal. All cache transfers use the burst protocol in the Pentium process, whereas, the 486 can perform cache Line-fills from memory that does not support burst transfers.

Table 5-2. Signals Shared by the 486 and Pentium Processors That Have Identical Functionality

Pentium and 486 Signal Having Same Functionality		
CLK	D31:D0	AHOLD
ADS#	DP3:DP0	HOLD
W/R#	A20M#	HLDA

Pentium and 486 Signal Having Same Functionality		
D/C#	INTR	BREQ#
M/IO#	NMI	FERR#
LOCK#	RESET	IGNNE#

Table 5-3. Signals Common to Both the Pentium Processor and 486 Whose Related Functionality has Changed with the Pentium Processor

Common Signals	Pentium Processor — 486 Description
A31:A3	A31:A3 are driven only once during a cache Line-fill — the 486 drives a new address for each transfer during a burst bus cycle.
BE3#:BE0#	BE3#:BE0# are driven only once during a cache Line-fill — the 486 drives new byte enables for each transfer during the burst. Note also that the Pentium processor asserts one or more of the byte enable lines only when one or more bytes are being addressed within the lower doubleword of an even quadword memory block, whereas, the 486 asserts one or more of the byte enable lines for every address.
EADS#	EADS# is not sampled while the processor is driving an address and invalidations are not allowed during each clock cycle — the 486 samples EADS# during each clock cycle, permitting invalidations during each clock.
KEN#	KEN# is sampled once by the Pentium processor during a cache Line-fill — the 486 samples KEN# twice during a cache Line-fill.
FLUSH#	The FLUSH# input is implemented as an interrupt with the Pentium processor and is recognized on the falling edge — the 486 recognizes FLUSH# when asserted low, and once setup and hold requirements have been satisfied, is recognized immediately.

Common Signals	Pentium Processor — 486 Description
BOFF#	When BOFF# is released the Pentium processor starts the bus cycle that was aborted from the beginning — the 486 restarts the aborted bus cycle from the point at which it was aborted.
PCHK#	The data parity checking has been extended in the Pentium processor. When a parity error is detected PCHK# goes active like the 486, but if PEN# is also asserted, the address and transaction type of the bus cycle in which the parity error was detected are stored in the new Machine Check Registers inside the Pentium processor. Additionally, if the MCE bit in the new CR4 register is set, a machine check exception is generated — the 486 has no machine check functionality when parity is detected, parity errors result only in the PCHK# signal being asserted.
BRDY#	The BRDY# signal indicates that the external device is ready to transfer data — the 486 BRDY# signal was used by devices that were capable of performing burst transfers. Those unable to perform burst transfers used the RDY# signal.

Table 5-4. The Pentium Processor's New Signals

AP	D63:D32	IERR#	PEN#
APCHK#	DP7:DP4	INIT	PRDY
BE7#:BE4#	EWBE#	INV	R/S#
BT3:BT0	FRCMC#	IU	SCYC
BUSCHK#	HIT#	IV	SMI
BP3:0/PM1:0	HITM#	JTAG Signals	SMIACT#
CACHE#	IBT	NA#	WB/WT#

Pentium Processor System Architecture

The Address Bus

The Pentium processor address bus consists of two sets of signal lines:

- the address bus proper, consisting of 29 signal lines designated A31:A3.
- the Byte Enable bus, consisting of the 8 signal lines designated BE7#:BE0#.

As demonstrated later in this chapter, the Pentium processor uses the address bus, A31:A3, to identify a group of eight locations, known as a quadword. The address identifies locations within memory or I/O space depending on the state of the M/IO# signal. Also, like the 486 and i386 microprocessors, the ADS# (Address Status) output goes active during address time (T1) when the address is output.

The Pentium processor uses the byte enable lines to identify one or more of the eight locations with which it actually wishes to perform a data transfer.

Like the Intel i386 and 486, the Pentium processor actually generates 32-bit addresses internally. A 32-bit address bus gives the processor the ability to address any one of 4GB (4 gigabytes, or 4096 megabytes) of memory locations. When the processor drives the address on the address bus, the three least-significant address bits, A2:A0, are stripped off. This is because these three address outputs don't physically exist on a Pentium processor.

When I/O locations are being addressed, one of 64KB individual I/O locations is identified with A15:A3. Address lines A31:A16 are driven to zeros during I/O addressing. The three least-significant address bits, A2:A0, are stripped off just as they are while addressing memory locations.

When designing a Pentium processor based system, one should always assume that whenever the processor outputs an address during a bus cycle, A2:A0 are always 0. Table 5-5 illustrates a number of addresses being output by the Pentium processor. Remember that address bits 0, 1 and 2 are stripped off during address output and are always assumed to be "0".

The result is that the Pentium processor is only capable of outputting every eighth address. It is physically incapable of addressing any of the intervening addresses. When the Pentium processor outputs an address, it is identifying a group of eight locations, called a quadword, starting at the address presented on the address bus.

Chapter 5: Pentium Signal Interface

In addition to identifying the quadword address via A31:A3, the processor also asserts one or more of its byte enable outputs, thereby indicating which of the eight locations it wants to communicate with during the current bus cycle. Asserting a byte enable line also identifies which of the Pentium processor's eight data paths will be used to communicate with the identified location(s) in the quadword.

The BE0# line is associated with the first location in the group of eight (quadword) and with the lowest data path, D7:D0. BE1# is associated with the second location in the quadword and with the second data path, D15:D8. BE2# is associated with the third location in the quadword and with the third data path, D23:D16. BE3# is associated with the fourth location in the quadword and with the fourth data path, D31:D24. BE4# is associated with the fifth location in the quadword and the fifth data path, etc. Table 5-6 illustrates this relationship.

Table 5-5. Example Addresses Output by a Pentium Processor

Address to be Output (h) (A31:A0)	Address Placed on Address Bus (h) (A31:A3 - A2:A0 presumed to be zero)
00000000	00000000
00000001	00000000
00000002	00000000
00000003	00000000
00000004	00000000
00000005	00000000
00000006	00000000
00000007	00000000
00000008	00000008
00000009	00000008
0000000A	00000008
0000000B	00000008
0000000C	00000008
0000000D	00000008
0000000E	00000008
0000000F	00000008
00000010	00000010

Address to be Output (h) (A31:A0)	Address Placed on Address Bus (h) (A31:A3 - A2:A0 presumed to be zero)
00000011	00000010
00000012	00000010
00000013	00000010
00000014	00000010
00000015	00000010
00000016	00000010
00000017	00000010

Table 5-6. Relationship of Pentium Processor Byte Enables, Data Paths and Locations in the Currently-Addressed Quadword

Byte Enable	Data Path Used	Location Addressed Within Quadword
BE0#	D7:D0	first
BE1#	D15:D8	second
BE2#	D23:D16	third
BE3#	D31:D24	fourth
BE4#	D39:D32	fifth
BE5#	D47:D40	sixth
BE6#	D55:D48	seventh
BE7#	D63:D56	eighth

Table 5-7 illustrates several example addresses and a description of how they are interpreted by external logic.

In the first example, the processor is identifying the quadword starting at location 00001000h. By asserting the BE0#, the processor indicates its intention to communicate with the first location in the quadword using the first data path (D7:D0).

Chapter 5: Pentium Signal Interface

Table 5-7. Pentium Processor Addressing Examples

Address(h) (A31:A3)	BE7#	BE6#	BE5#	BE4#	BE3#	BE2#	BE1#	BE0#	Location(s) addressed (h)	Data Path
00001000	1	1	1	1	1	1	1	0	00001000	0
FA026500	0	0	1	1	1	1	1	1	FA026506, FA026507	6,7
00000108	0	0	0	0	0	0	0	0	00000108-0000010F	0-7
01AD0F08	1	0	0	1	1	1	1	1	01AD0F0D, 1AD0F0E	5, 6

In the second example, the processor is identifying the quadword starting at location FA026500h. By asserting the BE6# and BE7#, the processor indicates its intention to communicate with the seventh and eighth locations in the quadword using the seventh (D55:D48) and eighth (D63:D56) data paths.

In the third example, the processor is identifying the quadword starting at location 00000108h. By asserting all eight of the byte enable outputs, the processor indicates its intention to communicate with all eight locations in the quadword using all eight data paths.

In the fourth example, the processor is identifying the quadword starting at location 01AD0F08h. By asserting the BE5# and BE6#, the processor indicates its intention to communicate with the sixth and seventh locations in the quadword using the sixth (D47:D40) and seventh (D55:D48) data paths.

The Pentium processor is capable of performing 8-, 16-, 24-, 32-, and 64-bit transfers. When asserting multiple byte enables, it may only assert adjacent byte enables.

Table 5-8. Example Instructions and Resultant Addresses

Instruction	Address h	BE7#	BE6#	BE5#	BE4#	BE3#	BE2#	BE1#	BE0#	Transfer Type
MOV AL,[0100]	00000100	1	1	1	1	1	1	1	0	8-bit transfer
MOV AL,[0101]	00000100	1	1	1	1	1	1	0	1	8-bit transfer
MOV BL,[0102]	00000100	1	1	1	1	1	0	1	1	8-bit transfer
MOV AH,[0103]	00000100	1	1	1	1	0	1	1	1	8-bit transfer
MOV AL,[0104]	00000100	1	1	1	0	1	1	1	1	8-bit transfer
MOV AL,[0105]	00000100	1	1	0	1	1	1	1	1	8-bit transfer
MOV BL,[0106]	00000100	1	0	1	1	1	1	1	1	8-bit transfer
MOV AH,[0107]	00000100	0	1	1	1	1	1	1	1	8-bit transfer
MOV AX,[0100]	00000100	1	1	1	1	1	1	0	0	16-bit transfer
MOV AX,[0102]	00000100	1	1	1	1	0	0	1	1	16-bit transfer

Instruction	Address h	BE7#	BE6#	BE5#	BE4#	BE3#	BE2#	BE1#	BE0#	Transfer Type
MOV AX,[0104]	00000100	1	1	0	0	1	1	1	1	16-bit transfer
MOV AX,[0106]	00000100	0	0	1	1	1	1	1	1	16-bit transfer
MOV EAX,[0100]	00000100	1	1	1	1	0	0	0	0	32-bit transfer

Table 5-8 shows the address and byte enables generated in the bus cycle caused by execution of the indicated instruction. All examples assume that the Data Segment register has 0000h in it and the processor is in real mode.

A20 Mask (A20M#)

A20M# allows the processor to emulate the address wrap-around at the 1MB boundary that occurs on the 8086/8088. This pin should only be asserted by external logic when the microprocessor is in Real Mode. The Pentium microprocessor masks physical address bit 20 (forces it to a zero) before performing a lookup to the internal cache or driving a memory bus cycle onto the buses. For additional information, see MindShare's *ISA System Architecture* book, published by Addison-Wesley.

Misaligned Transfers

A 24-bit transfer may occur if the programmer attempts to perform a transfer that crosses a quadword address boundary. If such an attempt is made, the processor will recognize its inability to address the entire object and run two bus cycles to access the locations specified. As an example, assume the data cache is configured for a write-through policy and the programmer attempts to execute the following instruction (in real mode) with the DS register set to 0000h:

```
MOV [0105],EAX
```

This instructs the Pentium processor to write the four bytes in the 32-bit EAX register to memory starting at location 00000105h (00000105h - 00000108h). Notice that locations 00000105h - 00000107h are in the quadword starting at address location 00000100h and that location 00000108h is in the next quadword starting at location 00000108h. Because it can't address two quadwords at the same time, the processor generates two back-to-back bus cycles.

To do this, the processor writes the most-significant byte in the EAX register to the first location in the quadword which starts at location 00000108h. It must then write the lower three bytes in the EAX register to locations 00000105h - 00000107h in the quadword starting at 00000100h.

During the first bus cycle, the processor identifies the quadword starting at memory location 00000108h along with BE0#, which tells external logic that the processor wants to communicate with the first location in the quadword, but not the upper seven. The most-significant byte in the EAX register is driven out onto the lowest data path, D7:D0, by the processor and is written into memory location 00000108h.

After the first bus cycle has completed, the processor automatically initiates a second bus cycle to address locations 00000105h - 00000107h. The processor places address 00000100h on address lines A32:A3 to specify the quadword (recall that A0, A1 and A2 are stripped off and should be thought of as being all zeros). Since the processor is addressing locations 00000105h - 00000107h, BE5#, BE6# and BE7# are asserted during the first bus cycle. This tells external logic that the processor wants to communicate with the upper three locations in the quadword (00000105h - 00000107h). The least-significant three bytes in the EAX register are driven out onto the upper three data paths by the processor and are written into memory locations 00000105h - 00000107h. This completes the second bus cycle and the execution of the MOV instruction.

The programmer should ensure that when transferring information to and from memory that all accesses are aligned within a quadword boundary. This prevents the processor from having to run two bus cycles to obtain a single data object from memory.

The Data Bus

The Pentium processor has a 64-bit data bus. It is more correct, however, to think of it as having eight 8-bit data paths:

- Data Path 0 is comprised of D7:D0
- Data Path 1 is comprised of D15:D8
- Data Path 2 is comprised of D23:D16
- Data Path 3 is comprised of D31:D24
- Data Path 4 is comprised of D39:D32
- Data Path 5 is comprised of D47:D40
- Data Path 6 is comprised of D55:D48

- Data Path 7 is comprised of D63:D56

Refer to Figure 5-2. Every quadword consists of eight locations and starts at an even address that is an integer multiple of eight. The processor communicates with the first location over Data Path 0 (D7:D0), the second over Data Path 1 (D15:D8), the third over Data Path 2 (D23:D16), the fourth over Data Path 3 (D31:D24), the fifth over Data Path 4 (D39:D32), the sixth over Data Path 5 (D47:D40), the seventh over Data Path 6 (D55:D48), and the eighth over Data Path 7 (D63:D56).

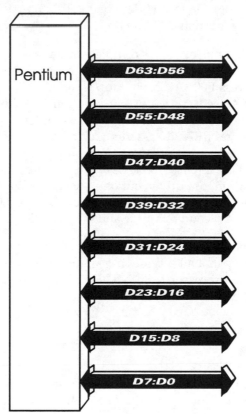

Figure 5-2. The Pentium Processor Data Bus

Chapter 5: Pentium Signal Interface

Communication with 8-,16-,32- and 64-bit Devices

Address Translation

The Pentium processor's address bus consisting of A31:A3 and BE7#:BE0# are designed to address 64-bit devices. The address required by other devices in the PC environment depends on their size as follows:

32-bit devices	A31:A2 and BE3#:BE0#
16-bit devices	A23:A1 and BHE#, BLE# (Bus High, Low Enable)
8-bit devices	A19:A0

Logic external to the processor must translate the address to the form expected by these different size devices as shown in figure 5-3. Notice that 64-bit devices require no translation of the address output by the Pentium processor. This means that no translation is needed for the external cache and main memory subsystem since they are 64-bit devices. The address translation is typically done in the expansion bus control logic for smaller devices that are integrated onto the system board or residing in expansion slots.

Data Bus Steering

External logic must also ensure that information read from and written to 8-, 16-, and 32-bit devices be transferred over the correct data path(s). Since smaller devices such as 8-bit devices connect to the lower data paths only and since the Pentium processor when reading from a device expects data from given locations to be transferred over their respective data paths, data from a specified address location must be directed or steered to the path over which the Pentium processor expects it. Conversely, when the Pentium processor writes data to a device, it assumes that the device is connected to all 8 data paths (that is, a 64-bit device). However, if the device is smaller that 64-bits the data paths used by the Pentium processor may not connect to the smaller devices, and again the data must be steered to the correct path. This is accomplished with a series of transceivers that can pass data from one path to another.

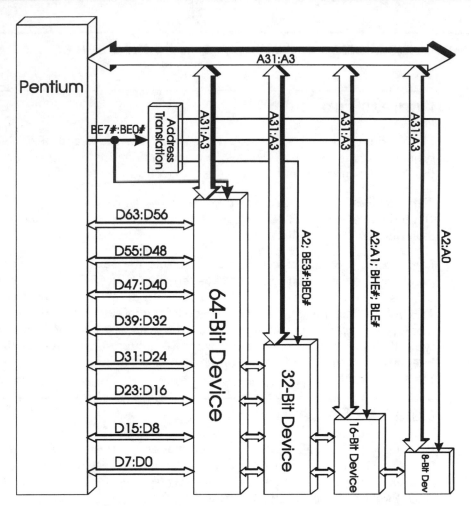

Figure 5-3. Address Translation for 8, 16, and 32-bit Devices

Data Bus Steering for 8-Bit Devices

Figure 5-4 illustrates the data bus steering logic required for 8-bit devices. Notice that an 8-bit device connects only to the lower data path (SD7:SD0). The operation of the data bus steering logic is an extension to the steering logic used in i386 systems. In i386 systems, data must be steered from data path 0 to data paths 1, 2, and 3. The Pentium processor requires additional transceivers to pass data from data path 0 to data paths 4, 5, 6 and 7.

For example, consider the following assembly language instruction:

```
MOV EAX, [D004]
```

Assume the memory access is to an 8-bit memory device. Since the target register (EAX) is a 32-bit register, the processor knows that it must retrieve 4 bytes of information from the starting memory address (D004h within the data segment). To execute this instruction, the processor runs a single memory read bus cycle to get the contents of the four locations starting at memory location D004h (within the data segment) and places them in the EAX register. The processor has no knowledge that the device being accessed is an 8-bit device capable of supplying only one byte of information over data path 0 in a single bus cycle. External logic is responsible for running multiple bus cycles to access the 8-bit device so that the processor's request for four bytes of data is satisfied. In the mean time, the processor waits for the bus cycle to complete, and not until all four bytes have been accessed and placed on the correct data path will BRDY# be sent to the processor, notifying it that valid data is present on its data bus and that the bus cycle can be ended.

The processor starts the bus cycle by placing the quadword address on the address bus (A31:A3) and asserting byte enables BE7#:BE4# to select the upper four bytes within the quadword starting at location D000h. Address translation logic converts the byte enables to A0, A1 and A2 which are required to address the 8-bit device. The byte enable signals also specify the data path over which the Pentium processor expects the data. (data paths 4, 5, 6 and 7).

Bus control logic on the system board samples the byte enables and determines that data paths 4 through 7 are to be used, and also detects that the device being addressed is an 8-bit device. The bus control logic knows that the Pentium processor expects all four bytes to be returned over data paths 4 through 7, but knows that the 8-bit device is not capable of supplying all four bytes at one time.

The First Byte Is Accessed

Address translation logic converts the quadword address output by the Pentium processor to a byte address required by the 8-bit device. Address translation results in address D004h being delivered to the 8-bit bus. The bus control logic detects when the 8-bit device is ready to complete the first transfer and activates the steering logic (Path 0/4 Transceiver) to transfer the contents of data path 0 to data path 4. (See figure 5-4.) The data then is latched into the latch on data path 4 and the steering logic is deasserted.

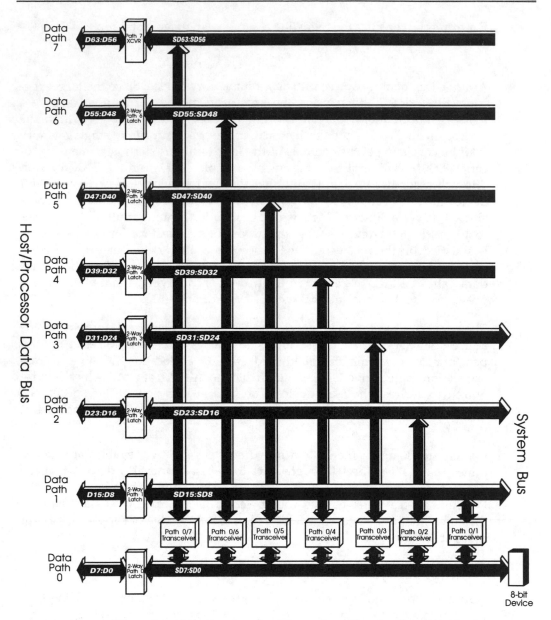

Figure 5-4. Data Bus Steering Transceivers Required by 8-Bit Devices

The Second Byte is Accessed

The bus control logic increments the address to select location D005h from the 8-bit device. Again data is delivered over path 0 and the steering logic is asserted (Path 0/5 Transceiver). When the device indicates that the data on the bus is valid, the bus control logic activates the data path 5 latch, which captures the data from location D005h, and the steering logic is deasserted.

The Third Byte is Accessed

Again the bus control logic increments the address, this time selecting location D006h. The steering logic directs the data accessed from the 8-bit device to data path 6 by activating the path 0/6 transceiver, and when the 8-bit device indicates that data is valid, the bus control logic activates the path 6 latch.

The Fourth Byte is Accessed

Once again the bus control logic increments the address to get the last byte requested by the processor. Location D007h is accessed from the 8-bit device and the steering logic activates the path 0/7 transceiver. When valid data is present on the bus, the bus control logic enables the latches on data paths 4 through 7 to transfer their contents to the processor. When all four bytes of data are present on data paths 4 through 7, the bus control logic asserts the BRDY# signal, telling the processor that valid data is present on the data buses. The processor latches the contents of data paths 4 through 7 and ends the bus cycle.

Data Bus Steering for 16-Bit Devices

Figure 5-5 illustrates the data bus steering transceivers required when the Pentium processor accesses a 16-bit device. Note that the transceivers needed to transfer data from the 16-bit device to the upper data paths include three transceivers that are also required for 8-bit device steering (paths 0/6, 0/4 and 0/2). However, three additional transceivers are required to transfer data from data path one to the upper data paths. These transceivers are for paths one to seven, one to five, and one to three.

When considering the previous example, (MOV EAX,[D004]) an access to a 16-bit device requires only two accesses since each transfer results in two byte being read. Once again the processor expects that to be returned on data paths four through seven and runs a single bus cycle. The bus control logic and data

Pentium Processor System Architecture

bus steering logic sample byte enables four through seven asserted and detect that the access if from a 16-bit device.

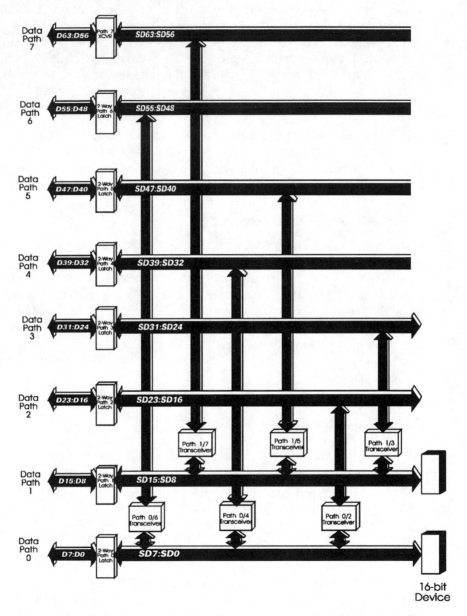

Figure 5-5. Data Bus Steering Transceivers Required by 16-Bit Devices

The First and Second Bytes are Accessed

Address translation logic converts the quadword address output by the Pentium processor to a word address required by the 16-bit device. Address translation results in address D004h and D005h being addressed. (Word address D004h is placed on the 16-bit address bus and both Bus Low Enable (BLE#) and Bus High Enable (BHE#) are asserted, addressing both bytes within the word starting at location D004h.) The 16-bit device delivers the contents of address D004h over data path 0 and the contents of address D005h over data path 1.

The bus control logic activates the data bus steering logic (Path 0/4 and path 1/5 transceivers) to transfer the contents of data paths zero and one to data paths four and five respectively. (See figure 5-5) The data then is latched into the latches on data paths four and five and the steering logic is deasserted.

The Third and Fourth Bytes are Accessed

The bus control logic increments the address to select locations D006h and D007h from the 16-bit device. Again, data is delivered over paths zero and one and the steering logic is asserted (Paths 0/6 and 1/7 Transceiver). When the 16-bit device indicates that the data on the bus is valid, the bus control logic enables the latches on data paths four through seven to output their latched data to be sent to the processor. The bus control logic then asserts BRDY#, telling the processor to latch the contents of data paths four through seven and end the bus cycle.

Data Bus Steering for 32-Bit Devices

Figure 5-6 illustrates the data bus steering transceivers required when the Pentium processor accesses a 32-bit device. Note that the transceivers needed to transfer data from the 32-bit device to the upper data paths includes two transceivers that have already used in the previous examples. The transceiver needed to transfer data between paths zero and four is also used with 8-bit devices and the transceiver needed to transfer data between paths one and five is also used with 16-bit devices. Two additional transceivers are required: one to transfer data from data path two to data path six and the other to transfer data from data path three to seven.

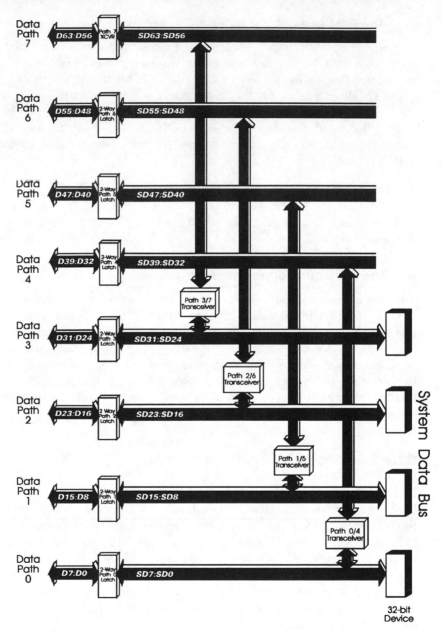

Figure 5-6. Data Bus Steering Transceivers Required by 32-Bit Devices

The 32-bit device is capable of accessing all four bytes within a single bus cycle. However, in the example move instruction, the data accessed from locations D004h through D007h is delivered over data paths zero through three, while the Pentium processor expects the data to be returned over data paths four through seven.

The quadword address output by the Pentium processor is translated into a doubleword address by the address translation logic. This resulting address placed on the 32-bit address bus indicates that the doubleword starting at location D004h is being addressed. Additionally, BE3#:BE0# are all asserted, telling the 32-bit device that all bytes within the doubleword are being requested.

When the bus control logic sees the processor's request for four bytes of data over the four upper data paths, and recognizes that a 32-bit device is responding, it activates the data bus steering logic to transfer all four bytes to the upper paths. The information is delivered over the upper four paths and BRDY# is returned to the processor.

Bus Cycle Control Signals

The Bus Cycle Control signals include those that are both driven and sampled by the Pentium processor during standard single transfer bus cycles and burst bus cycles. These signals are further categorized by function as follows:

- Address Status Output (ADS#)
- Bus Cycle Definition
- LOCK# AND SCYC
- Burst Bus Cycle Control
- Burst Ready Signal (BRDY#)

Address Status Output (ADS#)

At the start of a bus cycle, during "Address Time" (T1), the Pentium processor places the address on the address bus and the bus cycle definition on the control bus. It also activates the Address Status (ADS#) output to indicate that a valid address and bus cycle definition are present on the buses.

Bus Cycle Definition

To read data from or write data to an external location, the Pentium processor bus unit must run a bus cycle. During the bus cycle, the processor indicates the type of bus cycle by placing the proper pattern on the bus cycle definition signal lines. Table 5-9 defines each type of bus cycle and the respective pattern which will be output onto the bus cycle definition lines.

Table 5-9 Pentium Processor Bus Cycle Definition

M/IO#	D/C#	W/R#	CACHE#	Bus Cycle Type
0	0	0	1	Interrupt Acknowledge
0	0	1	1	Special Cycle
0	1	0	1	I/O Read
0	1	1	1	I/O Write
1	0	0	1	Code (Instruction) Read
1	0	0	0	Code Read (burst Line-fill) *
1	0	1	x	Reserved
1	1	0	1	Memory Data Read
1	1	0	0	Memory Data Read (burst Line-fill)*
1	1	1	1	Memory Data Write
1	1	1	0	Memory Write-back (burst cycle)

* Indicates burst cycle unless KEN# is sampled inactive

Special Cycles

The Pentium processor supports six types of special cycles. Table 5-9 shows the state of the bus cycle definition lines during a special cycle. To determine the type of special cycle being run, byte enable lines BE5#:BE0# must be decoded as shown in table 5-10.

Table 5-10. Special Cycle Decoding

Special Cycle Type	BE5#	BE4#	BE3#	BE2#	BE1#	BE0#
Shutdown	1	1	1	1	1	0
Flush	1	1	1	1	0	1
Halt	1	1	1	0	1	1
Write back	1	1	0	1	1	1
Flush Acknowledge	1	0	1	1	1	1
Branch Trace Message	0	1	1	1	1	1

Shutdown Special Cycle

The Shutdown special cycle in the Pentium processor is a superset of the 486 and earlier Intel processor implementations. Two conditions cause a shutdown cycle to be generated:

- **Triple Fault** - Like the earlier processors, the Pentium processor goes into a shutdown cycle when it encounters a triple fault condition. Specifically, if while handling a double fault exception, another fault is detected, the processor automatically shuts down.
- **Internal Parity Error Detected** - additionally, the Pentium processor goes into a shutdown condition when an internal parity error is detected.

The FLUSH#, SMI#, and R/S# signals are recognized by the Pentium processor during the shutdown state. Note also that the state of the internal caches is unchanged by a shutdown. As a result, modified data is not written back unless the FLUSH# signal is asserted or an inquire cycle is run.

The NMI, INIT, or RESET signals cause the Pentium processor to recover from a shutdown condition.

Flush Special Cycle

The flush special cycle is generated in conjunction with two instructions:

- **INVD** (invalidate instruction) - When the INVD instruction executes, the processor sets all cache entries to the invalid state and runs the flush special cycle. A flush special cycle notifies external logic that all internal cache lines have been invalidated, and tells the L2 cache (if present) that it should also invalidate its cache entries. Note that the INVD instruction does not force modified data to be written back to memory before the cache is invalidated; therefore, modified data is lost.

- **WBINVD** (write-back and invalidate) - The WBINVD instruction causes all modified data to be written back to memory prior the invalidating the cache entries. As each modified line is written back, the Pentium processor invalidates its entry. Once all lines are written back the processor runs a write back special cycle followed by a flush special cycle. This notifies external logic that all lines in the internal caches have been flushed and that the L2 cache should also invalidate its cache entries. (See "Write-back Special Cycle" later in this chapter for additional information.)

Halt Special Cycle

As with earlier Intel X86 processors, the halt special cycle is driven when a HLT instruction is executed. The Pentium processor leaves the halt state when any of the following signals are asserted:

- INTR (when maskable interrupts are enabled)
- NMI
- INIT
- RESET

Write-Back Special Cycle

The write-back special cycle is run after the WBINVD instruction executes to notify external logic that all modified lines in the internal, level one (L1) data cache has been written back to either memory or an external, level two (L2) cache. When all modified lines in the internal data cache have been written back, the write-back special cycle is run, followed by the flush special cycle. This forces the L2 cache to first, write-back its modified data, and second to invalidate all of its cache line entries.

Flush Acknowledge Special Cycle

A Flush-acknowledge special cycle runs in response to the FLUSH# signal being asserted. When the FLUSH# pin is driven low, the Pentium processor writes back all modified lines in the data cache and invalidates all cache line entries in both the code and data caches. The flush acknowledge special cycle is run to tell external logic that all modified lines have been written back and all cache entries invalidated. Note that the flush acknowledge special cycle indicates that the cache entries have been invalidated and not necessarily written back.

Branch Trace Message Special Cycle

The processor generates a Branch Trace Message Special cycle whenever a branch is taken and the trace bit (TR) in TR12 is set to one. The branch trace message cycle notifies external logic (and debugging tools) that the linear address of the branch target routine is being output. When a branch is taken, the IBT (Instruction Branch Taken) signal is driven active along with the following signals:

A31:A3   Bits 31:3 of the linear address

BT2:BT0   Bits 2:0 of the linear address (The normal method of deriving A2:A0 from the byte enable lines cannot be used during branch trace special cycles, because BE5#:BE0# define the type of special cycle being run.)

BT3   High if the default operand size is 32-bits
Low if the default operand size is 16-bits

LOCK# and SCYC

The Pentium processor asserts its LOCK# output while certain back-to-back transfers are in progress. This informs the bus arbitration logic that the external bus is owned by the processor and that it should not be granted to another bus master until the locked sequence has completed. The processor asserts LOCK# when the address and bus cycle definition are output during the initial cycle and it remains active until BRDY# is returned for the last bus cycle in the locked sequence. While LOCK# is asserted the processor ignores its HOLD input.

Locked transfers are typically generated by the processor when a read-modify-write operation is required. During a read-modify-write operation, the processor can read and modify a variable in external memory and be assured that the variable is not accessed by another bus master between the read and the write transfers. Additionally, when a locked transfer causes a misaligned transfer, the Pentium processor asserts a signal called Split Cycle (SCYC). This signal notifies external logic that the locked transfer requires twice the number of bus cycles expected since the access crosses a quadword boundary.

Conditions Causing LOCK#

The processor automatically generates locked transfers during the following types of bus transfers:

- During execution of an XCHG (Exchange) or a CMPXCHG instruction when one of its operands is memory-based.
- When a segment descriptor is read from memory and updated.
- When a page directory or page table entry read and updated.
- During the two interrupt acknowledge bus cycles that are generated in response to an external hardware interrupt request.
- Locked transfers are also generated when the programmer prefixes certain instructions with the LOCK prefix.

Recognition of LOCK#

While LOCK# is asserted, the Pentium processor will honor AHOLD and BOFF#, but not HOLD. In other words, the processor permits snooping, but will only give up control of the buses during a backoff condition. Note that LOCK# is guaranteed to be deasserted for one clock cycle between back-to-back locked sequences.

LOCK# Operation with Cache Enabled

The processor always propagates locked transfers through to the external memory. This is necessary to ensure locked transfers have their intended effect. Consider, for example, the possible problem if a read-modify-write sequence is allowed to complete within the processor's internal cache.

The Problem

Two programs executing on different CPUs that are competing to use the same system resource might implement a shared memory location (semaphore) to check for the availability of and establish ownership of that resource. To acquire ownership of the resource, the programmer must read and test the contents of the shared location to determine resource availability. If the resource is not in use (i.e. semaphore=0), the programmer sets the semaphore to a non-zero value and writes it back to memory. If the resource is in use, the programmer must continue to perform the read and test until the resource becomes available. If both CPUs perform the read and test operation at the same time, resource contention can result if the semaphore is found within the local data cache of both CPUs. Each CPU encounters a read hit to its internal cache, tests the semaphore and detects that the resource is available. Neither programmer has visibility that the other is also attempting to gain ownership of the resource and both determine it is available for their use. As a result, both programmers attempt to simultaneously use the same resource and contention occurs.

The Solution

The Pentium processor invalidates a cache line that is hit during a locked read transfer and runs the bus cycles to external memory. The locked read transfer is not converted into a cache Line-fill request, therefore the subsequent write misses the internal cache and also appears on the external buses. This behavior forces all locked transfers to occur on the external buses. Since only one CPU can own the external bus at a time, two locked transfers cannot be fulfilled simultaneously. The CPU that gains access to the external system buses first gains ownership first.

Note that a locked cycle that hits a modified line causes the processor to perform a write-back and invalidate on the modified line before starting the locked sequence. The LOCK# signal is not asserted during the write-back cycle.

LOCK# and Cache Coherency

To ensure cache coherency the processor must respond to the BOFF# signal during locked transfers. In a multiprocessing environment, if a locked read transfer is started by processor A, processor B must snoop the locked memory read. If processor B detects a snoop hit on a modified line, it asserts its HITM# signal. This causes Processor A's BOFF# signal to be asserted and the bus cycle is terminated without data transfer. Processor B then updates main memory by performing a burst cache write-back cycle. Following the write-back, BOFF# is deasserted and Processor A restarts the locked read transfer.

The processor also responds to external snoops (caused by another master accessing cacheable memory) during locked transfers. Support for external snoops during locked transfers is required when the processor has its own look-through L2 cache. A processor performing a locked transfer may not be able to gain immediate access to main memory (because the bus arbiter may have granted the buses to another bus master that currently has a higher priority). The L2 cache, having received the locked transfer from the processor, must wait for its arbitration grant so it can pass the bus cycle on to main memory. Meanwhile, the L2 cache must continue to snoop the system bus to ensure cache coherency is preserved. If a snoop hit occurs, the L2 cache may have to pass the snoop address on to the processor by asserting AHOLD and EADS#.

If the processor detects a snoop hit to a modified line while waiting for the locked read to complete, it asserts HITM#, causing the bus master to be backed off. Since the processor is currently running a locked read bus cycle, it must complete the read before performing the write-back. Once the locked read is completed, the processor then performs a burst write-back to update main memory , after which HITM# is deasserted (backoff is removed). LOCK remains asserted during both the locked read and write-back cycles. Following the write-back, the processor then performs the locked write bus cycle, thereby ending the locked sequence.

Burst Bus Cycle Control

Table 5-9 shows that all cacheable bus cycles result in burst bus cycles and that no other type of bus cycle is burstable. In short, only cache Line-fill cycles and cache write-back cycles will result in burst bus cycles. During cache Line-fills for either the instruction cache or data cache, the processor will activate the CACHE# bus cycle definition signal. The CACHE# signal notifies external memory that the processor wishes to perform a cache Line-fill, using a burst bus cycle. Despite the Pentium processor's request to perform a burst cache Line-fill, the bus cycle isn't converted to a burst Line-fill until the processor samples the Cache Enable (KEN#) signal asserted, indicating that the memory address is cacheable. The KEN# signal originates at the Non-Cacheable Address (NCA) logic, which is programmed to detect memory addresses that should be designated as non-cacheable.

During cache write-back cycles, the processor also asserts the CACHE# signal. However, KEN# does not have to be sampled active for the burst transfer to take place.

Chapter 5: Pentium Signal Interface

Burst Ready Signal

As with previous Intel processor systems, an external device signals the processor that a bus cycle is complete by activating the ready signal. Unlike the 486 processor, the Pentium processor uses only the Burst Ready (BRDY#) input. BRDY# indicates that the currently addressed device has presented valid data on the data bus pins in response to a read or that the currently addressed device has accepted data from the Pentium processor in response to a write.

Strong Write Ordering - EWBE#

The **External Write Buffer Empty** signal is used to ensure that memory operations occur in order of execution (strong memory ordering). Sometimes cache systems that employ write buffers permit read operations to be ordered ahead of buffered writes, causing bus cycles to be performed out of sequence from the actual execution sequence. The EWBE# signal provides a way to ensure that all buffered writes are completed before executing the next instruction, thus preserving the strong memory ordering.

Cache Control

The Pentium processor implements signal lines to control functions associated with the internal code and data caches. These signals are relevant only when the Pentium processor's internal caches are enabled. During reset, registers inside the Pentium processor are forced to specified values as shown under the "RESET" heading later in this chapter. The operation of the internal caches is determined by the values of the CD and NW bits in CR0. These bits during reset are both set to 1s, causing the internal caches to be disabled. Setting the CD and NW bits to 0s enables the internal caches and places the data cache in the write-back mode. These settings generally provide the highest performance configuration. The cache control signals fall into five groups:

- Cacheability - KEN#
- Data cache MESI state control - WB/WT#
- Flush Control
- Cache coherency (snooping)
- L2 cache control

Cacheability - KEN#

During each memory read bus cycle that misses the internal caches, the KEN# line is sampled by the Pentium processor to determine if the location being read is within cacheable address space. Non-Cacheable Address (NCA) logic is implemented to detect addresses that are designated as non-cacheable. If an address is not cacheable, the KEN# line is driven inactive telling the processor not to perform a cache Line-fill. As a result, a signal read cycle will be performed from the target location and it will not placed in cache memory.

The KEN# signal is sampled along with the first BRDY# or NA#, whichever occurs first.

Data Cache MESI State Control - WB/WT#

At the conclusion of each data cache Line-fill, the Pentium processor's data cache controller sets the MESI state bits for the line that has just been placed in cache. The state in which a cache line is initially stored in the data cache is either exclusive (E) or shared (S) and is controlled by the WB/WT# (Write-back or Write-through) input. When the WB/WT# line is set high the cache line is stored in the E state causing it to behave according to the write-back policy. When the WB/WT# line is set low, the cache line is stored in the S state, causing all writes to be transferred to external memory according to the write-through policy.

The WB/WT# signal is usually driven by the level two (L2) cache controller and is sampled by the processor along with the first BRDY# or NA#, whichever occurs first.

See the chapter entitled "Multiple Processors and the MESI Protocol", for an in-depth discussion of how the WB/WT# signal is typically implemented.

Snoop Control / Response

The snoop related signals consist of:

- AHOLD
- EADS#
- INV

- HIT#
- HITM#

AHOLD (Address Hold). When another bus master is either reading from or writing to memory, the Pentium processor must snoop the address bus to ensure that consistency is maintained between the internal write-back data cache, the read-only code cache, the external L2 cache and main DRAM memory. Since an external look-through cache controller resides between the Pentium processor and the system bus, it must control the snooping process.

The L2 cache must snoop the system address bus to monitor activity to system memory. The Pentium processor may at the same time access the L2 cache to perform a cache Line-fill or a write cycle. Since the Pentium processor might be in the process of reading from or writing to the L2 cache when another bus master accesses main memory, the L2 cache must force the processor to remove its address and prepare to receive a snoop address over its address bus. The L2 cache activates the processor's AHOLD input and the processor in response ceases to drive its address bus. The L2 cache then transfers the memory address from the current bus master from the system bus to the processor's local bus so that the Pentium processor can interrogate its internal cache directories to see if a copy of the address location being accessed by the bus master is contained within either of the internal caches.

Note that AHOLD does not need to be used when the processor connects directly to the system address bus. In other words, systems implemented without L2 caches or systems that use look-aside caches need not use AHOLD. In such systems, the processor will be in the HOLD state after having given up control of the buses to allow another bus master to access memory directly. When in the HOLD state, the processor is not able to run bus cycles and can therefore snoop the buses directly when EADS# is asserted.

EADS# (External Address Strobe). External logic must assert the EADS# signal to tell the processor that a valid address is on its local address bus and to go ahead and snoop it. When snoop goes active, the processor transfers the memory address from the address bus to the cache directories and the lookup takes place.

INV (Invalidate). External logic also drives the INV signal along with EADS# to tell the processor whether to leave the cache line valid or to mark it invalid in case of a snoop hit. The INV signal is generated by external logic to indicate whether the bus master is reading from or writing to a memory location. In general, when the snoop results from a memory read by another bus master, the INV signal is deasserted, causing the cache line to be left in a valid state. When a snoop results from a memory write by another bus master, the INV signal is asserted, resulting in the line being invalidated after it is pushed back.

HIT#. The Pentium processor asserts the HIT# signal when a snoop hit occurs on one of its internal caches. This signal can be used by external logic to notify other processors that have their own local caches, that the information they are reading from memory is shared by another cache in the system.

HITM#. The Pentium processor asserts the Hit Modified Line (HITM#) signal to indicate that a snoop operation has hit to a modified line in cache. This signal notifies external logic that the processor needs to perform a write-back operation.

L2 Cache Control

Two Pentium processor outputs provide a mechanism for controlling the L2 cache. The signal Page Cache Disable (PCD) signal controls cacheability of the L2 cache, while the Page Write-Through (PWT) signal specifies whether the L2 cache should use a write-back or write-through policy for the line being written to.

The state of the PCD pin is depends on several conditions as listed in table 5-11.

Table 5-11. State of the PCD Pin During Memory Accesses

Condition(s)	PCD Source	PCD Pin
Paging disabled	CR0, CD bit = 0	deasserted
	CR0, CD bit = 1	asserted
Paging enabled	CR0, CD bit = 1	asserted
Paging enabled, and CR0, CD bit = 0, when a page directory is being accessed	CR3, PCD bit = 0	deasserted
	CR3, PCD bit = 1	asserted
Paging enabled, and CR0, CD bit = 0, when a page table is being accessed	Page directory entry, PCD bit = 0	deasserted
	Page directory entry, PCD bit = 1	asserted

Condition(s)	PCD Source	PCD Pin
Paging enabled, and CR0, CD bit = 0, when a memory page is being accessed	Page table entry, PCD bit = 0	deasserted
	Page table entry, PCD bit = 1	asserted

The Page Write-Through (PWT) pin is asserted only when paging is enabled. With paging enabled, the state of PWT is determined as stated in table 5-12.

Table 5-12. State of the PWT Pin During Memory Accesses (with paging enabled)

Condition(s)	PCD Source	PWT Pin
Page directory is being accessed	CR3, PWT bit = 0	deasserted
	CR3, PWT bit = 1	asserted
Page table is being accessed	Page directory entry, PCD bit = 0	deasserted
	Page directory entry, PCD bit = 1	asserted
Memory page is being accessed	Page table entry, PCD bit = 0	deasserted
	Page table entry, PCD bit = 1	asserted

FLUSH#

The FLUSH# signal causes the data in the internal caches to be invalidated. Prior to flushing the contents of the data cache, all lines marked as modified are written back to memory. This ensures that updated information is not lost when the cache is invalidated.

Upon completing the write-back and flush operation, the Pentium processor runs a flush acknowledge special cycle to notify external logic that the flush operation has completed.

Bus Cycle Pipelining Control Signal

The Pentium processor has an input called NA# (Next Address). External devices that use pipelining are able to run back-to-back bus cycles that utilize the processor's buses to their fullest potential.

Devices that support bus cycle pipelining decode the address and latch the result, along with the transfer type. The device then requests the next bus cycle be sent over the buses (by asserting NA#) prior to the current cycle ending.

The results of the first access are latched and sent back to the processor over the data bus. At the same time the next access starts without having to wait for the current transfer to end. These back-to-back, pipelined bus cycles provide the highest bandwidth (transfer rate) bus transfers.

Interrupt Signals

Seven signals are implemented as interrupt inputs. These inputs are recognized on instruction boundaries, which the Pentium processor defines as the first clock of the execution stage in the instruction pipeline. This means that before an instruction enters the execution stage, the processor checks to see if any interrupt inputs are asserted. If an interrupt pin is asserted, the instruction pipeline is flushed and the interrupt is serviced. The order of priority in which the interrupt inputs are handled by the processor is:

1. BUSCHK# (Bus Check)
2. R/S# (Run/Stop)
3. FLUSH# (Internal Cache Flush)
4. SMI# (System Management Interrupt)
5. INIT (Processor Initialization)
6. NMI (Non-maskable Interrupt)
7. INTR (Maskable Interrupt Request)

BUSCHK#

The bus check (BUSCHK#) signal is asserted by system logic to notify the processor that the current bus cycle has not completed normally. The processor samples BUSCHK# with BRDY# and latches its value so that the processor can check its state on the next instruction boundary. The processor latches the address and control signals of the failed bus cycle that was running when BUSCHK# was asserted. This information is stored in the processor's machine check registers and a machine check exception (MCE) is also executed if the MCE bit in CR4 is set. Refer to the chapter entitled "Summary of Software Changes" for more information.

R/S#

This run/stop (R/S#) signal is used in conjunction with the Intel debug port. R/S# is implemented as a falling edge trigger. Once a trigger has been detected the processor is interrupted on the next instruction boundary. This interrupt causes the processor to stop execution under control of the debug tool and forces the processor to ignore all external interrupts. The Probe Ready (PRDY) signal is asserted by the processor to notify the debug tool that processor execution has stopped. The processor is now in Probe Mode and the debug tool can access internal registers via the Test Access Port (TAP). A low to high transition on R/S# permits the processor to continue executing code normally.

FLUSH#

When the FLUSH# pin is driven low, the Pentium processor writes back all modified lines in the data cache and invalidates all cache line entries in both the code and data caches. The flush acknowledge special cycle is then run to tell external logic that all modified lines have been written back and all cache entries invalidated.

SMI#

The system management interrupt causes the processor to enter system management mode. When SMI# is recognized asserted on an instruction boundary, it completes all buffered write transactions, awaits the assertion of the EWBE# signal and asserts SMI acknowledge (SMIACT#). The processor then saves its registers to system management RAM (SMRAM) and begins to fetch and execute SMM code. (See the chapter entitled "System Management Mode" for details.)

INIT

The processor's initialization (INIT) input causes the processor to perform a partial reset. The processor retains some information unlike RESET. Refer to the section entitled "System Reset and INIT" later in this chapter.

Pentium Processor System Architecture

NMI

The non-maskable interrupt (NMI) operates in the same manner as in earlier Intel processors. The processor reads the contents of entry two in the interrupt table to obtain the starting address of the NMI handler. The processor then saves the EFLAGS, CS and EIP registers and fetches and executes NMI handler.

INTR

The maskable interrupt request (INTR) operate the same as earlier x86 systems. When an INTR is asserted the processor performs two back-to-back interrupt acknowledge bus cycles to get the vector number assigned to the pending interrupt. The processor then reads the contents of the interrupt table entry specified by the vector number. Next the processor saves its place within the current program by pushing the EFLAGS, CS and EIP registers to the stack. The processor then begins to fetch and execute the interrupt service routine from the memory location obtained from the interrupt table.

Bus Master Signals

The bus master signals used by the Pentium processor are identical to those used by the 486 processor and include:

HOLD - The **Hold Request** input asks the processor to relinquish control of the buses.

HLDA - The **Hold Acknowledge** output is asserted by the Pentium processor to inform the requesting device that it now owns the buses. HLDA is not asserted until all outstanding bus cycles that have been previously pipelined have completed.

BREQ - The **Bus Request** output is asserted by the Pentium processor to inform the arbitration logic that is needs control of the buses to perform a bus cycle.

BOFF# - The **Back Off** input directs the Pentium processor to immediately release control of the buses during a bus cycle when a deadlock condition exists on the bus. In such situations, another bus master must gain control of the buses in order for the Pentium processor to complete the current bus cycle successfully. After the BOFF# signal is removed the Pentium processor restarts the bus cycle.

Floating-Point Error Handling

The Pentium processor has the same floating-point error-handling capability as the 486. The numeric exception (NE) control bit in CR0 allows the programmer to select the error-handling scenario to be used by the processor when a floating-point error is detected. The Pentium processor can use its native error-handling method or the PC-DOS compatible method.

The Pentium processor includes an input pin called IGNNE# (Ignore numeric error). If this pin is deasserted, the Pentium processor freezes immediately before executing the next floating-point instruction, causing an interrupt to occur If in native error-handling mode, an exception 16 is generated and FERR# (Floating-point Error) is asserted. If in DOS compatible error handling mode, only the FERR# signal is asserted.

If the processor's IGNNE# input is asserted and a Floating-Point error is encountered, the processor ignores the error and continues to execute floating-point instructions. This capability is provided to permit the processor to continue with program execution before the error has actually been cleared by the floating-point unit's interrupt service routine.

Native Error Handling

Setting the NE bit in CR0 to a "1" causes the processor to generate an internal Exception 16 interrupt when the Floating-Point Unit incurs an error and the IGNNE# is set inactive. This is the processor's native error handling method.

The error handling routine must have its starting address placed in entry 16d of the interrupt table. The processor reads the contents of entry 16d when a floating-point error occurs and jumps to the starting address of the floating-point error handler.

PC-DOS Error Handling

If the programmer wishes the processor to use the PC-DOS-compatible error reporting technique for Floating-Point errors, the NE should be set to 0. When a floating-point error occurs, the Pentium processor's FERR# signal is asserted. This signal goes to the interrupt controller's IRQ13 input, causing a maskable interrupt to occur. In response, the processor runs two interrupt acknowledge bus cycles to determine which of the 15 interrupts to service. IRQ13 causes the processor to read entry 75h in the interrupt table where DOS places the floating-point error handler entry point. The handler directs the external FPU to restart following an error condition by writing to an I/O register inside the FPU. However, the FPU inside the Pentium processor cannot be restarted in this fashion. Instead, external logic recognizes the I/O write, causing the IGNNE# signal to be asserted. This allows the Pentium processor's FPU to continue.

System Reset and Initialization

The RESET signal has the same function as with earlier processors, but the INIT signal has been added for performance gains when running code written for the 80286 processor. The INIT (Initialize) signal performs a reset but retains the contents of the internal caches and the floating-point state.

Some code written for the 80286 puts the processor in protected mode temporarily, usually to access extended memory, and sometime later returns to real mode to continue running DOS. This type of operation is typical of DOS extenders. Returning an 80286 to real mode requires that the processor be reset. The use of the RESET signal causes all data inside of the processor to be lost. However, the INIT signal can be used for this function in the Pentium processor, thereby retaining data and code that would otherwise have to be read from memory again. The processor state is the same after INIT as it is after RESET except the following retain their values they had prior to INIT:

- code cache
- data cache
- write buffers
- floating-point registers
- model-specific registers

- CD and NW bits of CR0 are unchanged and bit 4 is set to "1"

System Management Mode (SMI & SMIACT#)

The system management mode allows the processor to execute code from system management memory that is separate from the memory used by the operating system and applications. This permits the system designer to implement features such as power management that is transparent to the operating system. The Pentium processor implements two pins to support SMM.

- **SMI#** (system management interrupt) informs the processor that a system management handler, residing in System Management (SM) address space, needs to be executed.

- **SMIACT#** (system management interrupt acknowledge) informs external logic that the processor is in system management mode. The SMIACT# signal specifies access to system management RAM (SMRAM) so that SMRAM can be accessed.

Pentium Processor Reliability and Error Reporting

Address Parity (AP & APCHK#)

The address parity signal (AP) is driven along with the address during all processor generated bus cycles. Even parity is ensured for address lines A31:A5 (A4 and A3 are not included in the parity determination).

The Pentium processor checks address parity during inquire cycles, in the same clock period that EADS# is asserted. The AP signal is an input to the processor during inquire cycles to verify that even parity is returned with the snoop address. In the event of an address parity error, the processor activates its Address Parity Check output (APCHK#). APCHK# has no affect on program execution. The system designer is responsible for implementing address parity and taking the appropriate action when address parity errors are detected.

Data Parity (DP7:DP0, PCHK# & PEN#)

Even data parity is generated on all write bus cycles and is checked on all read bus cycles. Eight data parity bits are used, each one corresponding to one of the processor's eight data paths. (DP0 corresponds to data path 0 (D7:D0) ..... DP7 corresponds to data path 7 (D63:D56)). If a parity error is detected on a read operation, the Pentium processor asserts its PCHK# output, with no affect on program execution. Further action taken by the Pentium processor depends on the state of the Parity Enable input (PEN#).

When PEN# is sampled asserted during the same clock in which the parity error is detected, the address and control signals of the bus cycle causing the data parity error are latched in the processor's machine check registers. Additionally, a machine check exception is also generated when the machine check enable bit in control register four (CR4) is set to "1". The Pentium processor executes the machine check exception handler before executing the next instruction.

Internal Parity (IERR#)

IERR# is asserted when a parity error is encountered inside the Pentium processor. After the internal error has been reported to external logic, the Pentium processor enters the shutdown state, and performs a shutdown special cycle.

IERR# is also asserted by the Pentium processor when it is operating in "checker" mode and a mismatch is detected between the values sampled on the monitoring pins and the corresponding value computed internally.

Functional Redundancy Checking

Two or more Pentium processors can participate in functional redundancy checking. One processor (the master) fetches and executes instructions and performs bus cycles in normal fashion. One or more checker processors (connected directly to the master processor's buses) verify the correctness of the master processor's operations. The master processor fetches and executes instructions while the checker processor monitors all bus activity generated by the master. The checker is actually inputting the instruction stream being fetched by the master and executing each of the instructions, but doesn't drive the buses (with the exception of TDO and IERR#).

A Pentium processor selects its master/checker state on the trailing-edge of RESET by sampling the state of its FRCMC# (functional redundancy check master checker) input. A low selects checker mode, causing the processor to tri-state all of its outputs (except IERR# and TDO). A high on FRCMC# permits the processor to perform normally. The final state of FRCMC# when RESET is deasserted determines the mode each processor will be in.

Debug/Test Signals

Boundary Scan Interface (TAP)

Intel has implemented the IEEE 1149.1 Boundary Scan interface signals to permit in-circuit testing of the Pentium microprocessor. The related signals include:

- **TDI (Test data input)**. Used to supply data or instructions to the Pentium processor's TAP in a serial bit stream.
- **TMS (Test mode select)**. Used to select the mode of the Pentium processor's TAP controller.
- **TCK (Test clock)**. Used to shift serial information into the TAP on TDI or out of the TAP on TDO.
- **TRST# (Test reset)**. When asserted, forces the TAP controller into test logic reset state. In this state, all Pentium inputs and outputs operate normally.
- **TDO (Test data output)**. Used to output requested data or state out of the processor's TAP under the control of the TCK signal.

Execution Tracing

The Pentium processor provides a way to track the execution of instructions. This can be accomplished by monitoring external pins and by enabling the processor to perform branch trace message cycles.

Execution Completion

The external pins listed below are asserted to reflect execution of instructions within the processor. Each time the processor completes the execution of an instruction one or more of the following signals is automatically asserted by the processor.

- **IU.** The IU signal indicated that an instruction in the "u" pipeline has completed execution. The IBT signal cannot occur unless IU is active.

- **IV.** The IV signal indicated that an instruction in the "v" pipeline has completed execution. The IV signal cannot occur unless IU is also active, since and "v" pipeline instructions cannot complete independent of the "u" pipeline.

- **IBT (Instruction Branch Taken).** This signal is driven active for one clock cycle when the Pentium microprocessor executes an instruction resulting in an execution branch. When execution tracing is enabled, a branch trace special cycle will be run directly following the IBT signal.

Branch Trace Message Cycle

Branch trace message cycles can be enabled via Test Register 12 (TR12). When a branch is taken, the IBT signal is driven asserted and the branch trace message cycle is run by the processor to output the memory location that the instruction flow is branching to This message cycle notifies external logic (and debugging tools) that the linear address of the branch target routine is being output over the processor address bus A31:A3 along with the following signals:

BT3:BT0. The Branch Trace 3:0 lines are driven during a branch trace special cycle. BT2:BT0 provide address bits A2:A0 of the linear address for the branch target. BT3 specifies the default operand size: either 16-bits (low) or 32-bits (high).

Breakpoint/Performance Monitoring

The Pentium processor contains four debug registers that can be programmed with address and data breakpoints that the processor will monitor. If the processor encounters a match on the address or data it asserts the respective breakpoint pins (BP3:0).

The PM1:PM0 (performance monitoring) signals are multiplexed along with BP1:0 and are selected via control bits PB1:0 in the Debug Control register. Intel does not disclose the precise function of the performance monitoring pins.

Probe Mode

The system board designer may integrate a special debug port into the design to facilitate system/program debugging. Using the debug port signals, the programmer may remove the processor from run mode and place it into probe mode to access its debug and general registers. The signals used in conjunction with the Intel debug port include:

- **R/S# (Run/Stop)**. When set high, the processor is permitted to run normally. When R/S# transitions from a high to low state, the processor ceases to execute instructions. When PRDY is asserted in response the processor enters probe mode. This permits the debug tool to access the processor's debug registers through the boundary scan interface.

- **PRDY (Probe ready)**. Asserted by the processor when it has stopped execution as a result of the R/S# signal being asserted low. PRDY when asserted by the processor, notifies the debug tool that the processor is now in probe mode and ready to be accessed via the boundary scan interface.

Chapter 6

The Previous Chapter

The previous chapter detailed the Pentium processor's interface to the external environment (i.e., the address, data and control buses).

This Chapter

This chapter describes the operation of the Pentium processor's code cache and instruction pipelines. The discussion includes the code cache, dual integer pipelines and the floating-point pipeline.

The Next Chapter

The next chapter details the operation of the processor's L1 data cache and its relationship to the L2 cache and system memory. Cache line-fill, snoops and cache write-back bus operations are discussed in detail.

Introduction to the Code Cache and the Dual Instruction Pipelines

Much of the enhanced performance of the Pentium processor results from its dedicated code cache, dual integer pipelines and its pipelined floating-point unit. Another feature that provides performance gains is the branch prediction mechanism. This chapter describes the operation of the code cache, the branch prediction logic and the interaction of the key elements within the instruction pipelines.

The processor yields its best performance when:

- Instruction prefetches result in internal cache hits on the code cache, thereby reducing the probability that the execution units will stall while waiting for the next instruction(s).

- Sequential instructions are paired and proceed in parallel through the two instruction pipelines.
- Branch instructions are correctly predicted by the branch prediction logic.

The first part of this chapter focuses on instruction prefetching and the dual integer pipelines. The floating-point instruction pipeline is then discussed, followed by a detailed look at the code cache structure and operation. Note that this chapter does not discuss bus cycles performed by the Pentium processor. For details about bus cycle types, refer to the chapter entitled, "The Data Cache and Memory Accesses."

Overview

Figure 6-1 illustrates the Pentium processor block diagram. The Pentium processor incorporates two instruction pipelines designated the U and V pipelines. The U pipeline is the primary pipeline. Its execution stage incorporates a barrel shifter while the V pipeline's execution stage lacks this element. Only simple instructions can execute within the V pipeline, while all instructions can execute in the U pipeline. Both pipelines are supplied a steady stream of instructions by the prefetcher. The prefetcher is supplied code by either the code cache (in the event of a code cache hit) or by the bus unit (in the event of a code cache miss).

When the processor fetches a line of code from its internal cache, it transfer the line into the prefetch queue. Two instructions are then popped off the queue into the decode one, or D1, stage of each of the instruction pipelines. In the D1 stage of the two pipelines, the processor checks for instruction pairability and, if one of the instructions is a branch, predicts whether or not the branch will be taken when the branch instruction reaches the execution stage.

In the D2 stage, the instruction(s) is checked to see if it will access memory. If so, the target memory address is formed (offset added to segment start address), protection checks are performed, and, if necessary, protection exceptions generated.

The instruction(s) then proceeds to the execution stage for execution. If the execution of the instruction(s) requires access to memory, the memory access request is submitted to the data cache for a lookup. If a read request, the data is either supplied to the requesting execution unit by the data cache (on a hit) or by external memory (on a miss). If an execution unit issues a memory write request and the data is in the cache in the shared state, the cache is updated and the data is also written through to external memory. If the cache line is currently in the exclusive or modified state, the cache is updated, but the data is not written through to external memory. If a write miss on the data cache, external memory is updated. A complete description of the data cache's operation can be found in the chapter entitled, "The Data Cache and Burst Line Fills".

Finally, if the execution of an instruction requires the update of a processor register, the register is updated during the write-back stage.

The following sections provide a more detailed description of each stage in the instruction pipelines (to the extent that it is possible without engaging in too much speculation). It should be noted that Intel does not provide a great deal of detail regarding the exact implementation of the processor's internals (for obvious reasons).

Introduction to the Code Cache

The Pentium processor incorporates an 8KB, two-way set associative code cache dedicated to feeding instructions to the prefetcher. Both the code and data caches are disabled when the processor exits the RESET state. The Cache Disable (CD) bit and Not Write Through (NW) bits in Control Register zero (CR0) control operation of the internal caches. These bits are set to 1 when the processor begins to fetch and execute instructions causing the caches to be completely disabled. The POST programmer must enable the caches, by clearing the CD and NW bits to zero to enable the caches. See the chapter entitled, "Summary of Software Changes" for definition and interpretation of various CD and NW settings.

When the internal caches are first enabled, the internal code cache contains no valid information and the next prefetch results in a miss. This causes the code cache to submit a cache line-fill request to the bus unit for fulfillment. In response, the bus unit initiates a cache line-fill request from external memory. If the locations being read are cacheable, 32 bytes of code will be transferred back to the processor in a single burst cycle (four 8 byte transfers). When the L2 cache or the memory subsystem supplies the first quadword to the bus unit, the bus unit places it into its cache line-fill buffer and also routes it directly to the prefetcher. The first quadword returned will be the one requested by the prefetcher.

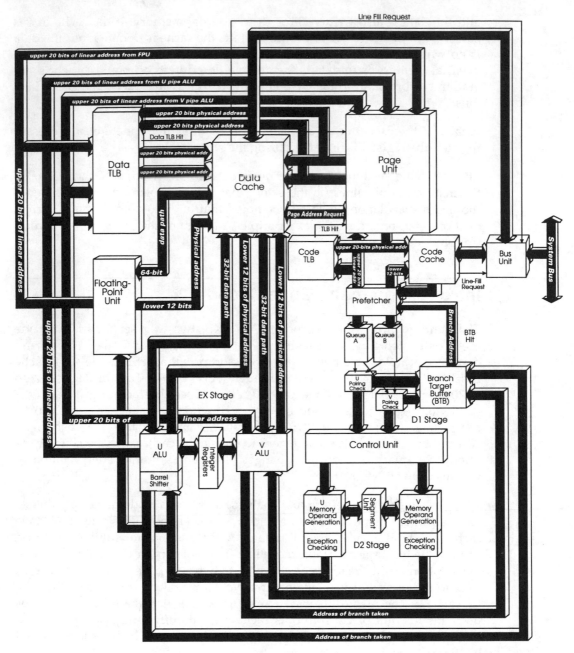

Figure 6-1. Overall Block Diagram of the Pentium Processor (Paging on)

Chapter 6: The Code Cache and Instruction Pipeline

As the remaining three quadwords become available, the bus unit places them into its cache line-fill buffer and also routes them to the prefetcher. When the entire line is assembled, the line is recorded in the code cache.

The Prefetcher

During normal operation with the cache enabled, the prefetcher receives a line of code from the bus unit, it places it into the active prefetch queue. The prefetcher has two prefetch queues, each of which can hold two lines, or 64 bytes, of information. Only one of the queues is active at a time. The prefetcher continues to fetch code from memory into the active queue sequentially until the branch prediction logic predicts that a branch will be taken when the branch instruction reaches the execution stage. The branch prediction logic then supplies the predicted branch target address back to the prefetcher. The prefetcher switches to the opposite prefetch queue and begins to fetch from memory sequentially starting at this new address. The newly active queue then supplies instructions into the two instruction pipelines immediately behind the jump instruction predicted to cause a branch.

If the branch is taken when the jump instruction reaches the execution stage, then the instructions immediately behind the jump in the instruction pipelines are the correct instructions. The execution unit doesn't stall. If, on the other hand, the branch is not taken, the instructions behind the jump in the pipelines and the current prefetch queue must be flushed. The prefetcher switches back to the other queue, which then begins to supply instructions (that were prefetched prior to the queue switch) into the pipelines. This flush and switch causes the execution units to stall briefly (three to four clocks) until the instruction stream from the new queue advances through the D1 and D2 stages to the execution stage. In addition, the branch prediction logic will update the branch's history bits to reflect that the branch was not taken this time.

If it is predicted that a branch currently in the D1 stage will not be taken, the prefetcher continues to prefetch sequentially into the current prefetch queue. If the prediction proves incorrect when the instruction reaches the execution stage, the instructions behind the branch instruction in the pipelines are incorrect. The processor must flush the instructions currently in the pipelines and instruct the prefetcher to begin fetching from the branch target address. In addition, the execution unit instructs the branch prediction logic to update the branch's history to indicate that the branch was taken this time.

Basic Function of the Decode One, or D1, Stage

In the decode one, or D1, stage the two instruction pipelines each receive instructions simultaneously from the active prefetch queue. In the D1 stage, two checks are performed:

- The two instructions are checked for pairability. If they are not pairable, the instruction in the V pipeline's D1 stage is deleted and the prefetcher will shift it into the U pipeline's D1 stage when the first instruction in the U pipeline's D1 stage moves on to the U pipeline's D2 stage. In other words, the instructions are serialized in the U pipeline.
- If either instruction is a branch instruction, the branch prediction logic makes a prediction as to whether the branch will actually be taken when the instruction reaches the execution stage. If predicted taken, the prediction logic will tell the prefetcher to switch queues and start fetching from the branch target address. If predicted not taken, the prefetcher will continue sequential code fetching into the current queue.

When paired, instructions in both pipes enter and leave each stage in the pipeline in unison. If the instruction in one pipeline stalls during a given stage, the instruction in the other pipeline is not sent on to the next stage until the other instruction is ready. Figure 6-2 illustrates the dual D1 stages.

Basic Function of the Decode Two, or D2, Stage

Figure 6-3 illustrates the D2 stages of the dual instruction pipelines. During the decode two, or D2, stage addresses are calculated for operands that reside in memory. The D2 stage performs the same functions as the segment unit does in the i486, but it has been enhanced in the Pentium processor so that addresses can be calculated more quickly. The Pentium processor can handle instructions containing both displacement and immediate values, or instructions using base and index addressing in a single clock cycle, whereas the i486 requires an additional clock cycle.

During the D2 stage, the processor also performs the segmentation protection checks required when the processor forming memory addresses in protected mode.

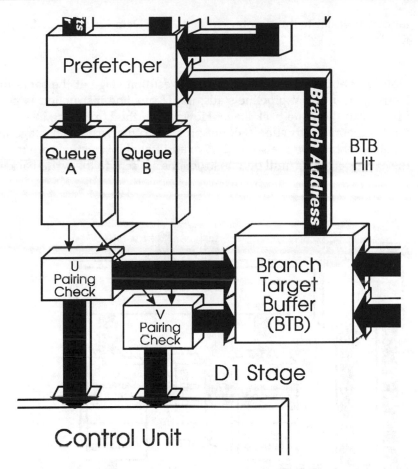

Figure 6-2. The Dual D1 Pipeline Stages

Basic Function of the Execution Stage

Figure 6-4 illustrates the execution stage of the dual instruction pipelines. The execution stage is comprised of the arithmetic logic unit, or ALU. As stated earlier, the U pipeline's ALU incorporates a barrel shifter, while the V pipeline's does not. It is obvious, then, that the U pipeline can handle instructions that cannot be handled in the V pipeline. When necessary, data cache accesses (on a cache hit) or memory accesses (on a miss) are performed in this stage. Access to the data cache can be made by the U pipeline and V pipeline simultaneously (refer to the chapter entitled, "The Data Cache and Memory Access" for details).

Note that both instructions enter the execution stage at the same time. If the instruction in the V pipeline stalls, the U pipeline instruction is permitted to proceed to the write-back stage. However, if the U pipeline instruction stalls, the V pipeline instruction will not proceed to the write-back stage until the U pipeline instruction is also ready. No additional instructions are transferred to the execution stage until both instructions are sent to the write-back stage.

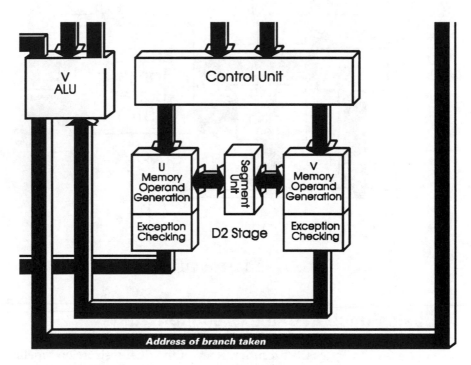

Figure 6-3. The Dual D2 Pipeline Stages

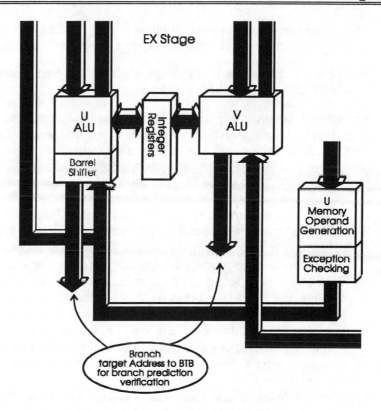

Figure 6-4. The Dual Execution Stages

The Write-Back Stage

As stated earlier, target registers are updated (when necessary) during the write-back stage. This would also include the update of the EFLAGS register (if necessary).

Rules for Integer Instruction Pairing

The Pentium processor can execute two integer instructions simultaneously, one in each of the instruction pipelines. The first instruction enters the u-pipeline and the next the v-pipeline. The u-pipeline is an enhanced version of the pipeline used in the i486 processor, while the v-pipeline has some limitations when compared to the u-pipeline (the V pipeline has no barrel shifter). As a result, some instructions will only execute in the U pipeline.

The prefetch queue currently in use delivers the first instruction to the U pipeline and the next to the V pipeline.

Not all instructions are pairable. If two sequential instructions are not pairable, then both must execute in the main U pipeline serially (as they would in the i486). Instructions are pairable only if the following criteria are met:

- Instructions must be simple. For more information, refer to the section in this chapter entitled, "Definition of Simple Instructions."
- Instructions must not have register contention. Special hardware has been added so that some exceptions to this rule are permitted, allowing pairing of some instructions that have explicit register contention.
- When entering the pipeline for the first time, an instruction is determined to be one byte in length. In this simple case, the prefetcher can easily determine the boundary between this instruction and the next. When a multi-byte instruction is executed for the first time, the instruction pipeline provides feedback to the code cache indicating the instruction's length. The code cache then stores this boundary information in the cache directory entry corresponding to the line the instruction was originally fetched from.
- When an instruction entering the pipeline has been fetched from the code cache before, the code cache also delivers its length. This permits the prefetcher to easily recognize the boundary between this instruction and the next.

Definition of Simple Instructions

Most simple ALU instructions are pairable and execute in a single clock cycle. These instructions are hardwired to execute quickly within the Pentium processor. Some instructions that require two or three clock cycles to complete are also considered simple and are therefore pairable. The following integer instructions are considered to be simple and are therefore pairable:

- mov reg, reg/mem/imm
- mov mem, reg/imm
- alu reg, reg/mem/imm
- alu mem, reg/imm
- inc reg/mem

- dec reg/mem
- push reg/mem
- pop reg
- lea reg, mem
- jmp/call/jcc near
- nop

Some instructions are only pairable if they are the first instruction in the pair (meaning that they must execute in the U pipeline). Others can execute in either the U pipeline or V pipeline, but can only be paired when they are the second instruction in the pair, so they only pair when run in the V pipeline. These restrictions exist primarily to eliminate register contention problems.

Register Contention

Register contention results if two instructions attempt to access the same registers during parallel execution. Two types of register contention exist: explicit contention and implicit contention.

Explicit Register Contention

Explicit register contention would occur if two instructions specified access to the same register. Examples of explicit register contention are listed in table 6-1.

Table 6-1. Examples of Explicit Register Contention

Instructions	Description of Contention
mov ax, 4b mov [bp], ax	Register write followed by read. When these two instructions execute sequentially, the first instruction updates the ax register with a value of 4b, and the second instruction reads this new ax value and writes it to memory at the location specified by [bp]. If paired, both instructions would execute in parallel. This means that the second instruction will read the contents of the ax register before the first instruction has updated it with the 4b value, creating invalid results.

Instructions	Description of Contention
mov ax, 4b mov ax, [bp]	Register write followed by write. In this example, both instructions write to the same register, preventing them from pairing.
mov al, 5 mov ah, A	Contention on subregisters within same 32-bit register. Two instructions that write to portions of the same 32-bit register cannot be paired. All register references are treated as an access to the entire 32-bit register.

Note that a pair of instructions that first reads from a register and then writes to the same register are pairable. For example, the following instructions can be paired:

mov ax, bx   This instruction executes in the U pipeline and reads from bx during the execute stage, and writes to the ax register during the write-back stage.

mov bx, [bp]   This instruction executes in the V pipeline and reads the contents of the memory location specified by [bp] during the execution stage, and writes to the bx register during the write-back stage.

Since the first instruction reads the contents of bx during the execution stage, which is prior to the second instruction writing to the same register during the subsequent write-back stage, no register contention exists. Furthermore, the instructions execute in parallel exactly and they would have executed serially.

Implicit Register Contention

Implicit register contention would occur if two instructions imply reference to the same register.

Exclusions to Implicit Register Contention Rule

Two exceptions to the rule for implicit register contention are:

1. Flags References -- Compare and Branch Operations. Examples would be a cmp followed by a jcc and an add followed by a jne.

2. Stack Pointer References -- Pushes and Pops. Examples would be: push reg/imm followed by push reg/imm; push reg/imm followed by a call; and pop reg followed by pop reg.

Instruction Branch Prediction

The Pentium processor includes branch prediction logic, allowing it to avoid pipeline stalls if it correctly predicts whether or not the branch will be taken when the branch instruction is executed. When a branch operation is correctly predicted, no performance penalty is incurred. However, when branch prediction is not correct, a three cycle penalty is incurred if the branch is executed in the U pipeline and a four cycle penalty if the branch is in the V pipeline. When a call or a conditional jump is mis-predicted, a three clock penalty is incurred in either instruction pipeline.

The prediction mechanism is implemented using a four-way, set-associative cache with 256 entries. This is referred to as the branch target buffer, or BTB. The directory entry for each line contains the following information:

*   A valid bit that indicates whether or not the entry is in use.
*   History bits that track how often the branch has been taken each time that it entered the pipeline before.
*   The source memory address that the branch instruction was fetched from.

If its respective directory entry is valid, the target address of the branch is stored in the corresponding data entry in the branch target buffer.

The branch target buffer, or BTB, is a look-aside cache that sits off to the side of the D1 stages of the two pipelines and monitors for branch instructions. Figure 6-5 illustrates the relationship of the D1 pipeline stages and the BTB. The first time that a branch instruction enters either pipeline, the BTB uses its source memory address to perform a lookup in the cache. Since the instruction has not been seen before, this results in a BTB miss. This essentially means that the branch prediction logic has no history on the instruction. It therefore predicts that the branch will not be taken when the instruction reaches the execution stage of the pipeline, and does not instruct the prefetcher to alter program flow. Even unconditional jumps will be predicted as not-taken the first time that they are seen by the BTB.

When the instruction reaches the execution stage, the branch will either be taken or not taken. If taken, the next instruction to be executed should be the one fetched from the branch target address. If the branch is not taken (e.g., if its qualifying conditions are not met), the next instruction executed should be the one fetched from the next sequential memory address after the branch instruction.

When the branch is taken for the first time, the execution unit provides feedback to the branch prediction logic. The branch target address is sent back and recorded in the BTB. A directory entry is made containing the source memory address that the branch instruction was fetched from and the history bits are set to indicate that the branch has been taken 100% of the times that it was executed (once, in this case). The history bits can indicate one of four possible states:

1. **Strongly taken.** The history bits are initialized to this state when the entry is first made. In addition, if a branch marked weakly taken is taken again, it is upgraded to the strongly taken state. When a branch marked strongly taken is not taken the next time, it is downgraded to weakly taken. On a lookup in the D1 stage, a hit on a strongly or weakly taken entry will result in a positive prediction (i.e., the branch is predicted taken).
2. **Weakly taken.** If a branch marked weakly taken is taken again, it is upgraded to the strongly taken state. When a branch marked weakly taken is not taken the next time, it is downgraded to weakly not taken. On a lookup in the D1 stage, a hit on a strongly or weakly taken entry will result in a positive prediction (i.e., the branch is predicted taken).
3. **Weakly not taken.** If a branch marked weakly not taken is taken again, it is upgraded to the weakly taken state. When a branch marked weakly not taken is not taken the next time, it is downgraded to strongly not taken. On a lookup in the D1 stage, a hit on a strongly or weakly not taken entry will result in a negative prediction (i.e., the branch is predicted not taken).
4. **Strongly not taken.** If a branch marked strongly not taken is taken again, it is upgraded to the weakly not taken state. When a branch marked strongly not taken is not taken the next time, it remains in the strongly not taken state. On a lookup in the D1 stage, a hit on a strongly or weakly not taken entry will result in a negative prediction (i.e., the branch is predicted not taken).

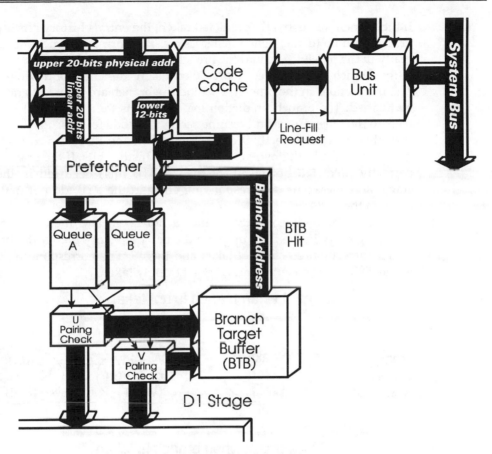

Figure 6-5. The Branch Target Buffer

If predicted not taken, no action is taken at this point. If predicted taken, the BTB supplies the branch target address back to the prefetcher and indicates that a positive prediction is being made. In response, the prefetcher switches to the opposite prefetch queue and immediately begins to prefetch from memory starting at the branch target address. The instructions fetched are supplied to the instruction pipelines immediately behind the branch instruction.

When the branch instruction reaches the execution stage, the branch will either be taken or not. The results of the branch are fed back to the BTB and the entry's history bits are upgraded or downgraded accordingly. The following list defines the BTB actions taken in each case when the branch instruction reaches the execution stage.

1. If the branch was correctly predicted taken, the entry's history bits are up-graded and no further action is necessary. The correct instructions are already in the pipelines behind the branch instruction.
2. If the branch was incorrectly predicted taken, the entry is downgraded. The instructions in the pipelines behind the branch are incorrect and must be flushed. The branch prediction logic instructs the prefetcher to switch back to the other queue and resume sequential code fetches.
3. If the branch was correctly predicted not taken and there is a corresponding entry in the BTB, downgrade the entry's history bits. If the branch was correctly predicted not taken (because a BTB miss occurred in the D1 stage) and there isn't a corresponding entry in the BTB, do not make an entry in the BTB.
4. If the branch was incorrectly predicted not taken and there is a corresponding entry in the BTB, upgrade the entry's history bits. If the branch was incorrectly predicted not taken and there isn't a corresponding entry in the BTB, make an entry and mark it strongly taken.

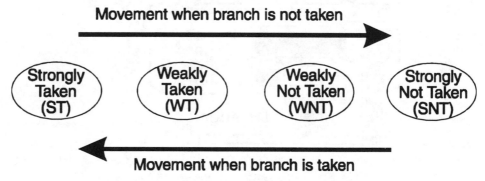

Figure 6-6. The Branch Target Buffer Branch History Bits

Code Cache Organization and Operation

The Code Cache Structure

Refer to figure 6-7. The code or instruction cache is 8KB in size, organized in a two-way set-associative configuration. The cache banks are referred to as way zero and way one. The cache is read-only and must therefore only implement a subset of the MESI protocol (S and I). Each cache line is 32 bytes wide, allowing 32 bytes to be delivered to the prefetch queue during a single prefetch.

Each cache way contains 128 cache lines. There is a separate 128 entry directory associated with each of the cache ways.

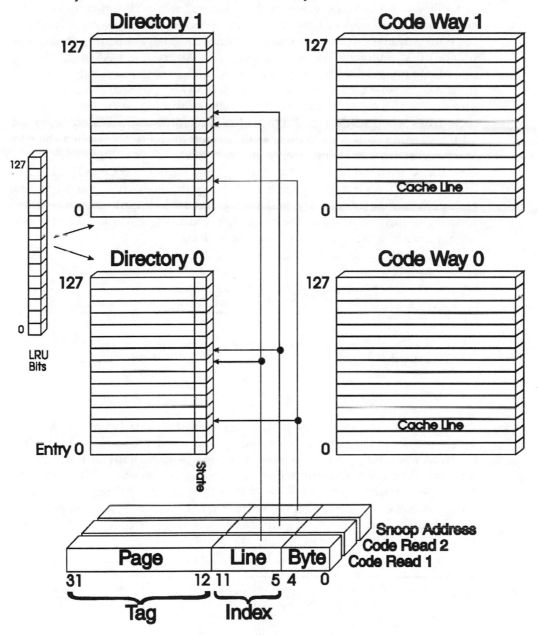

Figure 6-7. The Code Cache Structure

The cache directories are triple ported, allowing three simultaneous directory accesses (as shown in figure 6-7). Two of the ports support the split-line access capability described elsewhere in this chapter, while the other is used for snooping. Figure 6-8 illustrates the format of each directory entry. The 20-bit tag field within each directory entry identifies the page in memory (one of one million) that the cache line was copied from. Address bits A31:A12 identify one of one million 4KB pages within the 4GB address space. A single state bit indicates whether the line in the cache contains valid (Shared) or invalid (I) information. Also associated with each directory entry is a parity bit used to detect errors when reading each entry. The directories are accessed using the address issued by the prefetcher (as illustrated in figure 6-7). When the prefetcher initiates a split-line access, the two line addresses submitted to the code cache are labeled (in the illustration) Code Read 1 and Code Read 2. Address bits A11:A5 from the prefetcher identify the line where the target line resides in cache or in memory, and are used as the index into the cache directories. The lower portion of the prefetcher address (A4:A0) identifies a byte within the line and is not used during the look up.

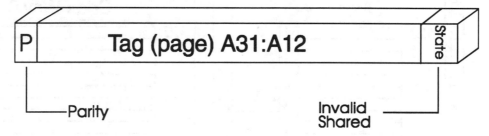

Figure 6-8. The Code Cache Directory Entry Format

As illustrated in figure 6-9, each cache line holds four quadwords of information. Accesses made to memory, caused by code cache misses, always result in the transfer of four quadwords from memory. As each quadword is received, it is placed in a cache line-fill buffer until the entire contents of the cache line have been acquired. When full, the contents of the line-fill buffer are transferred to cache memory and a directory entry is made to record its presence. As each quadword is received from memory, it is supplied directly to the prefetcher to fulfill its request as quickly as possible.

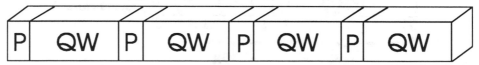

Figure 6-9. Organization of the Code Cache Lines

Chapter 6: The Code Cache and Instruction Pipeline

The code cache is designed to permit two simultaneous prefetch accesses: one to the upper half of one line and another to the lower half of the next line. Figure 6-7 illustrates an example of this split-line access capability where two addresses are issued by the prefetcher simultaneously. An instruction that straddles two adjacent cache lines can be accessed in a single cycle.

Figure 6-7 also shows a snoop address being presented to the cache directory at the same time that the split-line access is occurring. On a snoop hit, the snoop process does not read or write the cache lines, but can result in the invalidation of a cache line.

The Line Storage Algorithm

The code cache considers the 4GB memory space to be divided into 1,048,576 pages, each of which is 4KB is size. In addition, each page is subdivided into 128 lines, each of which is 32 bytes in length. By definition then, when the prefetcher issues a request for an instruction, the code cache must determine if it has a copy of that line from that page of memory space. If it doesn't, it must issue a cache line-fill request to the bus unit. The bus unit fetches the line from memory (the L2 cache or system memory) and then must place it in the cache and make a directory entry to track its presence.

Assume that the line was fetched from line eight in memory page twenty. The code cache uses the line number, eight, to index into entry eight of its twin directories and then takes one of the following actions:

- If either of the directory entries is marked invalid, the target page address, twenty, is saved in that directory entry as the tag address. The state bit is set to the shared state. The line fetched from line eight in memory page twenty is stored in line eight of the code cache way, or bank, associated with this directory. The LRU (least-recently used) bit associated with the pair of directory entries is set to indicate that entry eight in the opposite directory is now the least-recently used of the pair.
- If both of the entries are marked valid, the code cache will overwrite the entry currently pointed to by the LRU bit associated with this pair of directory entries. This is referred to as a cache line replacement. The target page address, twenty, is saved in that directory entry as the tag address. The state bit is set to the shared state. The line fetched from line eight in memory page twenty is stored in line eight of the code cache way, or bank, associated with this directory. The LRU (least-recently used) bit as-

sociated with the pair of directory entries is set to indicate that entry eight in the opposite directory is now the least-recently used of the pair.

Inquire Cycles

Inquire cycles are performed by the Pentium processor when another bus master either reads or writes system memory. This must be done to ensure cache consistency between the contents of the internal data and code caches and system memory. The code cache is a read-only cache, meaning that no line within it will ever be updated due to an internally-generated write operation. Therefore, the code cache need not implement the entire MESI protocol (because the modified and exclusive states are not required). The code cache implements only two of the MESI states: Shared and Invalid. The actions taken by the code cache when another bus master accesses system memory are detailed in the following sections.

Memory Writes by Another Bus Master

When another bus master initiates a write to a location in memory, external logic (either the L2 cache or the memory controller) directs the Pentium processor to snoop the address bus. When the processor's AHOLD line is asserted, the processor floats its address bus in preparation to receive the address currently being driven by the bus master. EADS# is then asserted by external logic, causing the internal code cache to use the address to snoop its directory. In addition to the EADS# signal, external logic also asserts INV, indicating that the snoop cycle is being caused by a write operation and the line should be invalidated in the event of a snoop hit. If the system does not incorporate an L2 cache, external logic need only assert EADS# to initiate the inquire cycle, since the address will already be present on the processor's address bus (being driven by the bus master).

The code cache performs a lookup to determine if it has a copy of the line that is being updated by the bus master. If a snoop miss results, no action is taken by the code cache. If, however, a snoop hit results, the cache line is invalidated (the directory entry's state bits change from the S to the I state because INV is asserted). The transition to the invalid state is necessary because the bus master is updating the line in memory and the cache line will then be stale. The processor asserts HIT# when a snoop hit is detected.

Chapter 6: The Code Cache and Instruction Pipeline

Memory Reads by Another Bus Master

The same action is taken by external logic when a memory read bus cycle is initiated by another bus master. INV is deasserted, however, indicating that it is not necessary to invalidate the entry in the event of a snoop hit. As a result, no action will be taken by the code cache for either a snoop hit or miss, except that the HIT# signal is asserted as a result of a snoop hit.

Internal Snooping

When the data cache initiates either a read or a write operation, the code cache snoops the address as it is passed from the data cache to the bus unit. If a snoop hit is detected, the code cache directory entry for that line is invalidated. Invalidation occurs for both read and write snoop hits. Invalidating a line in the code cache when the data cache reads the same line is necessary to maintain consistency when the processor is operating in write-back mode and modified code is being run.

Split-Line Access

In a complex instruction set computer (CISC), instructions are of variable length. The smallest instructions are one byte in length, while the maximum legal length of a Pentium instruction is fifteen bytes. A code cache miss always results in a 32-byte cache line-fill, if it's a cacheable address. Multi-byte instructions may straddle two sequential lines stored in the code cache. When the prefetcher determines that an instruction straddles two lines, it would appear that the prefetcher must perform two sequential cache accesses in order to get the instruction from the code cache. This would impact performance. The Pentium processor incorporates a split-line access feature, permitting the upper half of one line and the lower half of the next to be fetched from the code cache in one cycle. This split-line access capability permits an instruction that straddles line boundaries to be prefetched in a single clock cycle. When the split-line is read from the cache, the information is not correctly aligned (as shown in figure 6-10). The bytes of the instruction must be rotated so that the prefetch queue receives the instruction in the proper order.

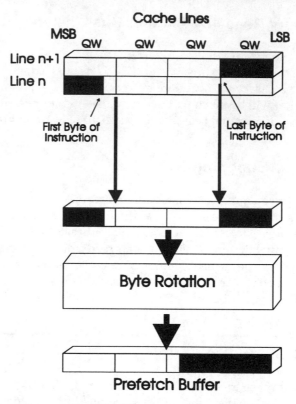

Figure 6-10. Split-Line Access from Code Cache

In order for split-line access to work efficiently, instruction boundaries within the cache line need to be defined. This permits the prefetcher to track where instructions start within a given line and to direct the code cache to either fetch an entire line, or the lower half of one and the upper half of the next. When an instruction is decoded for the first time, the length of the instruction is fed back to the code cache. Each code cache directory entry marks instruction boundaries within the line so that split-line accesses can be performed. Instruction boundaries are also required during the instruction pairing process.

The Floating-Point Pipeline

The floating-point unit in the Pentium processor has been significantly improved over the i486 floating-point unit. The new floating-point unit is heavily pipelined, permitting several instructions to execute simultaneously (under certain, predefined circumstances). Most floating-point instructions are issued singly to the U pipeline and cannot be paired with integer instructions. Only one instance of pairing is permitted with floating-point instructions (described below under the section entitled, "Floating-Point Pairing").

The Floating-Point Pipeline Stages

The floating-point pipeline consists of eight stages. The first four stages are shared with the integer pipeline, and the last four reside within the floating-point unit itself. The pipeline stages are listed in table 6-2.

Table 6-2. Floating-Point Pipeline Stages

Stage	Description
Prefetch	Identical to the integer prefetch stage.
Instruction Decode 1	Identical to the integer D1 stage.
Instruction Decode 2	Identical to the integer D2 stage.
Execution Stage (EX)	Register read, memory read, or memory write performed as required by the instruction (to access an operand).
FP Execution 1 Stage	Information from register or memory is written into a FP register. Data is converted to floating-point format before being loaded into the floating-point unit.
FP Execution 2 Stage	Floating-point operation performed within floating-point unit.
Write FP Result	Floating-point results are rounded and the result is written to the target floating-point register.
Error Reporting	If an error is detected, an error reporting stage is entered where the error is reported and the FPU status word is updated.

Floating-Point Instruction Pairing

Only the floating-point exchange instruction, FXCH, can be paired as the second instruction in the pair. Furthermore, pairing can only occur if the first instruction issued to the U pipeline is simple in nature. Simple instructions include the floating-point instructions listed below:

- FLD single or double precision
- FLD ST(i)

  and all forms of the following:

- FADD
- FSUB
- FMUL
- FDIVFCOM
- FUCOM
- FTST
- FABS
- FCHS

The ability to pair the FXCH instruction enhances floating-point performance considerably because operands used by floating point instructions must be on the top of the floating-point register stack in order to be accessed. This requirement results in a large number of FXCH instructions in floating-point code that is used to move the current operand to the top of the stack. The Pentium processor has been designed to allow faster access to registers permitting faster execution of exchanges. This faster access to registers along with the ability to execute the FXCH instruction in parallel with other floating-point instructions, results in improved performance.

FPU Pipelining

The resources within the floating-point unit can be allocated to more than one floating-point instruction at a time. This permits pipelined execution within the FPU itself. This capability is restricted as follows:

1. FDIV instructions require all of the FPU resources, so the FPU cannot execute any other instructions simultaneously with an FDIV.

2. Due to FPU resource limitations, two consecutive FMUL instructions cannot execute simultaneously.
3. One FMUL can be executed in parallel with one or two FADD instructions.
4. Three FADD instructions can be executed simultaneously.

Chapter 7

The Previous Chapter

The previous chapter described the operation of the Pentium processor's instruction pipeline, including the code cache, dual integer pipelines and the floating-point pipeline.

This Chapter

This chapter describes the operation of the Pentium processor's internal data cache. Interaction between the level two (L2) cache controller and the DRAM memory subsystem are also covered, along with the burst bus cycles that the Pentium processor is capable of running.

The Next Chapter

The next chapter summarizes the various types of bus cycles run by the Pentium processor.

Introduction to the Internal Data Cache

All instructions requiring access to memory are routed to the processor's internal data cache to determine if a copy of the target data is already on-board the processor. Most Pentium processor-based systems will employ a level two (L2) cache subsystem to increase performance when a miss occurs within the internal, or level one (L1) cache. The L2 cache provides a number of benefits described in the chapter entitled "Pentium Cache Overview." This chapter details the operation of the internal data cache and the interaction of the Pentium processor's internal data cache, the L2 caches and main system memory.

Pentium Processor System Architecture

Anatomy of a Read Hit

This example consists of a step-by-step description of two simultaneous reads submitted to the Pentium processor's internal data cache. Assume that two memory read instructions are being executed as follows:

```
MOV AX,[1056] ; Read in Pipeline U
MOV BX,[108C] ; Read in Pipeline V
```

Also assume that the processor is in protected mode, the data segment starts at memory location 002A0000h, and paging is turned off. The instruction in pipeline U tells the processor to read two bytes of information from locations 002A1056h and 002A1057h and place them in the AX register. The V-pipeline instruction causes two bytes of data to be read from locations 002A108Ch and 002A108Dh and placed in the BX register.

The Internal Cache's View of Main System Memory

Cache controllers view memory as being divided into pages equal in size to the cache ways. The Pentium processor has an 8KB, two-way set associative data cache so each cache way is 4KB is size. This means that the total 4GB of memory address space is viewed as 1,048,576 pages numbered 0 through 1,048,575, each of which is 4KB in size.

Each memory page is viewed by the internal cache controller as being organized like the cache ways. This means that each page in memory is viewed as having 128 lines, each containing 32 bytes of data. These lines are numbered 0 through 127.

The Pentium processor's data cache is interleaved on four byte (doubleword) boundaries to permit simultaneous doubleword accesses from both the U- and V-pipelines. As long as the two accesses do not target the same bank, two doublewords can be read from the data cache in a single clock cycle.

Each memory address sent to the internal cache controller is examined to determine the page, line and doubleword that contain the target memory location. Figure 7-1 illustrates how the data cache controller interprets the address sent from the execution pipelines.

Chapter 7: The Data Cache and Burst Bus Cycles

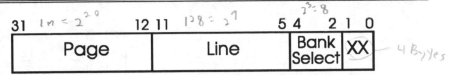

Figure 7-1. *The Address as Viewed by the Internal Data Cache Controller*

The example in Figure 7-1 shows that address lines:

- A31:A12 identify the page in which the target location resides
- A11:A5 identify the line that the target address occupies within the page (hence its position in the cache way)
- A4:A2 identifies which doubleword within the line that the target address occupies (hence the internal data cache bank in which the address data resides)
- A1:A0 are not used (don't care)

The Structure of the Internal Data Cache

Refer to figure 7-2. The 8KB internal data cache contains single-ported high speed static RAM. The cache RAM is organized into two 4KB ways referred to as way zero and way one. Each way consists of 128 lines numbered 0 through 127 and each line holds 32 bytes of data. Each data cache line consists of eight doublewords and the cache ways are interleaved on doubleword boundaries. Additionally, parity is generated for each byte within a line that is placed in the internal cache as shown in figure 7-3. When a byte of information is read from cache, parity is checked. If a parity error is detected, an internal parity error is signaled to external logic through the IERR# (Internal ERRor) output. In addition, the processor generates a special shutdown bus cycle and stops execution.

When a line of information is read from a page of external memory, the cache controller stores the line in one of the two internal cache memory ways (way zero or way one). Within the selected cache way, it is stored in the same line number as that which it came from within the page of external memory. The line number also selects the directory entry used to record the new entry. As an example, information from line 12 of any memory page is stored in entry 12 of one of the two cache banks.

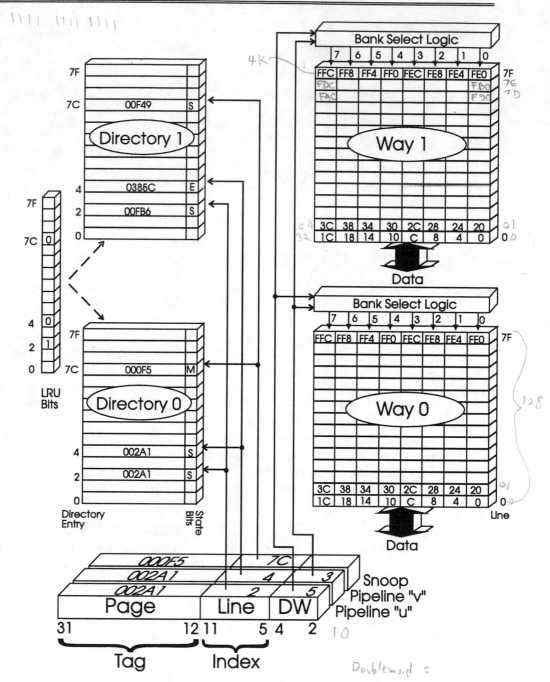

Figure 7-2. The Structure of the Internal Data Cache

Chapter 7: The Data Cache and Burst Bus Cycles

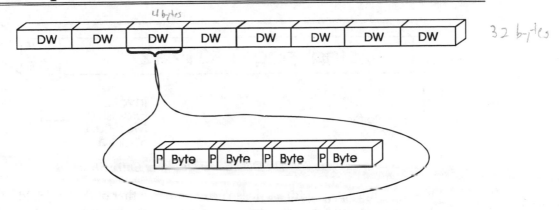

Figure 7-3. The Structure of Each Data Cache Line.

Refer to figure 7-4. Each directory entry has a tag (or page) field used to record the page number of the memory page that the line of information came from. When a line of information is read from memory, the cache controller indexes into the directory using the line number. It then examines the current setting of the entry's state bits If the state bits indicate that the line in way zero contains invalid information (I), no further checking is necessary for that line and the line in way one is checked. If the state bits are checked and the line is valid, the cache controller then compares the page portion of the memory address to the page address stored in the entry's tag field. If the memory page address compares with the tag field of either directory, this indicates that the cache has a copy of the addressed line stored within cache in the line associated with the entry.

As an example, if the processor were addressing line 5 in memory page 345, the cache controller would index into entry 5 in both directories and compare the target page number, 345, to the valid Tag field(s) in each entry. If the Tag field for directory 1, for instance, contained a valid Tag address 345, the cache controller has a copy of the desired information in line 5 of way one. The processor can then access the target information.

Note also that each directory entry has a parity bit that is generated and written each time the directory entry is updated. Parity is checked each time the entry is accessed to determine a hit or miss. An IERR# signal is asserted when a parity error is detected and a shutdown special cycle is run and the processor stops.

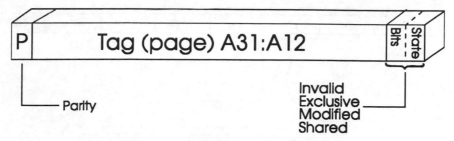

Figure 7-4. The Data Cache Directory Entry Structure

If the memory page address doesn't compare to either of the Tag fields, this is a cache miss and the cache controller issues a cache line fill request to the Bus Unit to fetch the desired information from external memory. When the requested line of information is fetched from external memory, the cache controller must place a copy of it in the cache and update the affected directory entry to reflect its presence and the MESI state in which it is stored. If both tag fields are currently in use, the cache controller must determine which of the two lines is the least recently and then overwrite that line with the line of new information. The cache directory entry must then be updated to reflect the presence and state of the new line of data. Under these circumstances, the current setting of the entry's LRU bit identifies which cache line is to be used to store the new data from external memory. The line from memory is then stored in the selected cache way, overwriting the line that was previously stored there. The page number, or tag, of the source memory page is then written into the selected tag field, and the entry's LRU bit is updated to reflect the change.

Setting the Cache Stage

The purpose of this section is to define the current state of the cache when the example memory read requests introduced earlier are submitted to the cache controller by the dual execution units.

In the example, the target memory addresses are 002A1056h through 002A1057h and 002A108Ch through 002A108Dh. The cache directories are triple ported to allow access from both pipelines and to permit an external snoop simultaneouly. For the purpose of this discussion, the following conditions are assumed in these entries at the moment of the access. Refer to table 7-1.

Chapter 7: The Data Cache and Burst Bus Cycles

Table 7-1. Data Cache Directory Entries Prior to Sample Reads

Directory Status	Entry 2	Entry 4	Entry 7C
LRU Bit	1	0	0
State Bits Directory 0	S	S	M
State Bits Directory 1	S	E	S
Tag Field Directory 0	002A1	002A1	000F5
Tag Field Directory 1	00FB6	0385C	00F49

The Internal Cache Look-up and Access

When the pipelines require operands from memory, they request information directly from the internal data cache. The address is examined by the data cache controller to determine if a copy of the target information is already in the internal cache. Figure 7-5 shows the interpretation of the addresses. Both the U- and V-pipe addresses reside in page 2A1h in memory. The U address is in line two of page 2A1h and the V address in line 4 of the same page. Address U resides within doubleword 5 of line 2, while address V resides in doubleword three of line 4. Since the operands (if present) will reside in the fifth and third doublewords, the same bank will not be accessed for both locations, therefore they can be accessed simultaneously.

When the data cache controller evaluates the state bits for the U pipeline access, the line two entry in directory zero shows that the data is shared (S) and entry two in directory one also has a shared (S) line. The data cache controller next compares the page portion of the address to the tag field stored in entry two of directory zero and finds a match. The controller now knows that the cache has a copy of the target address in line two of way zero; hence a read hit is detected. Since the address bits A4:A2 have a 5, the bank select logic activates bank 5 via the Bank Select Logic and the target locations are accessed and sent back to the U-pipe for register write-back.

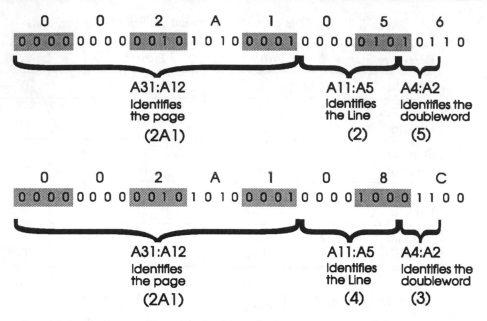

Figure 7-5. The Internal Data Cache Controller's Interpretation of the U- and V-pipe Addresses

Simultaneously, the data cache controller evaluates the state bits for the V-pipeline access. Entry four in directory zero shows that the data is shared (S) and entry four in directory one has an exclusive (E) line meaning that the line of information is not shared with another cache in the system other than the Pentium processor's own L2 cache. Since both entries have valid data, the cache controller compares the page portion of the address to the tag field stored in entry two of directory zero and directory one. The tag field in entry four of way zero matches the page portion of the V-pipe address, so the controller now knows that the cache has a copy of the target data in line four of way zero; therefore, a read hit is also detected for address V. Since the address bits A4:A2 have a 3, the bank select logic has activated bank three via the Bank Select Logic. The target locations are accessed and sent back to the V-pipe for register write-back.

LRU Update

The LRU bit for entry two and four must be updated to reflect the latest access to the cache ways. Since the LRU bit for entry two initially contained a "1" the LRU bit points to way one as having been least recently used. The current access was to way zero, so no change in the LRU bit is required ... way one is still least recently used. The LRU bit for entry four was originally a "0". Since the current access was to way zero, the least recently used cache way is now way one. The LRU bit is updated to a "1" to reflect this change.

The Snoop

In the example, another bus master is performing a read or write to a memory location contained in the Pentium processor's Level 2 (L2) cache while the data accesses are taking place. The L2 cache controller snoops that address and incurs a snoop hit to a modified line. The L2 cache backs the current bus master off and passes the snoop address to the Pentium processor so it can check the address to determine if it also has a copy of the target line. Since the data cache directory is triple ported, a snoop lookup can occur during the U- and V-pipe lookups.

The snoop address is interpreted by the cache controller which determines that the line resides in line 7Ch of some page in memory. The cache then checks the state bits and compares the page address from entry 7Ch within both directories. The state bits in directory zero indicate the line is modified and the tag portion of the directory entry matches the snoop page address. Therefore, a snoop hit occurs to a modified line, and both the HIT# and HITM# signals are asserted to notifiy the L2 cache that the L1 cache will perform the write-back.

Cache Structure and Performance
of Paired Instructions

The previous example illustrates an instruction pair simultaneously accessing internal cache memory in the same clock cycle. This is possible because the target data operands reside in different data cache banks. When a pair of instructions happen to access the same bank within the data cache (A4:A2 are the same), a bank conflict occurs because the banks are single ported and cannot respond to two simultaneous accesses. In such instances, the U-pipe access will complete first, while the V-pipe must wait. A bank conflict incurs a one clock penalty on the V-pipe instruction.

Pentium Processor System Architecture

Anatomy of a Read Miss

This example describes the sequence of events that occurs when both instruction pipelines request the contents of memory locations not found in the internal data cache. The two sample instructions used in this example are:

```
MOV EAX,[0054] ; Read into Pipeline U
MOV EBX,[008C] ; Read into Pipeline V
```

Again assume the processor is in protected mode, that the data segment starts at address is 00000000h and that the paging unit is turned off. The pipelines then are requesting two doublewords from locations 00000054h - 00000057h (U-pipe) and 0000008Ch - 0000008Fh (V-pipe).

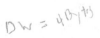

Set the Cache Stage

For the purpose of this discussion, assume that the internal data cache entries at the moment of the access are as listed in table 7-2, just where we left it in the previous example. See also Figure 7-6.

Table 7-2. Data cache entries prior to sample reads

Directory Status	Entry 2	Entry 4	Entry 7C
LRU Bit	1	1	0
State Bits Directory 0	S	S	I
State Bits Directory 1	S	E	I
Tag Field Directory 0	002A1	002A1	000F5
Tag Field Directory 1	00FB6	0385C	00F49

172

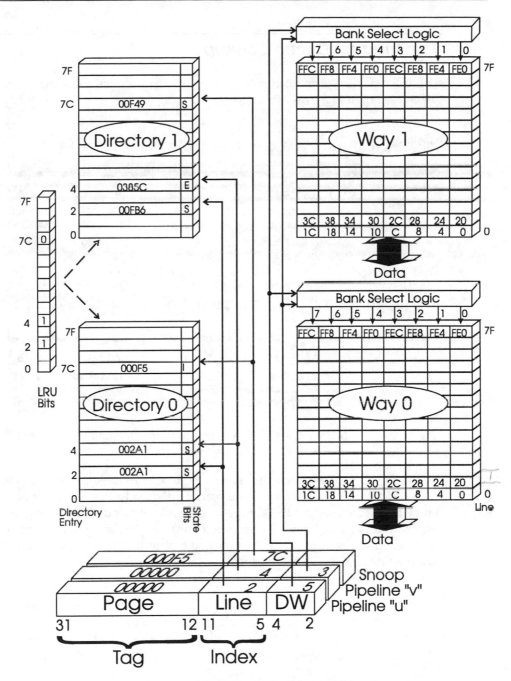

Figure 7-6. Internal Data Cache During Read Miss Example

The Internal Cache Lookup

The internal data cache controller interprets the address from the U- and V-pipes as shown in figure 7-7.

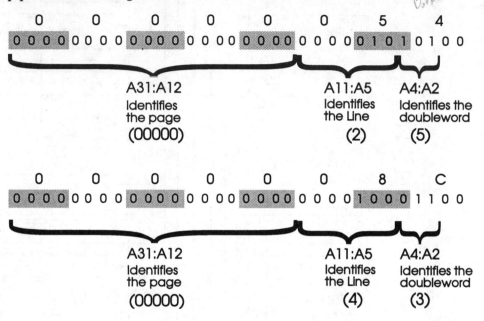

Figure 7-7. The Internal Data Cache Controller's Interpretation of the U- and V-pipe Addresses

The cache controller checks the state bits and compares the page portion of each address to the directory entries corresponding to the line being accessed. Entry two is checked for the U-pipe access and neither directory's tag matches the U-pipe page address, so it misses the internal cache. Similarly, entry four is checked in both directories during the simultaneous V-pipe access and again an internal cache miss results.

Chapter 7: The Data Cache and Burst Bus Cycles

The Bus Cycle Requests

When a miss occurs the internal data cache issues a cache line fill request to the bus unit which attempts to perform the line fill. In this case, two cache line fill requests are issued to the bus controller at the same time. The U-pipe read occurs first and the V-pipe is scheduled upon its completion.

The nature of the bus cycle run by the Pentium processor depends on whether the target location is cacheable, whether a copy of the target location is in the L2 cache, or whether an access must be made from the main memory subsystem. The following two scenarios assume that the requested locations are cacheable. The first scenario describes the bus cycles as they would look if the U-pipe request is found in L2 cache memory, and the V-pipe request is not found in the L2 cache. Both scenario one bus cycles assume no address pipelining. Scenario two assumes both U- and V-pipe requests hit the L2 cache and that address pipelining is active.

The Bus Cycle State Machine

The timing diagrams in this chapter show the processor's state machine operating in various states. The Pentium processor's bus unit has six bus states as follows:

Ti   **Bus idle state.**

T1   **Address Time**

T2   **Data Time**

T12   **Address Time (new cycle) and Data Time (cycle already is progress)**
Note: used during pipelined transfers.

T2P **Data Time (1st cycle pipelined) and Data Time (2nd cycle pipelined)**
Note: used during pipelined transfers.

TD   **Dead State (not shown in any of the timing diagrams)**

See the chapter entitled "Summary of Bus Cycles", for a more indepth discussion of the bus unit's state machine.

Scenario One: U-Pipe L2 Cache Hit / V-Pipe L2 Cache Miss

Figure 7-9 is a timing diagram of a U-pipe burst line fill from the external L2 cache. The V-pipe access results in an L2 cache miss and access to main DRAM memory. The timing diagram of the V-pipe line fill is shown in figure 7-10 and will be discussed following the U-pipe access.

The U-Pipe Access

The Bus Cycle Begins

The bus cycle begins when the processor outputs the address and the bus cycle definition. ADS# is asserted as the address is driven indicating that the address and bus cycle definition currently on the bus are valid.

When driving the address, the bus unit strips off the three least-significant bits of the address and converts them into the appropriate byte enable signals. The address output by the Pentium processor is shown in figure 7-8. Since the U-pipe request is for a doubleword from locations 00000054h through 00000057h, address lines A31:A3 indicate a starting quadword address of 00000050h in which location 54h through 57h reside. Byte enable lines BE7#:BE4# further specify that only the upper four bytes within the quadword are requested by the U-pipe instruction.

The Pentium processor also outputs the bus cycle definition lines along with the address. The bus cycle definition outputs indicate that a memory read line fill is being requested as shown in table Table 7-3.

The processor also sets its PCD (Page Cache Disable) output low, indicating to external memory that the address is within a page that is cacheable. Note that when paging is turned off, the state of the PCD output is determined by the state of the CD bit in control register zero (CR0). In this example the cache is enabled, thus the CD bit is set low. External memory now knows that the processor wants to perform a cache line fill.

Chapter 7: The Data Cache and Burst Bus Cycles

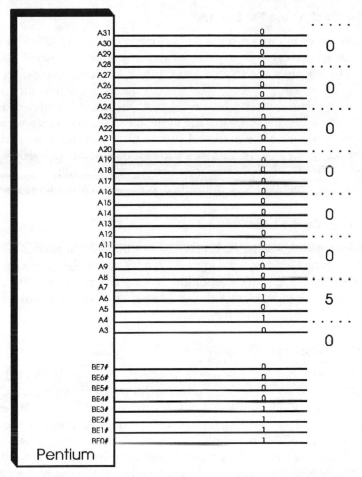

Figure 7-8. Pentium Processor Addressing Doubleword Starting at Location 54h.

Table 7-3. Bus Cycle Definition for Cache Line-fill Request

Signal	State	Description
M/IO#	1	this indicates that a memory cycle is being run.
D/C#	1	this indicates that a data access is being made.
W/R#	0	this indicates that a read cycle is being run.
CACHE#	0	this indicates that the processor wishes to perform a burst cycle (the location is cacheable).

The Cache Line Fill Defined

The intention of the processor is to perform a cache line fill via a burst transfer. The burst bus cycle is very similar to that performed by the i486 processor in that four transfers are required to fill the cache line. The target address locations 54h through 57h occupy the fifth doubleword within the cache line. To fill the cache line, the processor must read the eight doublewords that comprise the cache line that contains the target locations. This means that locations 40h through 5Fh must be read and placed in an internal data cache line. The Pentium processor's 64-bit data bus allows a quadword (8 bytes) of data to be transferred from external memory during each transfer; therefore, the Pentium processor requires four transfers to complete a line fill (as does the i486).

The L2 Cache Look-up

In this example, when the L2 cache receives the U-pipe address it performs a lookup in its cache directory and finds that a copy of the target line is resident in its cache SRAM. Upon determining that the target line is a hit, the L2 cache asserts the KEN# signal (since the address is obviously cacheable) and begins to access its fast SRAM memory.

The Cache Line Fill Confirmed

By default, all cache line fills are performed with burst cycles. The processor indicates its wish to perform a burst line fill by asserting the CACHE# signal and placing a low on the W/R# line. However, until the cache enable input (KEN#) is sampled asserted, the processor doesn't know if the address is cacheable. When KEN# is sampled asserted the processor performs the line fill using a burst transfer. If the processor samples the KEN# signal deasserted a single transfer is made from the target location(s) to supply the minimum requested data.

The processor samples KEN# when Burst Ready (BRDY#) is sampled asserted at the end of T2 time. The processor then knows that the transfer is cacheable, and since BRDY# is also asserted it captures the first quadword (locations 50h through 57h) that has been placed on the data bus by the L2 cache. The processor then proceeds with the rest of the burst transfer. More on burst transfers later. Notice that the processor also samples the WB/WT# signal low along with BRDY#. See "Controlling the MESI State-The Write-Once Policy" for an explanation of the WB/WT# signal.

Chapter 7: The Data Cache and Burst Bus Cycles

L2 Cache's Interpretation of the Address

Notice that the Pentium processor outputs a single target address and expects the L2 cache controller to interpret the address properly to complete the cache line fill. In this example, the target address output by the processor specifies that a doubleword be transferred (BE7#:BE4# are asserted, while BE3#:BE0# remain deasserted). When the L2 cache interrogates its cache directory with the target address, it recognizes that the line is in cache, and interprets the byte enable lines as if they are all asserted and an entire quadword is driven onto the processor's local data bus by the L2 cache.

The Burst Cycle

The L2 cache not only interprets the Pentium processor address as requesting 64 bits of valid data if the address is cacheable, but must also calculate the three additional addresses in the burst sequence necessary to complete the cache line fill. The address for the three additional quadwords will not be output by the processor. The burst sequence used with the Pentium processor is similar to that used by the i486, because both are based on two-way inter-leaved memory addressing. See "V-Pipe Access" for more details.

Figure 7-9 represents the fastest cache line fill possible. The entire 32 byte cache line is transferred from the L2 cache to the Pentium processor in five ticks of the processor's CLK. High speed L2 cache subsystems that can attain this performance virtually all use burst SRAM. These SRAM chips have built-in burst counters that automatically toggle address bits A3 and A4 to satisfy the line fill address sequence. If standard SRAM chips are used, the cache controller must supply the next burst address to the SRAM chips. The burst address sequence for the sample U-pipe instruction is:

50 - 57h   58 - 5Fh   40 - 47h   48 - 4Fh

BRDY# is initiated by the L2 cache and kept asserted until all four quadword transfers are completed, thereby satisfying the cache line fill request.

The First Quadword Read from L2 Cache

The target locations (54h - 57h) requested by the U-pipe are contained within the first quadword (50h - 57h) read from the L2 cache. After the processor latches the first quadword when BRDY# is sampled asserted, it sends the requested data operand to the U-pipe immediately and also stores the quadword in the 32 byte line-fill buffer.

The Last Three Quadwords Read from L2 Cache

Each of the remaining quadwords are placed in the line fill buffer as they are latched from the data bus. When the entire 32 byte line has been placed in the buffer, the entire cache line is written into cache memory and the cache directory is updated.

Line Entry and LRU Update

Refer to figure 7-6. The cache line read from the L2 cache (caused by the U-pipe read) must be placed in line two of the data cache. The LRU bit for entry two indicates that line two of way one has been least recently used, and must be replaced. Since entry two of directory one has its state bits set to "S", valid data exists in line two of way one. Therefore, valid data must be overwritten.

The contents of the line fill buffer is written into way one, and the LRU bit for entry two is updated to a "0" indicating that line two of way zero has been least used recently.

Controlling the MESI State — The Write-Once Policy

When a new line is read into the internal data cache, the initial state that it is placed in is determined by the L2 cache controller. Since the cache line requested by the U-pipe was found in the L2 cache, this means that the line had previously been requested by the processor and placed in the internal data cache, but was since overwritten by another line. The assumption made in this example is that the line read from the L2 cache was in the exclusive state. In response, the L2 cache controller drives the WB/WT# low (Write-through), directing the internal data cache to store the new line in the "S" state. This forces the internal data cache to perform a write-through to the L2 cache in the event of a processor write to any location in this line. This is necessary to enforce the write-once policy so that the L2 cache can be informed when the line has been modified by the processor. The L2 cache would then be able to snoop system bus activity correctly, to enforce the MESI protocol.

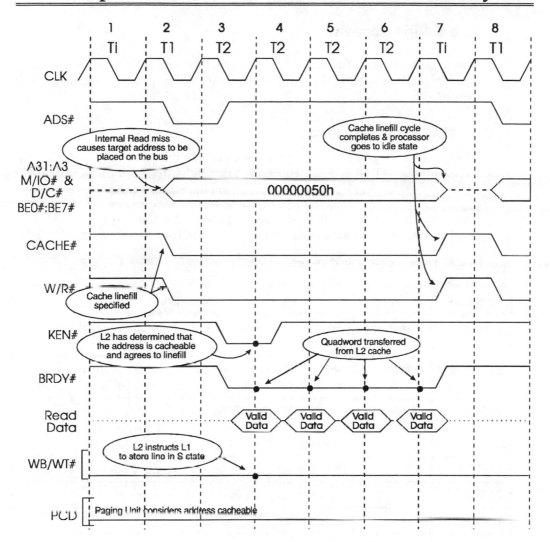

Figure 7-9. Burst Read Hit — L2 Cache

Note that during an internal data cache write-through, the L2 cache drives the WB/WT# signal high (write-back), directing the internal data cache to change the line state from "S" to "E". Subsequent writes to the internal cache line cause the state bit to be changed to M and no write-through is performed. This is possible because the L2 cache has already been notified that the cache line has been modified; therefore, the L2 cache is able to take the appropriate action when another bus master accesses a location within the modified line.

The V-Pipe Access

When the burst read finishes for the U-pipe, the Pentium processor inserts an idle state before starting the V-pipe burst read. Refer to the timing diagram in figure 7-10.

The Bus Cycle Begins

The bus cycle begins when the processor outputs the address and the bus cycle definition. ADS# is asserted as the address is driven indicating that the address and bus cycle definition currently on the bus are valid.

The processor outputs the address requested by the V-pipe (0000008Ch through 0000008Fh) along with the bus cycle definition as shown in table 7-4.

Table 7-4. Signals Output by the Processor When V-Pipe Access Begins

Signals	State	Description
A31:A3	00000088h	Address lines A31:A3 indicate the quadword address in which locations 8Ch through 8Fh reside.
BE7#:BE4#	0000b	BE7#:BE4# being asserted indicates that the upper four bytes within the target quadword is being addressed.
BE3#:BE0#	1111b	BE3#:BE0# being deasserted indicates that the lower four bytes within the quadword are not being addressed.
M/IO#	1	the processor is accessing a memory address location
D/C#	1	data is being accessed by the processor
W/R#	0	a read bus cycle is being run
CACHE#	0	the processor wishes to transfer an entire cache line via a burst bus cycle

The processor also sets its PCD (Page Cache Disable) output low indicating to external memory that the address is within a page that is cacheable. Note that when paging is turned off the state of the PCD signal is controlled by the CD bit in CR0. Since the cache is enabled CD is low, causing PCD to be low. External memory now knows that the processor wants to perform a cache line fill.

Chapter 7: The Data Cache and Burst Bus Cycles

The Cache Line Fill Defined

As with the U-pipe access, the intention of the processor is to perform a cache line fill via a burst transfer. The burst bus cycle is very similar to that performed by the i486 processor in that four transfers are required to fill the cache line. To fill the cache line, the processor must read all eight double-words that comprise the cache line associated with target locations 8Ch through 8Fh. This means that locations 80h through 9Fh must be read and placed in an internal data cache line.

The L2 Cache Look-up

When the L2 cache receives the V-pipe address, it performs a lookup in its cache directory and finds that the target line is not in its cache SRAM. Upon determining that the target location is not in its cache, the L2 cache transfers the bus cycle to the memory buses so that DRAM memory subsystem can be accessed.

The NCA Logic and Line Fill Confirmation

When the V-pipe access was initiated, the processor indicated its wish to perform a burst line fill by activating the CACHE# signal and placing a low on the W/R# line. However, the processor must sample the cache enable input (KEN#) to determine if the address is cacheable. When the address is cacheable, KEN# is sampled asserted and the processor performs a cache line fill using a burst transfer. When KEN# is sampled deasserted, the address is not cacheable and the target location(s) specified by the instruction are transferred with a single cycle.

When the L2 cache passes the bus cycle to the system bus, the NCA (Non-Cacheable Address) logic examines the address to verify that it is cacheable. The NCA logic asserts KEN# and passes it to the L2 cache. When the memory subsystem is ready to transfer data, the BRDY# signal is issued to the L2 cache, telling it that valid data is on the data bus. The L2 cache in turn issues BRDY#, KEN# and WB/WT# to the Pentium processor.

The processor samples KEN# and WB/WT# asserted when burst ready (BRDY#) is asserted. The processor now knows that the transfer is cacheable, that the line should be stored in the "S" state, and since BRDY# is asserted it latches the first quadword (locations 8Ch through 8Fh) that has been placed on the data bus by the DRAM subsystem.

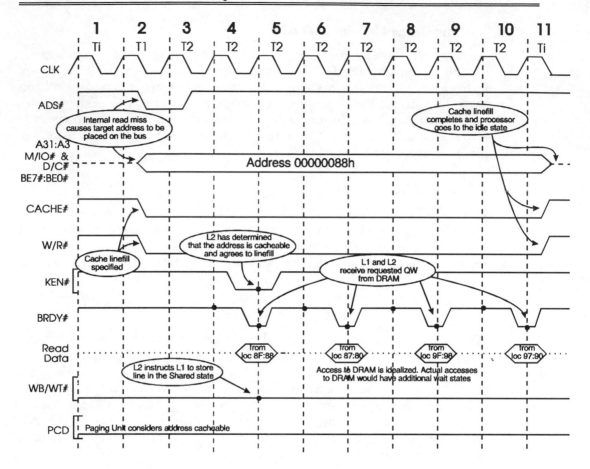

Figure 7-10. L2 Cache Miss — Burst Read from DRAM

DRAM System Memory's Interpretation of the Address

The Pentium processor outputs a single target address and expects the memory bus controller to interpret the address properly to complete the cache line fill. The target address output by the processor specifies only a doubleword (BE7:BE4 are asserted, while BE#:BE0 remain deasserted). When the memory subsystem recognizes that the line is in cache, it then interprets the byte enable lines as if they are all asserted, thus an entire 64-bit quadword is driven onto the system bus and back to the processors local bus.

Chapter 7: The Data Cache and Burst Bus Cycles

The Burst Sequence

The memory subsystem latches the Pentium processor's starting address and must calculate the three additional addresses in the burst sequence. The burst sequence used with the Pentium processor is the similar to that used by the i486, because both are based on two-way interleaved memory addressing. The burst address sequence for this example is:

88 - 8Fh   80 - 87h   98 - 9Fh   90 - 97h

The burst sequence can be satisfyed by toggling address bits A3 and A4. Following the first transfer, A3 is toggled to select the second quadword in the line fill. Following the second transfer both A3 and A4 are toggled to select the third quadword in the transfer. Following the third transfer A3 is again toggled to select the fourth and final quadword to complete the cache line fill addressing sequence.

Table 7-5. Quadword Address Sequences During Burst Transfers

1st Address Output	2nd Address Output	3rd Address Output	4th Address Output
80 - 87h	88 - 8Fh	90 - 97h	98 - 9Fh
88 - 8Fh	80 - 87h	98 - 9Fh	90 - 97h
90 - 97h	98 - 9Fh	80 - 87h	88 - 8Fh
98 - 9Fh	90 - 97h	88 - 8Fh	80 - 87h

The address sequence depends on which quadword within a cache line is being accessed first. The sample instruction for the V-pipe specifies access to location 8Ch through 8Fh, which is in the quadword starting at location 88h as shown above. Table 7-5 shows the address sequence that would occur when each of the quadwords are requested first.

The memory subsystem illustrated in figure 7-11 shows a conceptual implementation of a form of interleaving that, unlike true interleaved memory, accesses both 64-bit banks (banks A and B) simultaneouly. This permits the memory subsystem to read the first two quadwords requested by the processor in a single access. Since the processor's data bus width is 64-bits wide, the memory subsystem latches both quad words and transfers them to the processor in consecutive clocks. The memory controller enables the latch, which contains the first quadword in the line fill sequence, to output its contents. This latch is selected by the memory controller based on the initial state of A3 supplied by the processor. In this example, since the processor is addressing the quadword starting at address location 88h, A3 is initially a logical 1. This causes the latch associated with memory bank B to output its data first. The memory controller, having latched the processor's address, then toggles A3 to select the quadword residing in latch A (the quadword starting at location 80h).

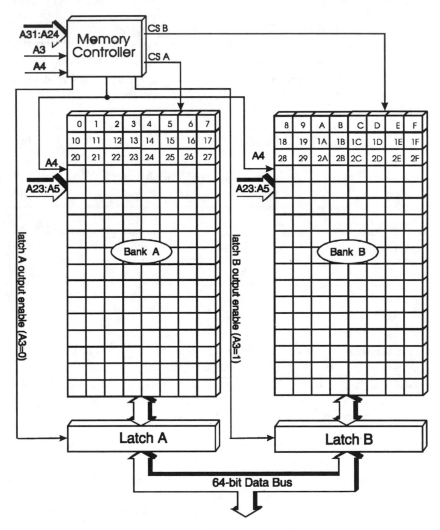

Figure 7-11. 64-Bit Two-Way Interleaved Memory

Chapter 7: The Data Cache and Burst Bus Cycles

Next, the memory controller toggles A4 causing the next two quadwords to be accessed. Note that this access can start as soon as the first 128-bits are latched. Once, the data is latched, the memory controller toggles A3 to select the contents of latch B (the quadword starting at location 98h). In the next clock, the memory controller transfers the final quadword, by toggling A3 again (selecting latch A).

The First Quadword Read from System Memory

The target locations (8Ch - 8Fh) requested by the V-pipe are contained within the first quadword (88h - 8Fh) read from memory. After the processor latches the first quadword when BRDY# is sampled asserted, it routes the target lo

cations requested by the instruction in the V-pipe directly to the specified register and also stores the quadword in the 32 byte line fill buffer.

The Last Three Quadwords Read from L2 Cache

Each of the remaining quadwords are placed in the line fill buffer as they are taken from the data bus. When the entire 32 byte line has been placed in the buffer, it then writes the line into the internal data cache memory and updates the directory entry.

Clean Line Replacement and LRU Update

The line read from main memory (caused by the V-pipe read) must be placed in line four of the data cache but valid data is already stored in line four of both cache ways. See figure 7-6. Since the LRU bit for entry four has a zero, it points to directory zero as having been least recently used, so the cache line is placed in line four of way zero. Line four of way zero, however, contains valid data since the state bits indicate that line four is shared (S). The current contents of line four are overwritten by data from the line fill buffer, and the LRU bit for entry four is updated to a "1" indicating that now line four of way one has been least recently used. Since the line to be replaced had not been modified by the processor, no write-back to external memory is required and the line replacement is said to be "clean."

Controlling the MESI State — The Write-Once Policy

When a new line is read into the internal data cache, its initial state is determined by the L2 cache controller. Since the cache line requested by the V-pipe was not found in the L2 cache, this indicates that the line had not been previously requested by the processor or that the copy of the requested line was overwritten by other entries in both the internal and L2 caches.

In this example, when the cache line fill occurs, copies of the cache line will end up in both in the internal and L2 caches. The cache line will be stored in the Exclusive state in the L2 cache. The L2 cache then drives the WB/WT# low directing the internal cache to store the new line in the S state. This forces the internal data cache to perform a write-through to the L2 cache the next time the processor writes to any location in this line. This is necessary to enforce the write-once policy so that the L2 cache can be informed when the line has been modified. The L2 cache can then correctly snoop system bus activity and enforce the MESI protocol. Note that during the internal cache write-through, the L2 cache drives the WB/WT# signal high (write-back), directing the internal cache to change the line state from "S" to "E." A subsequent write by the processor to the cache line causes the state bits to be changed to "M" and no write-through is performed.

Scenario Two: L2 Cache Hit (Pipelined access)

Figure 7-12 is a timing diagram of a U-pipe line fill followed by a V-pipe line fill from the L2 cache. The same U-pipe and V-pipe instructions are used for this example as in scenario one. However, scenario two assumes both the U-pipe and V-pipe accesses result in L2 cache hits and that address pipelining is enabled by the L2 cache. For the purposes of the following discussion, the U-pipe access is referred to as cycle A and the V-pipe access as cycle B. Pipelined transfers result in the fastest transfers that the Pentium processor is capable of performing.

Cycle A Begins

The first bus cycle begins when the processor outputs the address and the bus cycle definition. ADS# is asserted, indicating that the address and bus cycle definition currently on the bus are valid.

Chapter 7: The Data Cache and Burst Bus Cycles

The U-pipe request is for a doubleword from locations 00000054h through 00000057h. The Pentium processor drives the address and bus cycle definition lines for cycle A as shown in table 7-6.

Table 7-6. Signals Output when Cycle A Begins

Signal	State	Description
A31:A3	00000050h	Address lines A31:A3 indicate the starting quadword address in which locations 54h through 57h reside.
BE7#:BE4#	0000b	these asserted byte enable lines address the upper four bytes within the quadword.
BE3#:BE0#	1111b	these deasserted byte enable lines indicate that the lower four bytes within the quadword are not being addressed.
M/IO#	1	the processor is accessing a memory address location
D/C#	1	data is being accessed by the processor
W/R#	0	a read bus cycle is being run
CACHE#	0	the processor wishes to transfer an entire cache line via a burst bus cycle

The processor also sets its PCD output low as determined by the Cache Disable (CD) bit in CRO.

The L2 Cache Look-up (Cycle A)

In this example, when the L2 cache receives the U-pipe address, it performs a lookup in its cache directory and finds that a copy of the target line is in its cache SRAM. The L2 cache then asserts the KEN# signal (since the address is obviously cacheable) and begins to access its fast SRAM memory. At the same time, the L2 cache asserts the NA# (Next Address) signal requesting that the processor pipeline the next cycle early. The WB/WT# signal is also set low, telling the processor to store the cache line in the "S" state to enforce the write-once policy.

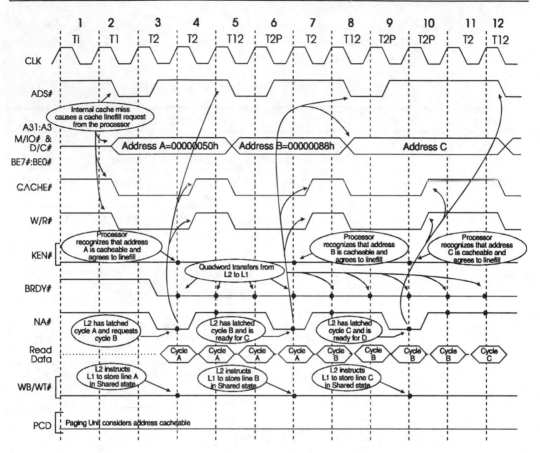

Figure 7-12. Pipelined Read Hit

Cache Line Fill Confirmed (Cycle A) and Pipelining Detected (Cycle B)

The processor always samples KEN# and WB/WT# on the leading edge of the clock in which either NA# or BRDY# is sampled asserted, whichever occurs first during the cycle. In this example, NA# and BRDY# are both asserted at the rising edge of the second T2 time (clock 4).

Since BRDY# is sampled asserted, the processor latches the first quadword (locations 50h through 57h) that has been placed on the data bus by the L2 cache. KEN# is also sampled asserted, telling the processor that the transfer is cacheable. WB/WT# is sampled low, directing the processor to store the line in the "S" state.

NA# sampled asserted tells the processor that the L2 cache supports pipelining and is granting permission to the processor to start the next cycle early. In response, the processor removes the address, CACHE# and W/R# signals for cycle A and prepares to start cycle B.

The Cycle A Transfer Continues

At the rising edge of each clock cycle, the processor samples the BRDY# signal to see if data is ready to be latched from the bus. In figure 7-12, BRDY# is sampled asserted on the next three consecutive positive clock edges (clocks 5, 6, and 7), thereby completing the cycle A transfer. When the last quadword is latched, the processor's line-fill buffer contents are stored in the least recently used line, and the state bits are set to "S" (because WB/WT# for cycle A was sampled low).

Cycle B Access Begins Early

When the Pentium processor samples the NA# signal asserted (trailing edge of clock 3), it waits one clock cycle and starts cycle B (the U-pipe access - clock 5). The L2 caches interrogates its cache directory and detects a cache hit. The L2 cache controller accesses its SRAM to satisfy the cycle B request as soon as the access for the U-pipe line fill (for cycle A) completes. The processor pipelines the cycle by outputting the signal shown in table 7-7.

Table 7-7. Signals Placed on the Bus During a Pipelined Cycle

Signals	State	Description
A31:A3	00000088h	Address lines A31:A3 indicate the starting quadword address in which locations 8Ch through 8Fh reside.
BE7#:BE4#	0000b	these asserted byte enable lines address the upper four bytes within the quadword.
BE3#:BE0#	1111b	these deasserted byte enable lines indicate that the lower four bytes within the quadword are not being addressed.

Signals	State	Description
ADS#	0	this signal notifies the L2 cache that a valid address and bus cycle definition are currently on the bus.
M/IO#	1	the processor is accessing a memory address location
D/C#	1	data is being accessed by processor
W/R#	0	read bus cycle is being run
CACHE#	0	the processor is requesting that an entire cache line be transferred via a burst cycle

The L2 Cache Look-up (Cycle B)

When the L2 cache receives the V-pipe access early, it accesses its directory and finds a copy of the target line. The cache then asserts NA# again to request the next cycle (Cycle C), and keeps KEN# and WB/WT# asserted low (clock 6). KEN# remains asserted because the address is cacheable, and WB/WT# is kept low, enforcing the write-once protocol.

Note that since the address for the V-pipe access (cycle B) has already been pipelined early, the Pentium processor need not insert an idle state between the U-pipe and V-pipe line fills.

Cycle B is Converted to a Line Fill and Cycle C is Requested

NA# is sampled asserted by the processor at the end of clock 6. The Pentium processor also samples KEN# and WB/WT# along with NA#. KEN# is sampled asserted indicating that cycle B is cacheable and WB/WT# is sampled low indicating that the cache line for cycle B should be stored in the "S" state.

Sampling NA# asserted tells the processor that external memory (the L2 cache in this case) is ready for the next bus cycle to be issued. In response to NA# being sampled asserted, the processor removes the CACHE# and W/R# signals for cycle B. One clock cycle later (clock 8) the processor outputs address C onto the bus and asserts the CACHE# and W/R# signals for cycle C. Note that the Pentium processor will not start the next bus cycle if two cycles have been issued by the processor and are currently pending completion. In this

Chapter 7: The Data Cache and Burst Bus Cycles

example, cycle A completes at the end of clock 6, therefore cycle C can be started at clock 8 since only cycle B is still pending completion.

The Cycle B transfer

The cycle B transfer begins in the clock cycle immediately following the completion of cycle A. Without pipelining, an idle clock period would be inserted between back-to-back bus cycles. In this instance, bus cycle pipelining allows the processor to start the next access early, allowing the first quadword to be transferred to the processor in the clock cycle immediately following completion of cycle A. Each subsequent quadword transfer for cycle B occurs in the next clock cycle until the cache line is filled.

The L2 Cache Look-up (Cycle C)

When the L2 cache receives cycle C, it accesses its directory and finds a copy of the target line. The L2 cache then asserts NA# to request the next cycle (Cycle D), and keeps KEN# and WB/WT# low. KEN# remains asserted because the address is cacheable, and WB/WT# is kept low, enforcing the write-once protocol.

Cycle C Converted to a cache line fill and Cycle D Requested

NA# is sampled asserted by the processor at the trailing edge of clock 9. The Pentium processor also samples KEN# and WB/WT# along with NA#. KEN# is sampled asserted indicating that cycle C is cacheable and WB/WT# is sampled low indicating that the cache line for cycle C should be stored in the "S" state.

NA# sampled asserted tells the processor that external memory (the L2 cache in this case) is ready for the next bus cycle to be issued. In response to NA# being sampled asserted, the processor removes the CACHE# and W/R# signals for cycle C. One clock cycle later the processor outputs the address and asserts the CACHE# and W/R# signals for cycle D. Note that the Pentium processor will not start the next bus cycle if two cycles are already outstanding. In this example, cycle B does not complete until the trailing edge of clock 10, therefore cycle D will not start until clock 12. At that point only cycle C is still pending completion.

Scenario Three: U-Pipe L2 Miss with Clean Replacement / V-Pipe L2 Hit

Scenario three assumes the same two accesses from the U-pipe (cycle A) and V-pipe (cycle B) used in scenarios one and two. In this example, the U-pipe access misses the L2 cache and the V-pipe access hits the L2 cache. Since cycle A misses the L2 cache, data must be accessed directly from the DRAM memory subsystem. Also assume that no room exists in the L2 cache to store the information being read from DRAM, therefore the least recently used data must be over-written. Overwriting the least recently used, but valid data may present a problem. Consider the following.

The Problem

To maintain cache coherency between the internal caches and the L2 cache, the policy of inclusion must be satisfied. In other words, the L2 cache must always contain a copy of the contents of the internal caches. Without this inclusion, a copy of valid information might reside in the internal cache but not in the L2 cache. In this instance, another bus master might write to a location in memory that in contained within the L1 cache but not the L2 cache. The L2 cache would snoop the address, experience a snoop miss and not generate an inquire cycle back to the Pentium processor. After the write cycle completed, the internal cache would have stale data.

The problem described above could develop when cycle A misses the L2 cache and a line in the L2 cache must be replaced to make room for the target line being read from memory. Since the L2 cache is typically many times larger than the internal caches, the organization of the internal caches, when compared to the L2 caches, will be quite different. In other words, the memory location stored in line two of one of the internal caches might be stored in line 130 of the L2 cache. As such, when the L2 cache replaces a line in its cache, a copy of the replaced line might also exist in one of the internal caches. The result -- valid data in the internal cache with no copy in the L2 cache. This situation must be prevented so that cache coherency can be maintained.

The Solution

When a cache line stored in the Shared or Exclusive state must be replaced, an inquire cycle (sometimes called a back-invalidation cycle) must be run to the Pentium processor with the invalidation (INV) signal driven high. This allows the internal caches to interrogate their cache directories to see if they have a copy of the information being replaced. If so, the internal cache line will be invalidated (since the INV signal is asserted), thus maintaining the "policy of inclusion".

When the L2 cache must replace a line stored in either the "E" or "S" states this is termed a "clean" replacement. When a cache line stored in the Modified (M) state must be replaced, it is termed a "modified" or "dirty" replacement. In this instance, a write-back cycle must be performed to store the modified data in DRAM memory prior to it being overwritten in the cache. (See Scenario 4.)

Cycle A Begins

Refer to figure 7-13. Cycle A begins with the Pentium processor driving the address and bus cycle definition onto the bus.

The L2 Cache Lookup (Cycle A)

The L2 cache detects the bus cycle and uses the address to interrogate its cache directory. The L2 cache does not find a copy of the target line in its directory, and also determines that the cache line into which the target information must be placed contains valid data that must be over-written when the new line is read from DRAM memory. The L2 cache then takes two actions:

1. passes cycle A to the memory bus to access DRAM memory
2. runs a back-invalidation (inquire) cycle to the Pentium processor to enforce the inclusion property

The address for cycle A is latched and transferred to the memory bus along with the bus cycle definition lines, starting the access to main memory.

In addition, the AHOLD signal is driven high to inform the processor that an inquire cycle is being run.

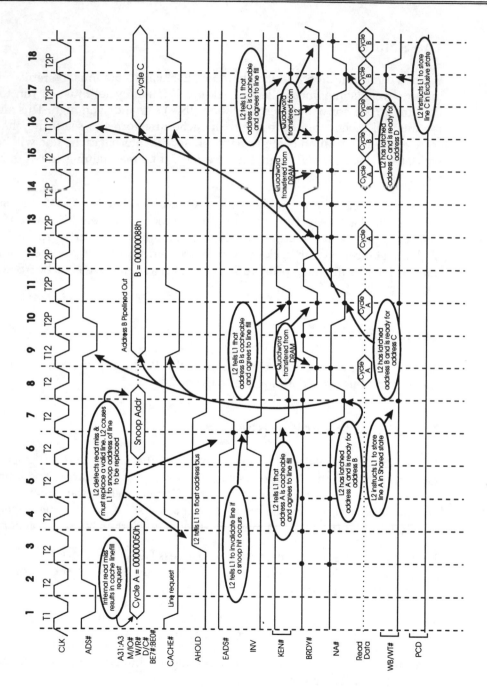

Figure 7-13. L2 Cache Miss with Clean Line Replacement

Chapter 7: The Data Cache and Burst Bus Cycles

The Processor Prepares for the Inquire Cycle

When the processor detects the AHOLD signal asserted, it floats its address bus, at the beginning of the next cycle, thereby removing the address for cycle A from the processor's local address bus.

The L2 Cache Initiates the Inquire Cycle

The L2 cache passes the address to be snooped to the processor (clock 6). The snoop address is the address of the line to be replaced in the L2 cache. When the address being passed to the processor is stable, the EADS# and INV signals are asserted.

The Pentium Processor Snoops the Address

EADS# commands the processor to use the address being presented on address lines A31:A5 to index into its cache directories to determine if a copy of the line is contained within the caches. If a snoop hit occurs to a line stored in either the "S" or "E" states, then the state bits will transition to "I", since the INV signal is asserted. If a snoop miss results, no further action is taken by the processor. The snoop cycle ends when the L2 cache removes the AHOLD signal. In this example, a snoop hit occurs to a line stored in the "S" state, therefore the state bits transition from "S" to "I".

When a hit is detected to a line in the "S" state, the HIT# signal is asserted, notifying external logic of a hit to a non-modified line. No action is taken by the L2 cache as a result of HIT# being sampled asserted.

Cache Line Fill Confirmed (Cycle A) and Pipelining Detected (Cycle B)

When the bus cycle first appears on the memory bus, the Non Cacheable Address (NCA) logic checks the address to see if it is cacheable. In this case, the address is cacheable and the KEN# signal is returned to the L2 cache indicating that cycle A is cacheable. Simultaneously, the address is seen by the memory subsystem's address decoder which recognizes the address and generates the appropriate chip select signals. The decoder also asserts NA# if the memory subsystem can take advantage of pipelining. In this example, it can. These two signals go to the L2 cache controller, which in turn delivers them to the Pentium processor as the back-invalidation cycle completes.

The processor samples NA# asserted, at the trailing edge of clock 7. As a result, KEN# and WB/WT# are also sampled to determine the cacheability of cycle A and to determine which MESI state the target location should be stored in. Cycle A is cacheable and the line should be stored in the "S" state.

Cycle B Begins

NA# indicates that the memory subsystem can take advantage of pipelining and is ready to receive cycle B while cycle A is still in progress. In response to NA#, the processor outputs cycle B onto its bus.

The Access to DRAM Memory (Cycle A)

When the snoop operation completes, the data accessed from slow DRAM will be transferred to the L2 cache and the processor. At the trailing edge of clock 8, the first BRDY# is returned, indicating that the first quadword for cycle A is present on the data bus. Both the L2 cache and the Pentium processor latch the information, and sample the BRDY# signal at the end of each clock period, awaiting the next three BRDY# signals to complete cycle A.

The L2 Cache Lookup (Cycle B)

When the cycle is pipelined at the leading edge of clock 9, the L2 cache interrogates its cache directory and finds a copy of the requested information. In response, the L2 cache controller asserts the NA# signal along with KEN# and WB/WT# is set low.

Cache Line Fill Confirmed (Cycle B) and Pipelining Detected (Cycle C)

The processor samples NA#, KEN#, and WB/WT# at the trailing edge of clock 10. KEN# tells the processor that cycle B is cacheable and WB/WT# being low directs the processor to store the cache line in the "S" state within the internal data cache. NA# indicates that the L2 cache controller supports pipelining and is requesting the next cycle pending be transferred early. Normally, the processor would drive cycle C onto the bus one clock cycle later. However, both cycle A and cycle B have already been pipelined, therefore the Pentium processor will not drive cycle C onto the bus until cycle A completes (trailing edge of clock 14).

Cycle A Completes and Cycle C Begins

After the last quadword for cycle A is transferred, the processor outputs cycle C onto the buses, at the leading edge of clock 16.

The L2 Cache Lookup -- Cycle C

When cycle C is pipelined at reference point 13, the L2 cache interrogates its cache directory and finds a copy of the requested information. In response, the L2 cache controller asserts NA# and KEN# and sets WB/WT# low.

The Cycle B Transfers

Cycle B transfers come directly from the L2 cache and can be delivered in the next clock cycle following the completion of the Cycle A transfers. The Pentium processor continues sampling the BRDY# signal at the end of each clock cycle. Since the data for cycle B are in the L2 cache, transfers occur every clock cycle.

Cache Line Fill Confirmed (Cycle C) and Pipelining Detected (Cycle D)

The processor samples NA#, KEN#, and WB/WT# at reference point 14. KEN# tells the processor that cycle C is cacheable and WB/WT# being high directs the processor to store the cache line in the "E" state within the internal data cache. NA# indicates that the L2 cache controller supports pipelining and is requesting the next cycle pending be pipelined out early. Normally, the processor would drive cycle D onto the bus one clock cycle later. However, two cycles (B and C) are already outstanding, therefore the Pentium processor will not drive cycle D onto the bus until cycle B completes.

Scenario Four: U-pipe L2 Miss with Modified Replacement

Scenario four details only the U-pipe transfer and assumes the target line is not in the L2 cache. Assume also, that the L2 cache must replace a cache line that has been modified. If the line were replaced without first writing its contents to DRAM memory, then the modified data would be lost. Also, since the line in the L2 cache must be replaced, a copy of the same line might also be stored in the internal data cache, and that line may have been modified more recently than the copy in the L2 cache. If this is the case, the processor should perform the write-back to DRAM memory. The timing diagram in figure 7-14 depicts the type of operation described above.

Bus Cycle A Begins

Cycle A begins with the Pentium processor driving the address and bus cycle definition onto the bus.

The L2 Cache Lookup (Cycle A)

The L2 cache detects the bus cycle and uses the address to interrogate its cache directory. The L2 cache does not find a copy of the target line in its directory, but determines that a modified line must be replaced in order to store the new line being read from DRAM memory. The L2 cache then performs three operatons:

1. passes bus cycle A to the system bus to access DRAM memory.
2. runs an inquire cycle to the Pentium processor to maintain the inclusion property and to determine if the processor has modified data in the internal data cache.
3. moves the modified data to a write-back buffer to make room for the line being acquired by bus cycle A.

The address for cycle A is latched and transferred to the memory bus along with the bus cycle definition lines, thereby starting the access to memory. In addition, the AHOLD signal is asserted to inform the processor that an inquire cycle is being run. The Processor in response removes the address for cycle A from the bus.

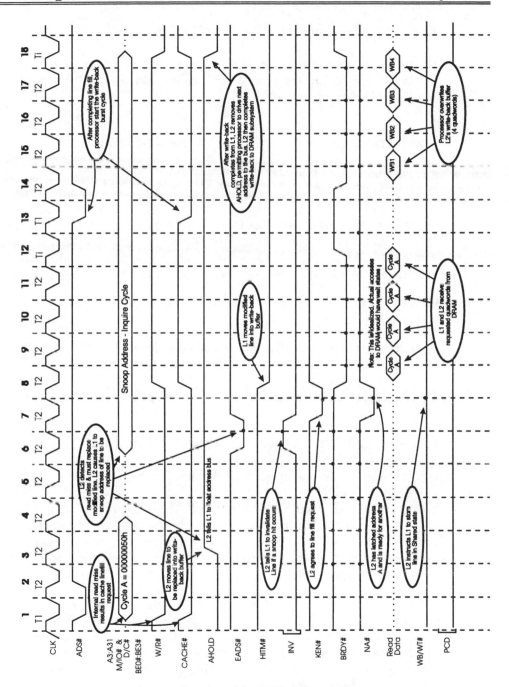

Figure 7-14. L2 cache miss with modified line replacement

The L2 Cache Initiates the Inquire Cycle

The L2 cache passes the address to be snooped (the address of the modified line to be replaced) to the processor. Once the address stablizes, the L2 cache asserts EADS# and INV.

The Pentium Processor Snoops the Address

EADS# commands the processor to use the address presented on address lines A31:A5 to index into its cache directories to see if a copy of the line is contained within the L1 caches. If a snoop hit occurs to a line stored in either the "S" or "E" states, then the state bits will transition to "I" (since the INV signal is asserted). In this example, a snoop hit occurs to a modified line in the data cache. The processor knows that it has the latest information within the modified line and must, therefore, perform a write-back to external memory.

When the Pentium processor detects a snoop hit to a modified line, it performs two operations:

1. Asserts HITM# to notify the L2 cache that its copy of the modified line is stale. The L2 cache is then made aware that the Pentium processor will perform the write-back.
2. Moves the copy of the modified line into its external snoop write buffer.

The Cache Line Fill Confirmed and Pipelining Detected

When the bus cycle first appears on the memory bus, the Non Cacheable Address (NCA) logic checks the address to see if it is cacheable. In this case, the address is cacheable and the KEN# signal is returned to the L2 cache, indicating that cycle A is cacheable. Simultaneously, the address is seen by the memory subsystem's address decoder, which recognizes the address and generates the appropriate chip select signals. The L2 cache also asserts NA#, signaling its readiness to perform a lookup on the next address.

The processor samples NA# at the trailing edge of clock 7. The processor samples KEN# and WB/WT# along with NA# to determine cacheability of cycle A and to determine which MESI state the target line should be stored in if cacheable. The processor determines that cycle A is cacheable (since KEN# is sampled asserted) and determine that the line should be stored in the "S" state (since WB/WT# is sampled low.

In response to NA# being sampled asserted, the processor ceases to drive bus cycle A. Note that the address for bus cycle A has already been removed due to the AHOLD signal. At the leading edge of clock 8, the CACHE# and W/R# lines are also removed.

Cycle A Completes

On the trailing edge of clock 8, the first quadword for bus cycle A is returned from the memory subsystem. Both the L2 cache and the Pentium processor receive the data and place it in their line fill buffers. In this example, the memory subsystem is able to complete the cycle A transfer in four consecutive ticks of the processor's clock. This is an idealized condition. Actual accesses to DRAM would have wait states.

The CPU Write-Back

When the processor recognizes that the cycle A transfer has completed, it starts the write-back bus cycle. The processor initiates the write-back by asserting ADS#, CACHE# and driving W/R# high at the rising edge of clock 13. Since AHOLD is still asserted, the processor cannot drive the address bus. Instead, the L2 cache continues to drive the snoop address (since the snoop address is the same as the write-back address). The first quadword of the write-back data is driven from the write-back buffer onto the data bus.

The L2 Cache Lookup (Write-Back Cycle)

The L2 cache sees ADS# asserted and knows that the processor has initiated the write-back cycle. The quadword in the processor's snoop write-back buffer is transferred to external memory using a burst transfer. The write-back data is received by the L2 cache and placed into its write-back buffer. The L2 cache asserts BRDY#, notifying the processor that the first transfer is complete. BRDY# is kept asserted by the L2 cache and the write-back completes in four consecutive clock cycles.

The Inquire Cycle Ends

When the processor's write-back transfer completes, the L2 cache removes the AHOLD signal to the processor, ending the inquire cycle. Subsequently, the L2 cache writes the contents of its write-back buffer to DRAM memory. When the inquire cycle ends, the Pentium processor is able to start the next pending bus cycle.

Anatomy of a Write Hit

When an instruction is executed that requires a write to memory, the internal data cache interrogates its internal directory to see if it has a copy of the information. If the target line is found in cache, the target location within the cache line is updated. Whether or not the Pentium processor writes the data on through to external memory depends on the state in which the line is stored in the internal data cache (as described below).

Write to a Line Stored in the "Shared" State

A write hit to a line in the internal data cache that is stored in the "S" state causes the processor to update the line in the internal cache and write the data through to external memory. The Pentium processor does not perform burst cycles when a write-through operation occurs. Burst write cycles only occur during write-back cycles. See the next chapter for a discussion of single cycle transfers.

Write to a Line Stored in the "Exclusive" State

When a write occurs to a location stored in the internal data cache and that line is stored in the "E" state, the location will be updated and no bus cycle will be generated. The state bits will, however, transition from the "E" state to the "M" state, indicating that the location has been modified but not written back to memory.

Chapter 7: The Data Cache and Burst Bus Cycles

Write to a Line Stored in the "Modified" State

When a write occurs to a location stored in the internal data cache and that line is stored in the "M" state, the location will be updated and no bus cycle will be generated. Since the state bits already indicate the location has been modified, no state transition is required.

Anatomy of a Write Miss

When one of the execution units performs a write operation and a copy of the location is not found in the internal data cache, a write bus cycle must be run to write the target information to external memory. The Pentium processor performs a single non-burst write transfer each time a memory write miss occurs.

When back-to-back memory write operations occur, the write buffers are used to increase performance. See the section entitled "Write Buffers" in the next chapter for additional information.

The Write-Back Buffers

Figure 7-15 shows the write buffers inside the Pentium processor. In addition to the write buffers discussed above, there are three additional write buffers dedicated to the write-back functions:

The External Snoop Write Buffer -- used to store write-backs caused by an external snoop hit to a modified line.

The Internal Snoop Write Buffer -- used to store write-backs caused by an internal snoop hit to a modified line during a code cache miss.

Line Replacement Write Buffer -- used to store write-backs caused by the replacement of a least-recently-used line that is modified.

Write cycles are driven to the bus in the following priority order:

- Contents of external snoop write buffer
- Contents of internal snoop write buffer

- Contents of replacement write buffer
- Contents of write buffers

Note that all write buffers are snooped during external snoop operations.

Inquire Cycles

External Snoop to a Modified Cache Line

The action taken by the Pentium processor during a snoop to a modified line results in a cache write-back. If a bus cycle is currently being run, the line to be written-back to memory is temporarily stored in the external write-back buffer until it can be written to memory using a burst transfer. MESI state transitions are determined by the INV signal generated by external logic.

- If INV=0, the line transitions to the "S" state
- If INV=1, the line transitions to the "I" state

Snoop to a Shared Cache Line

When a snoop hit occurs to a cache line stored in the shared state, the Pentium processor takes the following action:

- If INV=0, the line remains in the "S" state
- If INV=1, the line transitions to the "I" state

The Internal Snoop

The data cache snoops all read misses from the code cache. If a snoop hit occurs to a line stored in the "S" state, the line is invalidated in the data cache. If the snoop hits a line stored in the "M" state, then the read cycle completes to main memory and the code is stored in the code cache in the "I" state. The Pentium processor then performs a write-back from its "internal snoop write buffer". At the completion of the write-back, the code cache issues the read cycle again to obtain valid code.

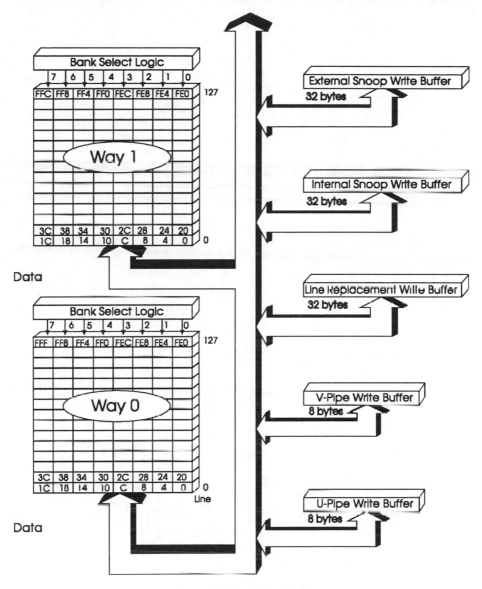

Figure 7-15. Write Buffers

Chapter 8

The Previous Chapter

The previous chapter described the operation of the Pentium processor's internal data cache, and the interaction between the Level 2 (L2) cache controller and the DRAM memory subsystem. Burst bus cycles required for cache line-fills and cache write-back burst cycles were also covered.

This Chapter

This chapter summarizes the various types of bus cycles run by the Pentium processor, with focus on non-burst transactions.

The Next Chapter

The next chapter discusses System Management Mode (SMM) feature implemented in the Pentium 60/66 processors.

Bus Cycle Overview

The Pentium processor runs several types of bus cycles as shown in table 8-1. The bus cycle type to be run is specified by the processor's bus cycle definition pins.

Three general categories of bus cycles are run by the Pentium processor.

- Burst Bus Cycle
- Single Transfer Bus Cycles (Non-Burst)
- Special Cycles
- Interrupt Acknowledge Bus Cycle

Pentium Processor System Architecture

This chapter details the timing of the bus cycle types and describes functionality and performance associated with each. For detailed examples of burst bus cycles see the previous chapter.

Table 8-1. Pentium Processor Bus Cycle Types

M/IO#	D/C#	W/R#	CACHE#	Bus Cycle Type
0	0	0	1	Interrupt Acknowledge
0	0	1	1	Special Cycle
0	1	0	1	I/O Read
0	1	1	1	I/O Write
1	0	0	1	Code (Instruction) Read
1	0	0	0	Code Read (burst line-fill) *
1	0	1	x	Reserved
1	1	0	1	Memory Data Read
1	1	0	0	Memory Data Read (burst line-fill)*
1	1	1	1	Memory Data Write
1	1	1	0	Memory Write-back (burst cycle)

* Indicates burst cycle unless KEN# is sampled inactive

Burst Bus Cycles

The Pentium processor runs burst bus cycles only when an entire cache line (32 bytes) is to be transferred to or from the Pentium processor. Specifically, the only burst bus cycles occur during cache line-fill operations (code reads or data reads) or cache line write-back operations. Notice that burst cycles can only be run when the processor asserts the CACHE# signal as shown in table 8-1.

Cache line-fill operations occur when an access to memory results in a data cache or instruction cache miss. When a cache miss occurs, a line-fill request is sent from the cache to the bus unit, which in turn initiates the burst bus cycle. A cache line-fill occurs when KEN# (the cache enable signal) is sampled asserted by the processor. If the processor samples KEN# deasserted, then no burst cycle nor cache line-fill occurs. Instead, a signal read transfer is performed from the target location specified.

Chapter 8: Summary of Pentium Bus Cycles

Write-back bus cycles occur when the processor must write an entire cache line back to memory. Write-backs occur for three different reasons:

1. An external snoop results in a hit to a modified line in the internal data cache. The modified line must be written back to memory for cache consistency to be maintained.
2. An internal snoop results in a hit to a modified line in the internal data cache. The modified line must be written back to memory for cache consistency to be maintained.
3. A modified line in the data cache must be replaced to make room for data being read from memory. The modified line must be written back to avoid losing modified data.

Detailed examples of burst cycles are covered in the previous Chapter entitled, "The Data Cache and Burst Line-Fills."

Single Transfer (Non-Burst) Bus Cycles

Single transfer cycles are run by the Pentium processor when accessing non-cacheable address space. Non-cacheable address space includes all I/O locations and memory locations that are designated as non-cacheable. Non-cacheable memory includes:

- all memory locations when the internal caches are disabled (the Cache Disable (CD) bit in Control Register zero (CR0) is set to "1").
- locations programmed as non-cacheable via the Non-Cacheable Address (NCA) logic (when the internal caches are enabled). In other words, the processor asserts its CACHE# output, informing external logic that it wishes to perform a cache line-fill (burst read) but KEN# is returned deasserted. When KEN# is sampled deasserted, the processor ends the bus cycle after a single transfer.
- locations within a page of memory, page table or page table directory that have been designated non-cacheable by the operating system (when the internal caches are enabled and the processor is in protected mode and paging is enabled).

Single transfer cycles can be categorized into four basic types:

- Non-cacheable memory reads (code reads and data reads)
- Non-cacheable memory writes
- I/O reads
- I/O writes

Additionally, each of these bus cycle types can be run in non-pipelined or pipelined mode.

Memory Read and Write Bus Cycles – Non-pipelined

Figure 8-1 illustrates the timing of a single cycle memory read followed by a memory write transfer. The memory read cycle illustrates a zero wait state transfer, while the write cycle illustrates a one wait state transfer. Both transfers are non-pipelined.

The Read. The memory read example assume that the internal caches are enabled and the Pentium processor has encountered a cache miss in either the code or instruction cache. The Pentium processor attempts to perform a burst cache line-fill, but samples KEN# deasserted, therefore, the bus cycle is not converted into a cache line-fill and a single transfer is made. the bus cycle begins in clock 2 when the processor asserts ADS# and drives the address and bus cycle definition lines onto its local bus. The processor samples BRDY# asserted on the trailing edge of clock 3, and also samples KEN# to see whether this bus cycle will be converted into a burst cache line-fill or not. Since KEN# is sampled deasserted, the processor knows that the address location is not cacheable and latches the data from the data bus and terminates the bus cycle with a single transfer.

The Idle State. Notice that the Pentium processor inserts an idle state (Ti) between all non-pipelined bus cycles to allowing for timing constraints associated with faster bus speed.

The Write. The memory write occurs as a result of either a cache hit or miss to the internal data cache. In either instance, a single transfer cycle is run by the Pentium processor. In clock 5, the Pentium processor drives the address and bus cycle definition onto its local bus and asserts ADS#. Note that the CACHE# output is driven deasserted, indicating that this will not be a burst transfer. As a result, KEN# is not sampled. At the beginning of the first T2 (clock 6) the processor drives the data over the path(s) required, based on the

Chapter 8: Summary of Pentium Bus Cycles

location(s) being addressed. The processor samples BRDY# deasserted on the trailing edge of clock 6, forcing the processor to insert another T2 time (1 wait state) into the bus cycle. On the trailing edge of the next clock (7), the processor samples BRDY# asserted indicating that the transfer has completed.

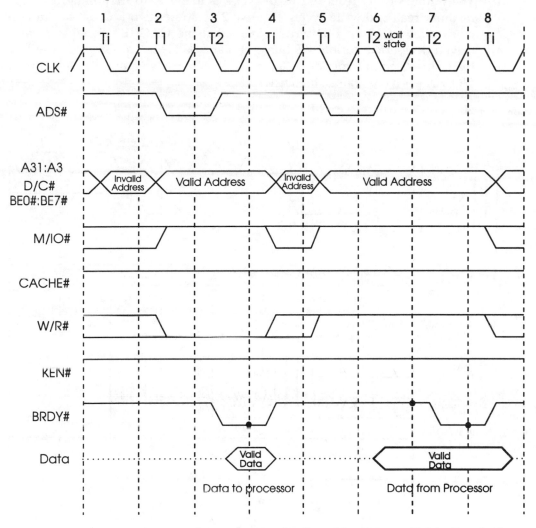

Figure 8-1. Timing of a Memory Read Followed by a Memory Write Bus Cycle (Non-Pipelined)

I/O Read and Write Bus Cycles – Non-pipelined

The timing of I/O read and write cycles is identical to the timing of single memory read and write cycles. Figure 8-2 illustrates two I/O cycles: An I/O read followed by an I/O write. Notice that the CACHE# signal is always driven deasserted during I/O bus cycles and KEN# is not sampled. The I/O read illustrated in figure 8-2 is a zero wait state transfer, and the subsequent I/O write is a one wait state transfer.

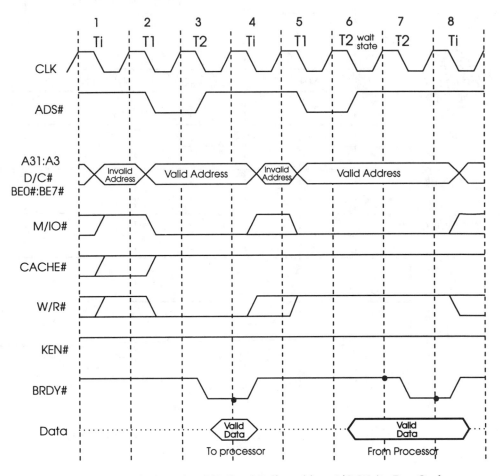

Figure 8-2. *Timing of an I/O Read Followed by a I/O Write Bus Cycle*
(Non-Pipelined)

Chapter 8: Summary of Pentium Bus Cycles

Single Transfer Bus Cycles (Pipelined)

When back-to-back cycles are run to memory or I/O devices that require one or more wait states to complete a transfer, pipelining can improve performance. These devices must decode the address and assert the NA# (Next Address) signal. When the processor samples NA# asserted, it drives the next pending bus cycle early, before the current bus cycle completes. This allows devices designed to take advantage of pipelining to decode the address early in preparation for the next transfer. These devices can also latch the current data access and return that data to the processor, while starting the next access during the current cycle.

Figure 8-3 illustrates two bus cycle transfer sequences, one without pipelining and the other with pipelining. The first sequence consists of three back-to-back bus cycles to a device requiring two wait states to complete each transfer. The processor samples NA# deasserted at all sample points, therefore the next cycle is not pipelined early. The second sequence consists of the same three back-to-back bus cycles. However, in this example NA# is sampled asserted by the processor. This causes the processor to start the next bus cycle prior to completing the first. Notice that the three pipelined cycles complete with four less clock cycles than the non-pipelined transfers.

Special Cycles

During special cycles, the address and data bus are floated except during the branch trace message cycle. ADS# is driven along with the bus cycle definition lines and byte enables BE5#:BE0#. When external logic detects a special cycle is in progress, then the byte enables are decoded to determine which special cycle is being run.

When branch trace message cycles are enabled and when a branch instructions is taken, the address bus contains the address of the branch target location. See the chapter entitled, "Test and Debug", for a discussion of the branch trace message cycle.

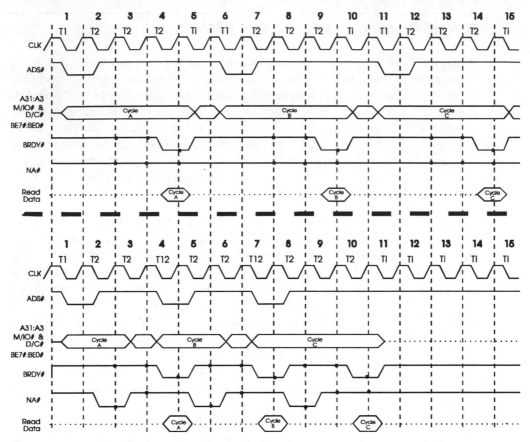

Figure 8-3. Comparison of Non-Pipelined Vs Pipelined Bus Cycles

Table 8-2. Special Cycles

Special Cycle Type	BE5#	BE4#	BE3#	BE2#	BE1#	BE0#
Shutdown	1	1	1	1	1	0
Flush	1	1	1	1	0	1
Halt	1	1	1	0	1	1
Write-back	1	1	0	1	1	1
Flush Acknowledge	1	0	1	1	1	1
Branch Trace Message	0	1	1	1	1	1

Chapter 8: Summary of Pentium Bus Cycles

Interrupt Acknowledge Bus Cycle

The Pentium processor performs two back-to-back interrupt acknowledge bus cycles when an interrupt request (INTR) is recognized (the same as earlier x86 processors). The processor uses these cycles to communicate with the interrupt controller(s). It is the responsibility of the system designer to insert wait-states into the interrupt acknowledge bus cycles to meet setup and hold requirements for the interrupt controllers.

The Bus Cycle State Machine

The Pentium processor's bus unit has six bus states as follows:

Ti **Bus idle state.** Like previous Intel 80X86 processors, the idle state indicates that no bus cycles are being run.

T1 **Address Time.** The first clock of a bus cycle when no other cycles are outstanding. The address and bus cycle definition are driven during T1 and ADS# is asserted. T1 indicates that this is the only bus cycle in progress. In other words, no bus cycle pipelining is occurring.

T2 **Data Time.** The second and subsequent clocks in a bus cycle. If a read bus cycle is being run, data is latched from the data bus when BRDY# is sampled asserted at the end of T2. During write bus cycles, data is driven during T2. During the T2 state no other cycles are currently running.

T12 **Address Time (2nd cycle pipelined) and Data Time (1st cycle already is progress).** T12 represents a pipelined state in which the address phase of a newly pipelined cycle and data time for the cycle already in progress occur simultaneously. Like T1, the address and bus cycle definition are driven during T12 and ADS# is asserted for the newly pipelined cycle. Also during T12, the cycle already in progress was initiated sometime in the past but has not yet completed. In short, the processor is still in the T2 state for the current cycle and has entered T1 state for the next pipelined cycle, hence the composite T12.

T2P **Data Time (1st cycle) and Data Time (2nd cycle pipelined).** This state represents two cycles that are outstanding on the bus and both are in the T2 state. During T2P, BRDY# is sampled for the first cycle initiated by the processor. When the first outstanding cycle completes, the state transitions to T2, indicating only one outstanding cycle.

Pentium Processor System Architecture

TD   **Dead State.** This state indicates there is one outstanding bus cycle, and BRDY# is not being sampled because the data bus transceivers need time to turn around (change direction) between consecutive reads and writes, or writes and reads. This state only occurs during pipelined transfers.

Bus State Transitions

Transitions occur between states as shown in the following state diagram (figure 8-4). The state transitions are described in table 8-3.

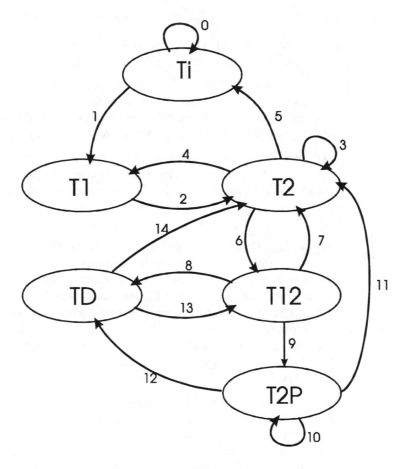

Figure 8-4. Pentium Processor's State Diagram

Table 8-3. Description of State Transitions

Ref #	State Transition Description
0	No request pending
1	The Pentium processor starts a bus cycle by driving the address and bus cycle definition onto the buses.
2	The processor always precedes from T1 to T2 unless BOFF# is asserted. In this case, the cycle is terminated and restarted when BOFF# is released.
3	The processor stays in T2 (adding wait states) until the last BRDY# is sampled, unless NA# is sampled asserted and another bus cycle is pending.
4	The processor transitions from T2 to T1 after the bus cycle ends, if another bus cycle is pending and the processor sampled NA# asserted. If NA# was not asserted the state transitions back to Ti.
5	The processor transitions from T2 to Ti after the bus cycle ends, if NA# was not asserted or if no other bus cycle is pending.
6	The processor transitions from T2 to T12 before the bus cycle ends, if NA# was asserted and another cycle becomes pending.
7	The state transitions from T12 back to T2 is the current bus cycle has ended and no dead clock is needed.
8	The bus state transitions from T12 to TD when the current bus cycle has completed and a dead clock is needed. A dead clock is needed when the first bus cycle has completed a read and the second is a write transfer, or when the first cycle is a write and the second is a read.
9	The bus state always transitions from T12 to T2P when the current bus cycle is still running and no BOFF# has been asserted. This indicates that two cycles are outstanding and both are in the data phase.
10	The Pentium processor stays in T2P until the first transfer completes.
11	The bus state goes from T2P to T2 when the first transfer completes, if no dead clock is needed. A dead clock is needed if the first transfer is a read and the second is a write or if the first is a write and the second a read.
12	The bus state transitions from T2P to TD when the first transfer (a read) has just completed and the second is a write, or when the first transfer just completed was a write and the second is a read.
13	The bus state leaves TD and returns to T12 when NA# is sampled asserted.
14	The processor transitions from TD to T2 is no bus cycle is pending in the processor or if NA# was sampled deasserted.

Chapter 9

The Previous Chapter

The previous chapter summarized the various types of bus cycles run by the Pentium processor, with focus on non-burst transactions.

In This Chapter

This Chapter discusses System Management Mode (SMM) feature implemented in the Pentium processors.

The Next Chapter

The next chapter covers the software changes introduced by the Pentium processor.

Introduction to System Management Mode

System management mode (SMM) simplifies system design when implementing control features such as power management. Early implementations of these features were not typically transparent to the operating system and application programs. As a result, power management implementations required customized software drivers and operating systems. SMM eliminates this requirement, since code used to perform power management is executed from a completely separate address space which is transparent to other system software (See figure 9-1).

A common implementation of power management is to turn power off to a device when it has been idle for a programmed amount of time. And when the device is accessed again, power is re-applied and the I/O instruction that caused the accessed is re-executed.

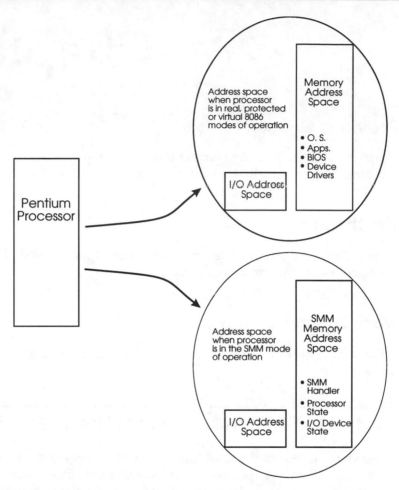

Figure 9-1. Address Space Available to Processor when Operating in Different Modes

Power management events (e.g.. a request to power down an inactive device) cause system management mode (SMM) to be invoked via the system management interrupt (SMI#) pin. The following steps introduce the actions taken by the processor when SMI# is asserted.

- The processor recognizes SMI# and asserts SMI acknowledge (SMIACT#).
- SMIACT# notifies the system that the next processor access will be to system management memory (SMRAM). This causes the system to enable access to SMRAM and disable access to normal system RAM.
- Current processor state information (internal registers) is saved to SMRAM via a series of memory writes.

Chapter 9: System Management Mode (SMM)

- The processor enters SMM after setting internal registers to their initial SMM state.
- The processor jumps to the entry point in SMRAM where the SMI handler resides.
- Power management status registers are checked by the SMI handler to determine what initiated the SMI request.
- The SMI handler services the power management request (e.g. saving the state of the inactive device to SMRAM and powering it down).
- The SMI handler upon completing its task issues the return from system-management mode (RSM) instruction.
- The processor retrieves and restores the saved processor state from SMRAM and continues normal program execution.

The following sections detail these steps.

System Management Memory (SMRAM)

The SMRAM Address Map

Figure 9-2 illustrates a typical layout for SMRAM. The processor pre-defines the range of addresses within SMRAM that are used to save the processor's state (context) when entering SMM. The processor also specifies the entry point of the SMI code. These locations are relative to the base address of the SMRAM. The other areas of SMRAM illustrated in figure 9-2 are implementation specific and left up to the SMM programmer to define.

The base address of SMRAM is set by the processor to a default value of 30000h. The processor defines a 512 byte region of SMRAM starting at location 3FFFFh (SMRAM base + FFFFh) downward to 3FE00h for saving the processor's context. Once the processor's context is saved, the processor jumps to the entry point of the SMI handler at SMM location 38000h (SMRAM base + 8000h). The SMI handler then executes its routine within SMRAM, using it to store data and stacks as required.

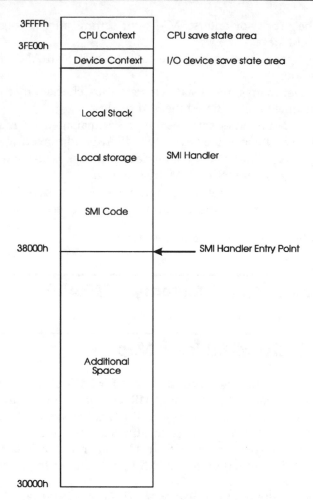

Figure 9-2. Sample Layout of SMM Memory

Figure 9-3 illustrates the processor's address space when SMM is both disabled and enabled. SMRAM is shown residing at its default location in SMM address space. The minimum amount of SRAM that can be implemented is from the SMRAM base + 8000h (38000h by default) to SMRAM base + FFFFh (3FFFFh by default). This 32KB address range encompasses the entry point to the SMI handler and the processor's state save address space. Note that when the processor enters SM mode, SMRAM overlays a region of physical memory that is normally accessible when not in SMM. All other physical memory is accessible to the SMI handler during SMM.

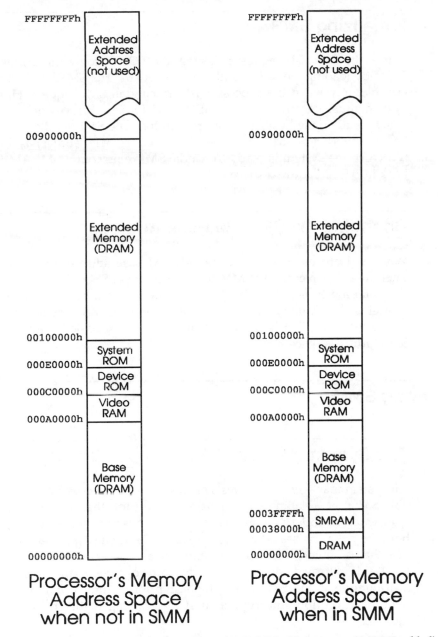

Figure 9-3. Typical PC Memory Map (SMM Disabled versus SMM Enabled)

Initializing SMRAM

Before the first SMI request is issued, the POST programmer must initialize SMM by loading the SMI handler into SMRAM. The SMRAM is normally accessible only when the processor is servicing an SMI request. However, the system must permit remapping SMRAM into the processor's real address space to allow the POST programmer to load the SMI handler into SMRAM, before entering SMM. Once the SMM code (SMI handler) is loaded into SMRAM, the system is ready to handle SMI request and SMRAM is mapped back into SMM address space.

Changing the SMRAM Base Address

When the processor RESETs, the SMRAM base address defaults to 30000h. Therefore, when entering SMM for the first time, SMRAM will be mapped to the default address. The SMI handler however, can relocate the SMRAM by changing the SMBASE Relocation slot in the processor's state save area. (See figure 9-4.) Any 32KB aligned location can be specified within the 4GB of SMM address space.

Entering SMM

The System Asserts SMI#

All system management requests are issued to the processor via the SMI# signal. SMI# is a falling-edge sensitive interrupt that is recognized on an instruction boundary. To guarantee that SMI# is recognized on the instruction boundary that causes access to an external location (e.g. access to an I/O device that is powered down), SMI# must be asserted at least three clocks before BRDY# is returned. When the processor recognizes SMI# asserted, it enters SMM mode if the SMI is the highest priority interrupt request currently pending execution. Interrupt request pins having higher priority than SMI# include:

- BUSCHK#
- R/S#
- FLUSH#

Chapter 9: System Management Mode (SMM)

These interrupt requests will be serviced by the processor prior to acknowledging the SMI#. However, an SMI request is latched by the processor and serviced when its priority comes up. The SMI# must be asserted for at least one clock cycle to be recognized, and must remain deasserted for at least four clock cycles before it is guaranteed to be recognized again.

Back-to-Back SMI Requests

After an SMI request is recognized, the SMI# pin is masked by the processor until the end of the SMI service routine (i.e. RSM is executed). If another SMI request is asserted while a current SMI is being serviced, it is latched and will be serviced when the current SMI completes. The second SMI request is recognized on the instruction boundary caused by the RSM instruction. As a result, back-to-back SMIs are run without returning to the program that was interrupted. Note that the processor can only latch a single SMI request at a time. In the previous example, if a third SMI request was asserted it would be lost.

SMI and Cache Coherency

As illustrated in figure 9-3, the default SMRAM address space overlaps a portion of main DRAM. The internal caches might have copies of the DRAM locations that SMRAM will overlay when the processor enters SMM. When the processor enters SMM, access to any of these cached locations results in cache incoherency. To prevent this from occurring the system designer must ensure that the caches are flushed prior to entering SMM. This can be accomplished by asserting the FLUSH# pin at the same time as SMI#. Since FLUSH# has a higher priority than SMI#, the internal caches will be flushed before the processor enters SMM. External caches must also be flushed in the same manner.

If normal memory and SMRAM do not overlap, then flushing the cache upon entry to SMM is not necessary. Similarly, if normal memory is not cacheable, then the caches do not require flushing.

See the section entitled, "Exiting SMM" regarding cache coherency when SMRAM is cacheable.

Pending Writes are Flushed to System Memory

Once the processor has entered SMM, some system memory may be hidden by SMRAM, if it overlays a portion of normal memory. Therefore, after SMI# is recognized by the processor and before it asserts SMIACT#, it completes all transfers to external memory including all buffered write operations. The processor also waits for the EWBE# signal to be asserted, indicating that all external buffers have also been flushed to memory. This ensures that data in the write buffers are written to normal memory, and not SMRAM.

SMIACT# is Asserted (SMRAM Accessed)

The processor asserts the SMIACT# signal to notify the memory controller that the processor in entering SMM. Typically, SMRAM overlays some portion of system memory. The memory controller must disable the normal system memory address range that SMRAM overlays before enabling SMRAM.

Processor Saves Its State

The first action taken by the processor when entering SMM is to save the current state, or context, of the processor. All registers listed in figure 9-4 are written to SMRAM in a stack-like fashion from the top of the state save address location downward. The offsets shown in figure 9-4 are relative to the SMI entry point.

Note that some of the locations within the state-save map can be written to by the SMI handler. When the processor exits SMM the state-save information is restored to the processor's registers, thereby loading the changed values.

Three entries within the state-save map are specific to SMM:

- Auto-HALT Restart Slot
- SMM Revision Identifier
- SMBASE Slot

Offset	Bits 31 ... 0	
7FFC	CR0	
7FF8	CR3	
7FF4	EFLAGS*	
7FF0	EIP*	
7FEC	EDI*	
7FE8	ESI*	
7FE4	EBP*	
7FE0	ESP*	
7FDC	EBX*	
7FD8	EDX*	
7FD4	ECX*	
7FD0	EAX*	
7FCC	DR6	
7FC8	DR7	
7FC4	Reserved	TR
7FC0	Reserved	LDT Base
7FBC	Reserved	GS
7FB8	Reserved	FS
7FB4	Reserved	DS
7FB0	Reserved	SS
7FAC	Reserved	CS
7FA8	Reserved	ES
7FA7–7F98		
7F94	IDT Base	
7F93–7F8C	Reserved	
7F88	GDT Base	
7F87–7F04	Reserved	
7F02	Reserved	Auto HALT Restart Slot*
7F00	Reserved	I/O Instr. Restart Slot*
7EFC	SMM Revision Identifier	
7EF8	SMBASE Slot*	
7EF7–7E00	Reserved	

31 · · · · · · · · · · Bits · · · · · · · · · · 0

Offset from
SMRAM Base

* Locations are writable

Figure 9-4. The Processor's SMM State-Save Map

Auto-HALT Restart

This slot in the state-save map indicates whether the processor was in the HALT state when entering SMM. Bit 0 is the only bit defined within the Auto-HALT Restart slot and is set as follow:

- If the processor was not in the HALT state when it entered SMM, then bit 0 is reset to 0. When this value is restored, the processor returns to the next sequential instruction. Setting bit 0 to a 1 causes unpredictable behavior.
- If the processor was in the HALT state when the SMI# pin was asserted, then bit 0 is set to 1. When this value is restored, the processor returns to the HALT state and performs a HALT special cycle. The SMI handler can change bit 0 to a 1 causing the processor to return to the next instruction following the HALT instruction.

SMM Revision Identifier

The SMM revision identifier is read-only and indicates the SMM version and extensions supported by this processor. Figure 9-5 illustrates the contents of the revision identifier.

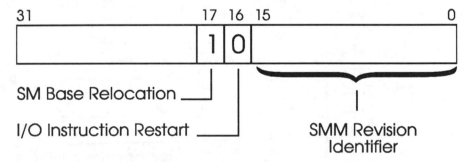

Figure 9-5. SMM Revision Identifier Definition

The lower sixteen bits define the revision level of the SMM architecture. The upper sixteen bits are used for indicating support for available extensions.

- I/O Instruction Restart (bit 16=0) — indicates that the Pentium 60/66 processors do not support this feature.
- SM Base Relocation (bit 17=1) — indicates support for relocating the SMRAM base address in memory.

Chapter 9: System Management Mode (SMM)

SMBASE Slot

This slot is used to identify the starting address of SMRAM as specified by bit 17 of the SMM revision identifier. The SMRAM base address defaults to 30000h when the processor RESETs. However, the SMI handler can move the SMRAM base address to any 32KB aligned location within the 4GB of SMM address space. This is accomplished by writing the new address into the SMBASE slot in the state-save area. Note that the SMI handler must relocate its code to the new entry point before exiting SMM. When the processor executes the RSM instruction and restores the state-save map, the new SMBASE address takes effect. The next time SMI# is asserted the processor calculates the new SMI entry point and the location of the state-save map as follows:

- SMI Entry Point = SMRAM base + 8000h
- State-Save location = SMRAM base + [8000h + 7FFFh]

The Processor Enters SMM

When the SMI# pin is asserted the processor may be executing code in any one of the processor's other modes of operation: Real mode, VM86 mode, or protected mode. Once the processor saves its current state to SMRAM, it initializes its internal registers in preparation for entering SMM mode. Table 9-1 shows the initial core register contents upon entry to SMM.

Table 9-1. Initial Core Register Values for SMM

Register Name	Contents
General Purpose Registers	Unpredictable
EFLAGS	00000002h
EIP	00008000h
CS Selector	3000h
CS Base	00030000h (default)
DS, ES, FS, GS, SS Selectors	0000h
DS, ES, FS, GS, SS Bases	00000000h
DS, ES, FS, GS, SS Limits	FFFFFFFFh
CR0	Bits 0,2,3 & 31 cleared (PE, EM, TS & PG); others are unchanged

Register Name	Contents
DR6	unpredictable
DR7	00000400h

The operating conditions of the processor based on these values are as follows:

- CR0, bit 0 (protected mode enable) is cleared, therefore the processor uses real mode address calculation.
- CS:IP values result in the SMI entry point of 38000h.
- All segment and limit values (except CS) define a 4GB segment (i.e. the segment base address of 00000000h and the limit of FFFFFFFFh creates a single 4GB segment).
- CR0, bit 2 (EM) is cleared so that no floating-point exceptions are generated.
- CR0, bit 3 (task switch) and 31 (paging enable) are cleared, since SMM does not operate in protected mode.
- CR0, bit 8 (trap or single-step flag) is cleared disabling the single-step exception.
- CR0, bit 9 (interrupt enable) is cleared disabling the processor's INTR input.
- DR7 is cleared to disable debug traps. (Bit 10, set to 1, is reserved)

When in SMM, the processor uses real mode addressing, however some aspects of the processor's operation differs from standard real mode operation. The following sections highlights the processor's capabilities when in SMM.

Address Space

When in SMM mode, the processor is capable of accessing all I/O address space and can access the entire 4GB of memory address space. The ability to access the entire 4GB of address space must be accomplished with 32-bit offsets within a segment whose start address must be within the first 1MB of address space.

Chapter 9: System Management Mode (SMM)

Exceptions and Interrupts

Upon entry to SMM the processor blocks NMIs and disables INTRs. These interrupts are disables because the interrupt routine is not aware of the existence of SMRAM. For the same reason, debug and single-step traps are also disabled. An SMM programmer wishing service interrupts or use these traps within SMM, must ensure that the routines called do not conflict with SMRAM. Note that software interrupts are permitted in SMM, however, the same potential conflicts and solutions apply.

Executing SMI Handler

Once the processor has initialized itself, it enters SMM and jumps to the entry point where the SMI handler resides. The SMI handler first checks status registers to determine the nature of the SMI request. Once the request is identified, the handler then executes the specified management routine designed to handle the request. The SMI handler may be designed to handle a wide variety of requests. Typical requests might include:

- Saving the state of a device
- Powering down an idle device
- Powering up a device that has been accessed
- Stopping or slowing down oscillators and clocks
- Saving state information for entire system (to non-volatile memory) and powering the system down.
- Managing security protection

When the SMI handler completes its task, it executes the Return from System Management mode (RSM) instruction, thereby returning the processor to normal program flow.

Exiting SMM

The processor exits SMM by executing the RSM instruction. The RSM instruction is only valid when in SMM mode. Any attempt to execute this instruction in any other modes results in an invalid op-code error.

The RSM instruction causes the processor flushes all write buffers and to wait for the EWBE# signal to be asserted. Then the processor restores the state-save map, returning the processor to the same exact state (except for the control slots) that it was in prior to the system management interrupt request. Next the processor deasserts the SMIACT# signal and the interrupted program can continue execution.

Two control slots implemented within the state-save map allow modifications to the information restored to the processor. These are the:

- **The Auto HALT Restart control slot**. This slot gives the SMM handler the ability to specify how the processor should exit SMM if the processor was halted upon entry to SMM. The default condition is to return the processor to the HALT state when exiting SMM. In this case, the processor performs a halt special cycle to notify external logic that it is entering the HALT state. This default action occurs if the Auto HALT Restart control slot is not modified by the SMI handler. If the control slot is reset to zero, the processor returns to the instruction following the HALT instruction, permitting program execution to continue.
- **The SMBASE Relocation slot**. The SMI handler may also change the SMRAM base address, causing the processor to vector to a new SMI handler entry point the next time an SMI request is serviced.

If the processor recognizes invalid information restored from the state-save map, it enters the SHUTDOWN state and the processor performs a shutdown special cycle. This occurs when:

- the SMBASE slot contains a value that is not 32KB aligned.
- a reserved bit of CR4 is set to 1 on a write to CR4.
- CR0 contains an illegal bit combination.

Note that the processor recognizes SMI# when in the SHUTDOWN state, however Intel recommends that SMI# not be asserted during SHUTDOWN.

Chapter 10

The Previous Chapter

The previous chapter discussed the System Management Mode (SMM) features implemented in the Pentium processors.

This Chapter

This chapter provides an overview of the changes within the software environment. The changes cover those software items that have changed from 486 environment.

The Next Chapter

The next chapter focuses on the Pentium features associated with test and debug.

Introduction

The changes covered in this chapter include the following:

- New Definition for Control Register zero (CR0), CD and NW bits
- Addition of Control Register 4 (CR4)
- Additions to the EFLAGS register
- Data parity checking and bus checks incurred during a bus cycle
- Virtual paging extensions
- Virtual 8086 mode extensions
- Debug extensions
- New exception
- New instructions
- Incompatibilities

Interpretation of CR0, CD and NW Bits

Operation of the internal code and data caches are controlled by the CD and NW bits within CR0. When RESET is removed from the processor, CD and NW are set to 1, and all invalid bits are set causing the internal caches to be disabled. The caches behave according the to CD and NW setting shown in table 10 - 1.

Table 10 - 1. Interpretation of the CD and NW Bits within CR0

CD	NW	Description
1	1	Read hits access the cache.
		Read misses do not cause line fills.
		Write hits update the cache, but not external memory.
		Write hits cause Exclusive (E) state lines to change to Modified (M) state.
		Shared lines remain in the Shared (S) state after write hits.
		Write misses access memory.
		Inquire and invalidation cycles do not effect the cache contents or state.
1	0	Read hits access the cache.
		Read misses do not cause line fills.
		Write hits update the cache
		Writes to S state lines and write misses update external memory
		Writes to S state lines change to the E state when WB/WT#=1
		Inquire and invalidation cycles effect the cache contents and state.
0	1	Illegal combination; results in General Protection (GP) fault 0
0	0	Read hits access the cache.
		Read misses cause line fills if CACHE# and KEN# are asserted.
		Cache lines are initially entered in the E or S state depending on the state of WB/WT# (E = 1, S=0).
		Write hits update the cache.
		Only writes to S state lines and write misses access external memory.
		Writes to S state lines change to E state when WB/WT#=1
		Inquire and invalidation cycles effect cache contents and state.

Chapter 10: Summary of Software Changes

Control Register 4 (CR4)

Control Register four, or CR4, has been added. Figure 10-1 illustrates its usage.

- Machine check enable, or MCE, is discussed in the section entitled, "Parity and Bus Cycle Verification."
- Page sized extensions, or PSE, is discussed in the section entitled, "Virtual Paging Extensions."
- The debugging extensions, or DE, are discussed in the section entitled, "Debugging Extensions."
- Time stamp disable, or TSD, used in conjunction with performance monitoring. (considered proprietary by Intel).
- Protected mode virtual interrupts, or PVI, is considered proprietary by Intel and is not discussed.
- Virtual 8086 mode extensions, or VME, is discussed in the section entitled, "VM86 Extensions."

Control Register 4 (CR4)

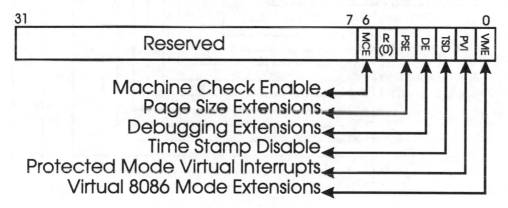

Figure 10-1. Control Register 4 (CR4)

EFLAGS Register

Figure 10-2 illustrates the EFLAGS register. The bits added in the Pentium are:

- ID bit. Refer to the section in this chapter entitled, "CPUID" for more information.
- Virtual Interrupt Pending, or VIP, bit. Refer to the section in this chapter entitled, "VM86 Extension" for more information.
- Virtual Interrupt Flag, or VIF, bit. Refer to the section in this chapter entitled, "VM86 Extension" for more information.

EFLAGS

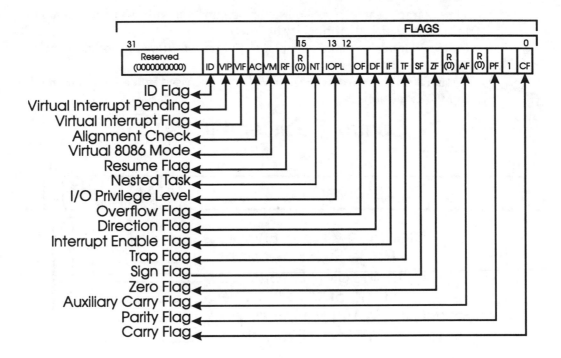

Note: all bits shown with a one or a zero are Intel reserved. They must always be set to the values previously read from them.

Figure 10-2. The EFLAGS Register

Chapter 10: Summary of Software Changes

Parity and Bus Cycle Verification

When the MCE bit in CR4 is zero, the Pentium processor is inhibited from generating a machine check exception (exception 18d, or 12h). The MCE bit is cleared to zero when RESET is asserted. If the MCE bit is set to one, the processor is enabled to generate a machine check exception. This will occur under two circumstances:

- Detection of a data parity error during a read bus cycle. This occurs only when the processor samples the PEN# signal asserted during BRDY# of a given read cycle. PEN# is asserted by the system to request that the processor latch the contents of the address and control signals associated with the bus cycle in the event that it returns invalid parity. An even parity check is performed on the returned data.
- The processor's BUSCHK# input is sampled asserted at the end of a bus cycle (on the last BRDY#), indicating that the bus cycle was not completed successfully. The processor latches the address and bus cycle type into the machine check registers, and the machine check exception is generated.

Figures 10-3 and 10-4 illustrate the machine check registers. These sixty-four bit registers are new in the Pentium and are read using the RDMSR, read model-specific register, instruction. The MCAR, machine check address register, contains the physical address present on the address bus during the failed bus cycle. The MCTR, machine check type register, indicates the type of bus cycle that failed. The CHK bit in the MCTR will be set to one if the MCTR and MCAR contain valid information.

Machine Check Type Register (MCTR)

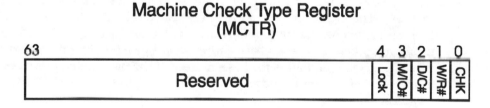

Figure 10-3. The Machine Check Type Register, or MCTR

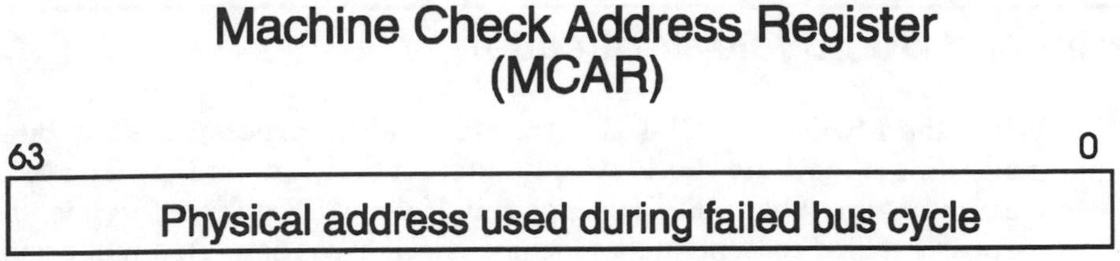

Machine Check Address Register (MCAR)

63   0

Physical address used during failed bus cycle

Figure 10-4. Machine Check Address Register

Virtual Paging Extensions

The paging unit incorporated in the 386 and 486 processors defines a page size as 4KB. If the PSE (page size extension) bit in CR4 is set to zero, the paging unit is backwardly compatible with the 486 paging unit. If the PSE bit is set to one, the paging unit permits the operating system programmer to define a page as either 4KB or 4MB in size.

Intel has not publicly documented this feature, but information in publicly available documentation reveals enough to figure out most, if not all, of its operational characteristics.

When a linear address is presented for a lookup, the respective page directory entry is read and the state of bit seven, the page size (PS) bit, is checked. Figure 10-5 illustrates the Page Directory entry. If the PS bit is set to zero, the entry defines a Page Table and the Page Table entries identify 4KB pages in memory. The 4KB page base address consists of bits 31:12, not shown. If the PS bit is set to one, the entry defines a 4MB memory page. Bits 31:22 define the upper ten bits of the page's base address and bits 8:0 define the pages attributes. The paging unit adds the base address of the page to the offset specified in bits 21:0 of the linear address to produce the physical memory address to be accessed.

As an example of its usage, a 4MB page would be handy for defining one contiguous, high-resolution display frame buffer in memory.

Page Directory Entry

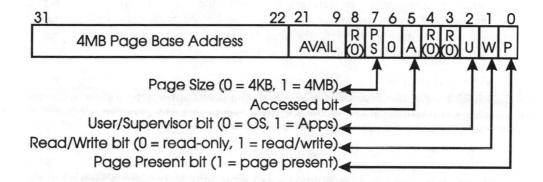

Figure 10-5. The Page Directory Entry

Note: If page size = 4MB (bit 7 = 1), bits 31:22 indicate the physical start address of the 4MB page in memory. Bit 4 of CR4, the Page Size Extension (PSE) bit, must be set to enable 4MB pages. Else, a 4KB page size is defined and bits 31:12 indicate the physical start address of the 4KB page in memory.

VM86 Extensions

Interrupt Redirection

General

When an interrupt or exception occurs while the processor is running an MS-DOS task in VM86 mode, the operating system programmer can handle the request in one of three ways:

- Pass the request to the interrupt/exception handler routine that the MS-DOS task normally uses. The pointer to this routine is in the respective entry in the real mode interrupt table found within the task's 1MB of linear address space.
- Execute a protected mode service routine to service the request.
- Perform a task switch to the task designed to handle the request.

The 386/486 Handling of Interrupt Redirection

The 386 and 486 processor's implement VM86 mode, but do not have any hardware mechanism to determine whether the request should be handled through the protected mode IDT or should be redirected through the task's real mode interrupt table to the real mode interrupt service routine that is normally used in the MS-DOS environment.

When an interrupt or exception occurs while the processor is operating in VM86 mode, the processor will obtain the interrupt vector (either from the 8259A interrupt controller, the software interrupt instruction, or from its exception detection logic) and jump through the protected mode IDT to the protected mode routine or separate task designed to handle the request. In this routine, the programmer determines if the processor was operating in VM86 mode at the point of interruption by examining the state of the VM86 bit in the EFLAGS register at the point of interruption. If the VM86 bit is set to one, the processor was in VM86 mode at the point of interruption. The interrupt handler can then determine whether to handle the request in protected mode or to vector through the interrupted task's real mode interrupt table to the interrupt or exception handler routine that normally handles this type of event.

This method implies quite a bit of software overhead and therefore impacts the performance of the interrupt servicing procedure.

Pentium Processor Handling of Interrupt Redirection

The Pentium processor has added some extensions that permit a more expeditious handling of interrupts that occur while the processor is in VM86 mode. Intel has declined to publish a detailed description of these extensions, but the functions provided can be discussed. The VM86 mode extensions are implemented using the following new elements:

- The virtual mode extensions, or VME, bit in CR4.
- The protected mode virtual interrupts, or PVI, bit in CR4.
- The virtual interrupt pending, or VIP, bit in EFLAGS.
- The virtual interrupt flag, or VIF, bit in EFLAGS.
- The interrupt redirection bitmap in the TSS.

It must be stressed that this discussion of Pentium handling of interrupt redirection is based on speculation (hopefully of the intelligent variety).

Chapter 10: Summary of Software Changes

When an interrupt or exception occurs, the processor obtains the interrupt vector and then determines if the currently-executing task is operating in protected or VM86 mode. If it is in protected mode, the processor uses the interrupt vector to index into the IDT and jumps to the protected mode service routine (if the IDT entry contains an interrupt or trap gate descriptor) or switches to the servicing task (if the IDT entry contains a task gate).

If the processor is operating in VM86 mode and the VM86 extensions are not enabled, interrupt redirection is handled as described in the previous section.

If the processor is operating in VM86 mode and the VM86 extensions are enabled, the processor uses the interrupt/exception vector to index into the interrupt redirection bit map in the VM86 task's TSS. This is a thirty-two byte bit map (pictured as a subset of figure 10-6) that defines the VM86 mode action to be taken for each of the two hundred and fifty-six interrupt vectors (32 bytes x 8 bits/byte = a 256 bit map). It checks the state of the bit corresponding to the vector and determines whether to vector through the IDT or to redirect the request through the respective entry in the VM86 task's real mode interrupt table in the first 1KB of the task's linear address space.

If it is to vector through the task's real mode interrupt table, it performs the following steps:

1. Multiply the vector by four to obtain the linear address of the entry in the task's real mode interrupt table.
2. Performs a four byte read from memory starting at this linear address to obtain the CS:IP values. The page unit will remap this read to the correct memory locations in physical memory.
3. The new values are placed into CS:IP, causing the processor to jump to the real mode interrupt/exception service routine.

The Pentium's method for handling interrupt redirection involves far less software overhead than was necessary in the 386/486 environments, resulting in faster interrupt servicing.

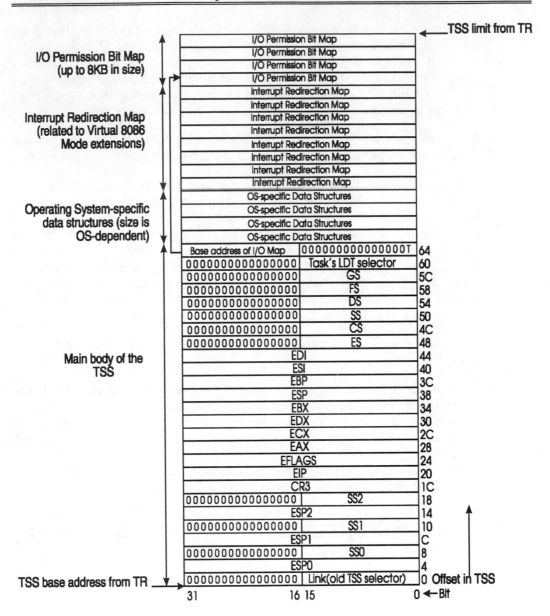

Figure 10-6. The TSS Format

Chapter 10: Summary of Software Changes

Enable/Disable Interrupt Recognition

General

Under some conditions, an MS-DOS task may not function correctly if it is interrupted during the execution of certain critical instruction sequences. In order to prevent recognition of interrupts during this period of time, the programmer would execute a CLI instruction before the sensitive instruction sequence and an STI instruction afterwards. The CLI instruction clears the IF bit in the EFLAGS register, disabling recognition of maskable interrupts. When the STI instruction is executed, it sets the IF bit to a one, reenabling interrupt recognition. In a single-tasking environment, the disabling of interrupt recognition for brief periods of time is acceptable because only one program is being run by the operating system. In a multitasking environment, allowing one program to disable interrupt recognition can be dangerous. Although disabling interrupt recognition may be desirable from the perspective of the currently-running program, time-critical interrupts may occur that must be serviced by another task. Having the IF flag bit clear would prevent the timely servicing of interrupts related to currently-suspended tasks.

When an MS-DOS task attempts to execute a CLI instruction in a multitasking environment it must not be permitted to do so. In some manner, the processor and/or operating system must note the fact that this program prefers not to be interrupted while still permitting certain, high-priority interrupts to be serviced. The 386/486 processors have limited hardware support for this type of protection, while the Pentium processor includes an extended ability to implement it with a minimum of software overhead.

The 386/486 Processor

When operating in VM86 mode, the 386/486 processors will trap to the VMM (virtual machine monitor) when an attempt is made to execute an instruction that would alter the state of the processor's IF flag bit. As stated earlier, the processor cannot permit the IF flag bit to be altered. It is entirely up to the 386/486 operating system software to emulate the CLI and STI instructions by implementing a software version of the IF bit. How this is accomplished is operating system-specific. Typically, the operating system programmer would define a bit in the OS-specific data structure area of the task's TSS. This would represent the task's desired state for the actual IF bit in the EFLAGS register.

When an attempt to execute the CLI instruction is detected, the VMM will clear the virtual IF bit in the TSS, rather than the actual IF bit in the EFLAGS register. Detection of an attempt to execute the STI instruction will cause the OS to set the virtual IF bit to a one.

When an interrupt occurs while the processor is executing a task in VM86 mode, the VMM is invoked. It checks the state of the task's virtual IF bit to determine if the task is sensitive to interrupts. If the virtual IF bit in the TSS is zero, the operating system will only service certain, high-priority interrupts immediately and will defer servicing of other, lower-priority interrupts until the next time the task is interrupted or suspended and its virtual IF bit is set to one. The operating system will then service outstanding interrupt requests.

The Pentium Processor

As indicated earlier, the Pentium processor implements extensions to VM86 mode to facilitate interrupt servicing with a minimum of software overhead. *As noted earlier, Intel has chosen not to publish the particulars regarding these extensions. Consequently, the following discussion of the Pentium implementation is based on speculation and hints in the published documentation.*

When the Pentium's VM86 mode extensions are enabled, two new EFLAGS bits are available:

- The virtual interrupt flag, or VIF, bit.
- The virtual interrupt pending, or VIP, bit.

When operating in VM86 mode with the extensions enabled, the Pentium processor operates differently when an attempt is made to execute an instruction that would alter the state of the processor's IF flag bit. As stated earlier, the processor cannot permit the IF flag bit to be altered by an application. When an attempt to execute the CLI instruction is detected, the processor will clear the virtual IF bit in the EFLAGS register, rather than the actual IF bit in the EFLAGS register. Detection of an attempt to execute the STI instruction will cause the virtual IF bit in EFLAGS to be set to one.

When an interrupt occurs while the processor is executing a task in VM86 mode, the VMM is invoked. It checks the state of the task's virtual IF bit (in EFLAGS) to determine if the task is sensitive to interrupts. If the virtual IF bit is zero, the operating system will only service certain, high-priority interrupts immediately. Servicing of other, lower-priority interrupts will be deferred until the next time the task is interrupted or suspended, and the operating system will set the VIP bit in EFLAGS to indicate that one or more interrupts have been deferred. The operating system will service deferred interrupt requests when both the VIP and VIF bits are set. This indicates that one or more interrupts are pending and the MS-DOS task doesn't mind being interrupted.

Protected Mode Virtual Interrupts

The details of this feature have not been published and the published documentation provides too little information to speculate intelligently at this point in time.

Debug Extensions

Figure 10-7 illustrates the Pentium processor's debug registers. DR7 is the debug control register. It is used to enable/disable each of up to four breakpoints and to specify the type of breakpoint. The Pentium processor has added the ability to break on I/O reads or writes.

The debug mode control register is new. It is used to specify the usage of the PM0/BP0 and PM1/BP1 Pentium processor output pins. They can be configured to output debug breakpoint match or performance monitoring information. Intel considers the information regarding these two pins to be proprietary (it isn't published in the public domain).

Figure 10-8 illustrates Test Register 12 (new in the Pentium). This register contains four bits used to enable special test functions: These bit are defined as:

- **NPB (No Branch Prediction)** – the usage of this bit is under non disclosure, however, its name seems to clearly indicate that dynamic branch prediction can be disabled by setting this bit.
- **TR (Tracing)** – this bit permits execution tracing. The branch trace message special cycle to be enabled or disabled. When the TR bit is a one and a branch is taken, the processor generates a branch trace special cycle and the IBT, instruction branch taken, output is asserted. If the TR bit is a zero and a branch is taken, the processor's IBT output is asserted, but the branch trace special cycle is not generated.

- **SE (Single Pipe Execution)** – the usage of this bit is under non-disclosure, however, its name seems to clearly indicate that the V pipeline can be disabled by setting this bit, thereby permitting single pipe execution.
- **CI (Cache Inhibit)** – Its use is also under non-disclosure, but the name certainly indicates that setting this bit to a one will inhibit caching by the internal caches.

Debug Registers

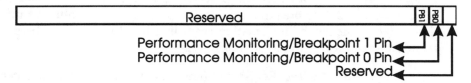

31 30	29 28	27 26	25 24	23 22	21 20	19 18	17 16	15 14	13 12	11 10	9	8	7	6	5	4	3	2	1	0	
Control	LEN3	R/W3	LEN2	R/W2	LEN1	R/W1	LEN0	R/W0	0 0	GD 0	0 1	GE	LE	G3	L3	G2	L2	G1	L1	G0 LO	DR7
Status	1 1	1 1	1 1	1 1	1 1	1 1	1 1	1 1	BT BS	BD 1	1 1	1	1	1	1	1	1	B3	B2	B1	B0	DR6

Reserved	DR5
Reserved	DR4
Breakpoint 3 Linear Address	DR3
Breakpoint 2 Linear Address	DR2
Breakpoint 1 Linear Address	DR1
Breakpoint 0 Linear Address	DR0

Debug Mode Control Register

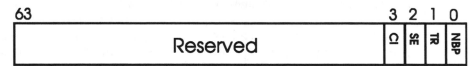

Reserved   PB1 PB0

Performance Monitoring/Breakpoint 1 Pin
Performance Monitoring/Breakpoint 0 Pin
Reserved

Figure 10-7. The Pentium Debug Registers

Test Register 12
(TR12)

63		3	2	1	0
Reserved		CI	SE	TR	NBP

Figure 10-8. Test Register 12

Chapter 10: Summary of Software Changes

New Exceptions

The machine check exception is the only new exception that has been added to the Pentium. It's described earlier in this chapter in the section entitled, "Parity and Bus Cycle Verification."

New Instructions

RDMSR and WRMSR

The **read and write model-specific register** instructions are used to access the contents of a selected 64-bit model-specific register (MSR.) The Pentium processor implements numerous MSRs that control functions related to:

- testability
- execution tracing
- performance monitoring
- machine check errors

When either the RDMSR or WRMSR instruction is executed, the value in the ECX register specifies access to one of the processor's model-specific registers. If reading from a specified register, its contents are deposited into the register pair EDX:EAX. When writing to the register, the current contents of EDX:EAX are written to the target MSR. The only MSR registers defined by Intel in their public-domain documentation are the:

- machine check address register, or MCAR (ECX=00h)
- machine check type register, or MCTR (ECX=01h)
- test register 12, or TR12 (ECX=0Eh)

Intel specifies that ECX values of 03h, 0Fh and all values above 13h are reserved. Details regarding other registers that can be accessed via the RDMSR and WRMSR instructions are provided by Intel with the appropriate nondisclosures.

Many developers, in an attempt to define the undocumented registers, have probed Pentium systems and uncovered the function of several of the MSRs. This information is now publicly available in numerous sources outside Intel. Since these MSRs provide considerable insight into performance monitoring, the authors have included a summary of some of these registers.

- time stamp counter (ECX=10h) – Reading this register gives the number of processor clocks (PCLKs) since reset. New start values can also be wri•tten to the counter using the WRMSR instruction.
- hardware statistics index register (ECX=11h) – This register allows the programmer to select two of thirty-eight known internal hardware statistics (see table 10 - 2) that can be accessed via the respective hardware statistics counter (counter 1 or 2).
- hardware statistics counter 1 (ECX=12h) – Provides a count of the number of hardware events that have occurred. The hardware event is selected via the hardware statistics index register.
- hardware statistics counter 2 (ECX=13h) – Provides a count of the number of hardware events that have occurred. The hardware event is selected via the hardware statistics index register.

Table 10 - 2. Internal Hardware Statistics and Index Number

Index	Hardware Function	Index	Hardware Function
0	Data Read	15	Pipeline Flushes
1	Data Write	16	Instructions Executed
2	Data TLB Miss	17	Instructions Executed in V pipe
3	Data Read Cache Miss	18	Bus Utilization (clocks)
4	Data Write Cache Miss	19	Pipeline Stalls due to Write-back
5	Write Cache Hit to M or E line	1A	Pipeline Stalls due to Data Read
6	Cache Write-Backs	1B	Pipeline Stalls due to Write (E or M lines)
7	Data Cache Snoops	1C	Locked bus cycles
8	Data Cache Snoop Hits	1D	I/O read or write cycles
9	Memory Accesses to U & V pipes	1E	Non-cacheable memory access
A	Data Cache Bank Conflicts	1F	AGI (Address Generation Interlock)
B	Misaligned Memory Accesses	22	Floating-point operations
C	Code Reads	23	Breakpoint match (DR0)
D	Code TLB Miss	24	Breakpoint match (DR1)
E	Code Cache Miss	25	Breakpoint match (DR2)
F	Segment Register Loads	26	Breakpoint match (DR3)
12	Branches	27	Hardware Interrupts
13	BTB Hits	28	Data read or write
14	Branches Taken	29	Data read miss or write miss

Chapter 10: Summary of Software Changes

CMPXCHG8B

The compare and exchange eight bytes instruction can compare two eight-bytes data objects. The instruction performs as follows:

- Compares the sixty-four bit value in EDX:EAX with the value specified in memory.
- If equal, the value in ECX:EBX is stored into the specified memory operand.
- If unequal, the contents of the memory operand is copied into EDX:EAX.

CPU ID

The CPU identification instruction provides software with information regarding the vendor, family, model and stepping of the processor. The programmer uses a value in the EAX register to identify the information desired. The defined EAX input values are:

- 00000000h in EAX returns 00000001h in EAX for the Pentium processor and the ASCII representation of the string "GenuineIntel" is returned in EBX:EDX:ECX.
- 00000001h in EAX returns the information illustrated in figure 10-9 in the EAX register. EBX and ECX are set to zero. 3Fh is returned in the EDX register, indicating features supported by the processor. Feature bit zero is the only one currently defined: a one returned in this bit indicates that the FPU is present on-chip.
- If any other input value is used in EAX with the CPUID instruction, EAX, EBX, ECX and EDX are all returned with zeros.

The programmer can determine if the processor supports the CPUID instruction by attempting to set and clear the ID bit, bit 21, in the EFLAGS register. If it can be set/cleared, the processor supports the CPUID instruction.

CPU ID Information

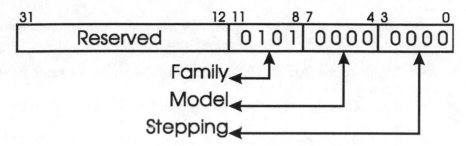

Figure 10-9. EAX Register Contents After Request For Family, Model and Stepping Information

RSM

Execution of the resume from system management mode instruction causes the processor's state (register set) to be restored from system management memory (SMM). The only registers not affected are the model-specific registers. Restoring the register set allows the processor to resume the interrupted application at the point of interruption. If, during the register reload, any of the processor state information is found to be faulty, the processor will enter the shutdown state. Faulty information that would cause a shutdown on exit from SMM are:

- The value stored in the state dump base field is not a 32KB-aligned address.
- Any reserved bit in CR4 is set to one.
- Any combinations of bit settings in CR0 that are recognized to be illegal. Two cases would be: paging enabled but protected mode disabled; and caching enabled but write-through disabled (write-back selected).

Chapter 10: Summary of Software Changes

Incompatibilities

Accessing the Test Registers

ICE and debugger applications require access to the processor's test registers. In the 386 and 486 processors, the move instruction, MOV, is used to access the test registers.

In the Pentium processor, the new WRMSR instruction is used. This means that ICE/debugger software written for the 386/486 processors must be re-written in order to run on the Pentium processor.

Use of Reserved Bits

Intel has always cautioned software developers not to use reserved bits in any form. They should be treated as undefined. This means that they should be masked out when a register is read from. If a software application depends upon the reserved bits remaining in a defined state from one processor to another, the possibility of improper operation is very high.

The reason that this subject is mentioned here is that certain applications that ran on the 386/486 processors may not run on a Pentium based system. This is due to the fact that the state of some bits designed as reserved in the 386/486 processors has changed in the Pentium environment. Since Intel has always stressed caution in this area, the fault lies with the software developer, not with Intel.

Chapter 11

The Previous Chapter

The previous chapter provided an overview of the changes within the software environment. The changes cover those software items that have been modified or added since 486 processor.

This Chapter

This chapter focuses on the Pentium features associated with test and debug.

The Next Chapter

The next chapter discusses the primary changes introduced by the Pentium P54C processors.

Pentium Processor Hardware Test-Related Features

The Pentium processor incorporates a set of features that facilitate system test during normal operation and extended test capabilities during manufacturing-level diagnostics. The following sections define these capabilities.

Customer Environment Test Features

General

This section describes the test mechanisms provided by the Pentium processor to facilitate testing of the Pentium processor and its associated system board support logic in the customer environment. These testing mechanisms do not require that special test equipment be connected to the system under test.

The next section after this one describes the test mechanisms provided to facilitate testing in the manufacturing and depot repair environments.

Built-In Self Test, or BIST

The Pentium processor incorporates a built-in self-test, or BIST. The BIST is initiated if the processor samples its INIT input asserted on the trailing-edge of RESET. The BIST tests approximately 70% of the processor's internal logic and takes approximately 524,288 clocks to complete. The processor initiates no bus cycles during the BIST.

The BIST is divided into two parts:

- During the hardware self-test, the microcode and all large PLAs, or programmable logic arrays, are tested. All possible input combinations are tested. The microcode ROM is tested using stored checksums.
- During the microcode self-test, the constant ROMs are tested, as well as the Branch Target Buffer, or BTB, the Translation Lookaside Buffers, or TLBs, the Prefetch Buffer, the code cache, and the data cache. During the first pass, data patterns are written in all buffers and caches and are read back and verified. During the second pass, the complement of the original data patterns are written, read and verified.

The EAX register contains the results of the BIST. If the BIST has been invoked when the system is powered-up, the programmer should verify that EAX contains all zeros at the start of the POST. If EAX is non-zero, the Pentium processor is faulty and the system is not usable. If any internal parity errors are detected during the BIST, the processor will assert its internal error output, IERR#, and will enter the shutdown state.

The BIST may also be initiated through the test access port. This capability is described in this chapter under the heading, "The Test Access Port."

Parity Error Detection

General

This section describes the parity check logic incorporated within the Pentium processor. This logic facilitates the detection of three types of errors:

- **Internal parity errors** detected while reading data from internal caches or buffers.
- **Data parity errors** detected during the data transfer phase of a bus transaction.
- **Address parity errors** detected by a target device during a bus cycle initiated by the processor or by the processor while snooping an address generated by a bus master.
- **Detection of a Bus Check**. Non-parity errors (detected by external logic) during a bus transaction, preventing a bus transaction from completing correctly.

Internal Parity Error Detection

All of the Pentium processor's internal memory arrays are protected by parity. This provides parity protection for 53% of the on-chip logic. The on-chip parity logic includes:

- Parity bit per byte in the data cache.
- Parity bit per directory entry in the data cache's tag SRAM.
- Parity bit per quadword (one quarter of a line) in the code cache.
- Parity bit per directory entry in the code cache's tag SRAM.
- Parity bit per entry in both the data and code TLBs.
- Parity bit per directory entry in both the data and code TLBs.
- Parity bit per entry in the microcode ROM.

The Branch Target Buffer is also covered by the parity check logic.

Whenever a parity error is detected on a read from an internal memory array, the processor will assert its internal error output, IERR#, for one clock during each clock that a parity error is detected. In addition to the assertion of IERR#, the processor will also enter the shutdown state, indicating that it is not safe to proceed. Logic external to the processor should monitor IERR#. If detected, system operation should be terminated (because the processor is not functioning correctly).

Whenever the processor has to perform a write-back, it must first read the line to be written from the data cache. If an internal parity error is detected during this read, the line will still be written back to external memory. For this reason, the system designer should monitor the processor's IERR# output during a write-back to verify the integrity of the line being written.

Parity Error Detection During Bus Transactions

During a bus transaction, parity errors may be detected under the following conditions:

- The processor is driving a corrupted address onto the address bus. This can occur during any read or write transaction.
- The processor is driving corrupted data onto one or more data paths during a write transaction.
- The processor detects corrupted data on one or more data paths during a read transaction.
- The processor detects a corrupted address during an inquire cycle.

Table 11-1 defines the actions to be taken when each type of parity error is detected.

Table 11-1. Bus Transaction Parity Error Action Table

Condition Detected	Recommended Action(s)
Processor driving corrupted address onto address bus.	When the processor initiates a bus cycle, it drives an address onto the address bus. In addition, the processor's bus unit also computes even parity on address lines A31:A5 and drives the resulting parity bit onto its address parity output, AP. It is the responsibility of external logic to verify that the address contains correct parity. The AP signal has the same timing as the address being driven onto the bus by the processor. If the processor is generating corrupted addresses, it is unsafe to continue operation. It is the responsibility of the system board logic to take the appropriate action (e.g., generate a BUSCHK# to the processor, illuminate an LED, assert RESET to the processor, etc.).

Condition Detected	Recommended Action(s)
The processor is driving corrupted data onto one or more data paths during a write transaction.	When performing a write transaction, the processor drives a data byte onto its respective data path and simultaneously drives the parity bit (DPn) associated with the data path. Even parity is generated. External logic should be designed to check the validity of the data byte. If a parity error is detected, it is the responsibility of the system board designer to take the appropriate action (e.g., generate a BUSCHK# to the processor, illuminate an LED, assert RESET to the processor, etc.).
The processor detects corrupted data on one or more data paths during a read transaction.	When a parity error is detected on one or more of the data paths during a read transaction, the processor will assert its PCHK# output. In addition, if external logic asserts PEN# to the processor, the processor latches the bus transaction's address into the machine check address register, or MCAR, and the transaction type into the machine check type register, or MCTR. The MCTR CHK bit is set to one, indicating that MCAR and MCTR contain valid information. IF PEN# is asserted and the machine check enable bit, MCE, in CR4 is a one, a machine check exception (exception 18d) will be generated. In the exception handler, the programmer may examine the contents of MCAR and MCTR to determine the appropriate action to be taken. Figures 11-1 and 11-2 illustrate the format of the MCAR and MCTR registers.
The processor detects a corrupted address during an inquire cycle.	External logic asserts EADS# when driving an address to be snooped into the processor. When EADS# is sampled asserted by the processor on the rising-edge of PCLK, the processor samples the address on A31:A5 and the state of the parity bit on its AP input. If the parity is not even, the processor asserts its APCHK# output two clocks after EADS# is sampled asserted. It is the responsibility of the system board logic to take the appropriate action when APCHK# is sampled asserted (e.g., set a readable, external status bit and generate an NMI to the processor).

Machine Check Address Register (MCAR)

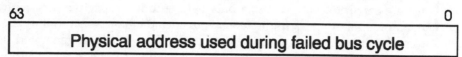

Figure 11-1. Machine Check Address Register

Machine Check Type Register (MCTR)

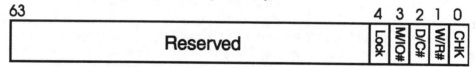

Figure 11-2. Machine Check Type Register

Bus Check

The BUSCHK# input to the processor is used by logic external to the processor to report unsuccessful completion of a bus transaction. Examples would be:

- Detection of an address parity error during a read or write transaction.
- Detection of a data parity error during a write transaction.

The processor samples the state of BUSCHK# when the last BRDY# of a transaction is sampled asserted. In response to a bus check, the processor latches the bus transaction's address into the machine check address register, MCAR, and the transaction type into the machine check type register, MCTR. In addition, if the machine check enable bit, MCE, in CR4 is set to one, the processor will generate a machine check exception (exception 18d). If BUSCHK# is asserted prior to the sample point, the processor will remember it (latch it), but will not respond to it until the final BRDY# of the transaction is sampled asserted.

Machine Check Exception Summary

The machine check exception (exception 18d) was not implemented in x86 processors prior to the Pentium processor. It will only be generated if the machine check enable bit, MCE, in CR4 is set to one and one of the following conditions is detected:

- A data parity error is detected by the processor during a read transaction and the processor's PEN# input is asserted by logic external to the processor.
- The processor detects a bus check at the end of a transaction.

In both cases, the processor latches the bus transaction address and type into the machine check address register (MCAR) and machine check type register (MCTR), respectively. In addition, the processor sets the CHK bit in MCTR to indicate that MCAR and MCTR contain valid information.

Functional Redundancy Checking

In a multiprocessing environment where two or more Pentium processors are present in the system, one of the processors may be configured to verify the correctness of all of the other processor's operations. The master processor fetches and executes instructions while the checker processor monitors all bus activity generated by the master. The checker is actually inputting the instruction stream being fetched by the master and executing each of the instructions, but doesn't drive the buses (with the exception of TDO and IERR#).

In order to initiate functional redundancy checking, the master and checker must both be connected to all bus pins with the exception of TDO and IERR#. A Pentium processor selects its master/checker state on the trailing-edge of RESET by sampling the state of its FRCMC# (functional redundancy check master checker) input. A low selects checker mode, causing the processor to tri-state all of its outputs (except IERR# and TDO). A high on FRCMC# permits the processor to perform normally. The final state of FRCMC# when RESET is deasserted determines the mode each processor will be in.

This feature can be implemented so that the processors can be placed into the master/checker configuration during testing, but may operate independently during normal operation (in order to achieve high system performance through multiprocessing). This would require a set of tri-stateable buffers to be placed between the two sets of processor buses. During functional redundancy checking:

- The buffers would be enabled, permitting one processor to monitor the bus activity generated by the other processor.
- One processor would be configured as the master and the other as the checker.
- The checker's L2 cache is disabled to prevent it from handling requests issued by the master processor.

During normal operation:

- The buffers would be disabled, allowing the two sets of processor buses to run separately and concurrently. This permits the two processors to run separate programs concurrently.
- Both processors would be configured as masters so that both may generate the bus transactions necessary to run their respective programs.

Figure 11-3 illustrates this configuration.

Development/Manufacturing Test Features

The test features described in this section were designed to facilitate testing in the manufacturing and/or depot repair environments. They require external test equipment.

Tri-Stating the Processor

Background

In the manufacturing or depot repair environments, the Pentium processor-based system board may be tested on a tester with a bed-of-nails vacuum test fixture. In order to test the driveability and interconnect of the circuit traces connected to the processor, the test hardware/software may need to electrically disconnect the Pentium processor from the system board circuitry. Having forced the processor to disconnect from the remainder of the system board logic, the tester may then drive all of the signals normally driven by the processor. This permits the tester to drive the system board traces and verify the effects of the tester's programmed stimulus of each signal line.

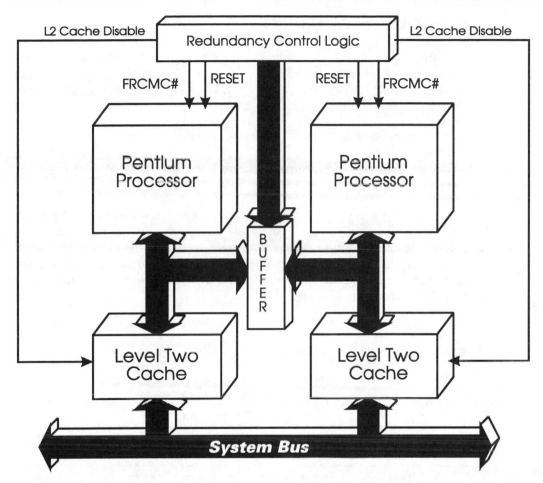

Figure 11-3. Multiprocessing System Permitting Functional Redundancy Check

Implementation

When the RESET signal is deasserted by logic external to the Pentium processor, the processor samples its FLUSH# input. If FLUSH# is sampled asserted on the falling-edge of RESET, the processor floats all of its output-only and input/output pins. This is known as tristate test mode. The only signal excluded is the processor's TDO output. The processor will remain in tristate test mode until the RESET input is toggled again and FLUSH# is sampled deasserted on RESET's falling-edge.

The Test Access Port, or TAP

The Pentium processor implements the IEEE 1149.1 TAP and boundary scan architecture. It should be noted that a detailed discussion of the TAP and boundary scan is outside the scope of this publication. This decision was made for two reasons:

- The Intel Pentium processor data book contains a discussion of these features.
- The test engineering community is already well-acquainted with the IEEE 1149.1 specification.

The TAP provides access to both the boundary scan interface and the Pentium processor's probe mode instruction and data registers. Probe mode is used to facilitate implementation of debug tools used to debug the system and software. A detailed discussion of probe mode remains under five year non-disclosure by Intel, but the section following this one provides speculation on its function and implementation.

The BIST may be initiated by issuing the RUNBIST command to the TAP.

The signals associated with the TAP are briefly described in table 11-2.

Table 11-2. TAP-Related Signals

Signal	Description
TDI	**Test data input**. Used to supply data or instructions to the Pentium processor's TAP in a serial bit stream.
TMS	**Test mode select**. Used to select the mode of the Pentium processor's TAP controller.
TCK	**Test clock**. Used to shift serial information into the TAP on TDI or out of the TAP on TDO.
TRST#	**Test reset**. When asserted, forces the TAP controller into test logic reset state. In this state, all Pentium inputs and outputs operate normally.
TDO	**Test data output**. Used to output requested data or state out of the processor's TAP under the control of the TCK signal.

Chapter 11: Test and Debug

Probe Mode and the Debug Port

General

The system board designer may integrate a special debug port into the design to facilitate system/program debugging. Using the debug port signals, the programmer may remove the processor from run mode and place it into probe mode to access its debug and general registers. They can then be remotely programmed by the debug tool to detect up to four types of accesses to four different addresses. The debug registers are described in the section in this chapter entitled, "Hardware Breakpoint Support." After setting up between one and four breakpoints using the debug tool, the user can switch the processor back into run mode and resume program execution. When the processor detects a breakpoint compare, it automatically exits run mode, enters probe mode and signals this event to the debug tool. The tool then accesses the processor's debug status register, determines the breakpoint detected and displays the pertinent information.

Table 11-3 defines the signals on the debug port connector and suggested pinouts.

Table 11-3. Example Debug Port Connector Pinouts

Signal	Direction	Pin	Description
TDO	Output	13	**Test data output.** Used to output requested data or state out of the processor's TAP under the control of the TCK signal.
TDI	Input	12	**Test data input.** Used to supply data or instructions to the Pentium processor's TAP in a serial bit stream.
TMS	Input	14	**Test mode select.** Used to select the mode of the Pentium processor's TAP controller.
TCK	Input	16	**Test clock.** Used to shift serial information into the TAP on TDI or out of the TAP on TDO.

Signal	Direction	Pin	Description
TRST#	Input	18	**Test reset.** When asserted, forces the TAP controller into test logic reset state. In this state, all Pentium inputs and outputs operate normally.
BSEN#	Input	20	**Boundary Scan Enable.** Asserted by the debug tool to select the mux's A set of inputs to gate to the processor's boundary scan interface inputs. This permits the debug tool to use the boundary scan interface to access the processor's TAP port.
R/S#	Input	7	**Run/Stop.** When set high, the processor is permitted to run normally. When set low, the processor ceases to execute instructions (in other words, it freezes) and enters probe mode. This permits the debug tool to access the processor's debug registers through the boundary scan interface.
PRDY	Output	11	**Probe ready.** Intel has provided too little information on this signal, so the authors decline to speculate on its exact function.
INIT	Output	1	**Initialization.** This is an input to the Pentium processor and to the debug tool. When asserted by the system board reset logic, it has the same effect on the processor as RESET except that the internal caches, write buffers, model specific registers and floating point registers retain their contents. Program execution starts at the power-on restart address, FFFFFFF0h. When asserted, it also initializes the debug tool logic to a known state. The debug tool could indicate the state of the INIT signal with an LED.

Signal	Direction	Pin	Description
RESET	Output	3	This is the **reset** signal generated by the system board reset logic. It resets the system logic as well as the debug tool logic.
DBRESET	Input	2	**Debug tool reset**. When the engineer wishes to reset the system, a debug reset switch on the debug tool is depressed. In response, the tool generates debug reset to the system board reset logic. This causes the system board reset logic to assert RESET to all system board logic.
SYSR/S#	Output	9	**System Run/Stop**. This signal is an input to the debug tool from the system board's debug port logic (pictured in figure 11-4). If the debug tool isn't installed, this signal is not used.
DBINST#	Input	19	**Debug tool installed.** Connecting the debug tool to the system board causes this signal to be grounded, asserting it. It disables the R/S# signal open collector driver so that the debug tool can control the processor's R/S# input.
Vcc		6	Power
Gnd		4,8,1 0,15, 17	Ground
SMIACT#	Output	5	**System Management Interrupt Active** is an input from the system board. It permits the debug tool to detect when the processor enters system management mode.

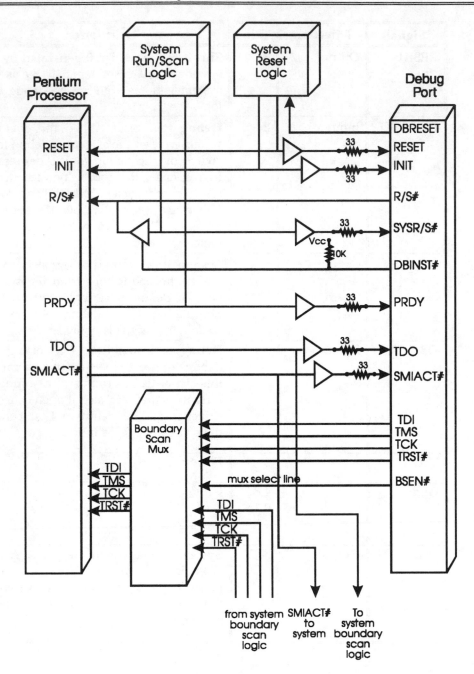

Figure 11-4. Suggested Debug Port Logic

Operational Description

The run/stop signal, R/S#, is an input to the processor. When the debug tool is not installed, the pullup resistor on the debugger installed signal, DBINST#, enables the open collector driver. This allows the system board run/stop logic to supply the run/stop signal to the processor. When the debug tool is installed, the debugger installed signal, DBINST#, is grounded, disabling the open collector driver and blocking the system board's run/stop logic from supplying the R/S# signal to the processor. Instead, the debug tool controls the processor's run/stop input, R/S#, directly. The debug tool may monitor the state of the system board's run/stop signal on its SYSR/S# input.

When the engineer wishes to access the processor's TAP controller, the debug tool sets the R/S# and BSEN# lines low. Setting the R/S# signal low causes the processor to freeze on the next instruction boundary. The PRDY signal is asserted by the processor to inform the debug tool that is has stopped execution. Asserting boundary scan enable (BSEN#) selects the boundary scan mux's "A" set of inputs to be gated to the processor's boundary scan TAP inputs. The tool may then access the processor's TAP controller to access the processor's debug registers and set up one or more breakpoints. In order to prevent the program from accessing the debug registers after they've been set up by the debug tool, the GD bit should be set in the debug command register, DR7.

After the breakpoint(s) is set and the engineer wishes to let the processor resume normal operation, the tool deasserts BSEN# and sets R/S# high. The high on R/S# takes the processor out of boundary scan mode and the deassertion of BSEN# disconnects the tool's boundary scan outputs from the processor and gates the system board's boundary scan signals to the processor's boundary scan inputs.

When in probe mode the debug tool can use the boundary scan interface to access the processor's debug status register, DR6, to ascertain which breakpoint was detected (see the description of the BD status bit in table 11-9) and then displays a visual indication to the engineer. Through the TAP, the engineer may access and display any of the processor's internal registers.

The debug tool may monitor the processor's SMIACT# output to determine when the processor is in system management mode.

Program Debug Features

The Pentium processor implements features that facilitate program/system debug. These features can be divided into three groups:

- A special interface to facilitate the implementation of a system debugger. This is referred to as the probe port and will remain under non-disclosure for fifteen years.
- A set of signals to facilitate program tracing by an in-circuit emulator, or ICE.
- A superset of the 386, 486 processor debug registers to provide hardware support of memory and I/O breakpoints.

ICE Support

The purpose of an ICE is to trace instruction execution without interfering with program execution. The Pentium processor implements three signals, a special bus transaction type, and a special register to facilitate ICE interfacing. The signals associated with the ICE interface are described in table 11-4.

Table 11-4. ICE-Specific Signals

Signal	Description
IU	Asserted by the processor when an **instruction completes in the U instruction pipeline**.
IV	Asserted by the processor when an **instruction completes in the V instruction pipeline**.
IBT	**Instruction branch taken**. Asserted by the processor when a branch instruction has been executed and the branch has been taken.
PM/BP0	**Performance monitoring bit 0 or breakpoint bit 0**. The function of this output and that of PM/BP1 (see next entry) is controlled by the PB0 and PB1 bits in the debug mode control register. When these bits are set to zero (default), PM/BP0 and PM/BP1 signal performance monitoring information. When PB0 is set to one, PM/BP0 is asserted by the processor if breakpoint zero is detected. For more information, refer to the section entitled, "Hardware Breakpoint Support (the Debug Registers)."

Signal	Description
PM/BP1	**Performance monitoring bit 1 or breakpoint bit 1**. When PB1 is set to one, PM/BP1 is asserted by the processor if breakpoint one is detected. For more information, refer to the section entitled, "Hardware Breakpoint Support (the Debug Registers)" and to the previous entry in this table.
BP2	**Breakpoint bit 2**. Asserted by the processor if breakpoint two is detected. For more information, refer to the section entitled, "Hardware Breakpoint Support (the Debug Registers)."
BP3	**Breakpoint bit 3**. Asserted by the processor if breakpoint three is detected. For more information, refer to the section entitled, "Hardware Breakpoint Support (the Debug Registers)."

Table 11-5 defines the interpretation of the IU, IV and IBT outputs.

Table 11-5. Interpretation of IU, IV and IBT Outputs

IU	IV	IBT	Interpretation
0	0	0	No instruction completed.
0	0	1	Does not occur.
0	1	0	Does not occur.
0	1	1	Does not occur.
1	0	0	Non-branch Instruction completed in the U pipeline.
1	0	1	A branch was taken by an instruction in the U pipeline.
1	1	0	Instructions completed in the U and in the V pipelines. Neither was a taken branch.
1	1	1	Instructions completed in both pipelines and the instruction in the V pipeline was a taken branch.

If the trace bit, TR in TR12, is set to one, the processor generates a branch trace message special cycle whenever a branch is taken. The processor also asserts IBT. Figure 11-5 illustrates test register 12 (TR12). The processor indicates that is running a special cycle by setting M/IO# to zero, D/C# to zero and W/R# to one. It indicates that it is the branch trace message version of the special cycle by asserting BE5# and deasserting the other byte enable outputs.

Test Register 12
(TR12)

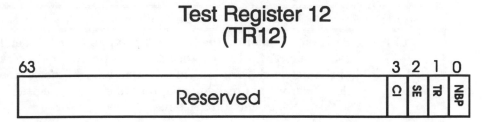

Figure 11-5. Test Register 12, or TR12

TR 12 contains three other bits used to enable special test functions: These bits, permit new internal hardware features to be disabled, to aid in debugging code. Note that the exact behavior of the processor is not disclosed by Intel.

- **NPB (No Branch Prediction)** - the usage of this bit is under non-disclosure, however, its name seems to clearly indicate that dynamic branch prediction can be disabled by setting this bit.
- **SE (Single Pipe Execution)** - this bit clearly indicate that the V pipeline can be disabled by setting this bit, thereby permitting single pipe execution.
- **CI (Cache Inhibit)** - Its use is also under non-disclosure, but the name certainly indicates that setting this bit to a one will inhibit caching by the internal caches.

Hardware Breakpoint Support (the Debug Registers)

Like the 386 and 486 processors, the Pentium processor provides hardware breakpoint detection. This is implemented using the processor's debug registers. These registers are illustrated in figure 11-6. Other processor functions associated with debug include:

- The debug exception, exception one. This exception is generated when the processor encounters a breakpoint match on a condition specified in the debug registers.
- The breakpoint instruction exception, exception three. This exception is generated when the processor executes the breakpoint instruction.
- Trap bit in a task's TSS. Causes a debug exception when a task switch occurs to a task with this bit (the T bit) set to one.
- The resume flag bit in the EFLAGS register. When set to one by the debugger (by executing an IRETD instruction), prevents the processor from

generating a debug exception again when it returns to an instruction that already caused a debug exception.

- The trap flag bit in the EFLAGS register. When set to one, the processor generates a debug exception after the execution of each instruction. This permits single-stepping through a program.

The debug control register, DR7, is used to enable one or more breakpoints. Table 11-6 describes the bits in DR7.

Debug Registers

	31 30	29 28	27 26	25 24	23 22	21 20	19 18	17 16	15 14	13 12 11 10	9 8	7	6	5	4	3	2	1	0	
Control	LEN3	R/W3	LEN2	R/W2	LEN1	R/W1	LEN0	R/W0	0 0	GD 0 0 1	GE LE	G3	L3	G2	L2	G1	L1	G0	L0	DR7
Status	1 1	1 1	1 1	1 1	1 1	1 1	1 1	1 1	BT BS BD	1 1 1 1	1 1	1	1	1	1	B3	B2	B1	B0	DR6

Reserved	DR5
Reserved	DR4
Breakpoint 3 Linear Address	DR3
Breakpoint 2 Linear Address	DR2
Breakpoint 1 Linear Address	DR1
Breakpoint 0 Linear Address	DR0

Debug Mode Control Register

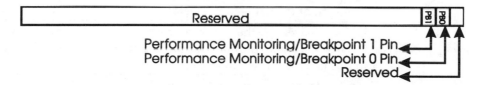

Reserved	PB1	PB0

Performance Monitoring/Breakpoint 1 Pin
Performance Monitoring/Breakpoint 0 Pin
Reserved

Figure 11-6 The Debug Registers

Using the Pentium processor's DR7, DR0, DR1, DR2 and DR3 registers, the programmer may enable the processor to detect any of four different types of accesses to up to four different addresses specified in DR0-DR3. *The Pentium processor has added the capability to monitor for read or write accesses to I/O ports.* The 386 and 486 processors do not possess this capability.

When a breakpoint is detected, the processor generates a debug exception (exception one) and jumps to the debug exception handler routine. In addition, the processor will set the appropriate bits in the debug status register, DR6. Table 11-9 describes the bits in DR6.

Table 11-6. Definition of DR7 Bits Fields

Field	Definition
R/W0	Defines the **type of access** to the address specified in DR0 that the processor will look for a match on. Table 11-7 defines the interpretation of the value in this field.
LEN0	Defines the **size of the access** to the address specified in DR0 that the debug logic will monitor for. The interpretation of the value in this field is defined in table 11-8.
L0	**Enable local breakpoint 0**. When set to one, a debug exception will be generated if the debug logic detects a match on an access of the type and length specified in the R/W0 and LEN0 fields to the address specified in DR0 while in the current task. This bit is automatically cleared when a task switch occurs. This prevents the generation of a debug exception on an access match while in another task.
G0	**Enable global breakpoint 0**. When set to one, a debug exception will be generated if the debug logic detects a match on an access of the type and length specified in the R/W0 and LEN0 fields to the address specified in DR0 while in any task.
R/W1	Defines the type of access to the address specified in DR1 that the processor will look for a match on. Table 11 - 7 defines the interpretation of the value in this field.
LEN1	Defines the size of the access to the address specified in DR1 that the debug logic will monitor for. The interpretation of the value in this field is defined in table 11-8.
L1	**Enable local breakpoint 1**. When set to one, a debug exception will be generated if the debug logic detects a match on an access of the type and length specified in the R/W1 and LEN1 fields to the address specified in DR1 while in the current task. This bit is automatically cleared when a task switch occurs. This prevents the generation of a debug exception on an access match while in another task.
G1	**Enable global breakpoint 1**. When set to one, a debug exception will be generated if the debug logic detects a match on an access of the type and length specified in the R/W1 and LEN1 fields to the address specified in DR1 while in any task.

Field	Definition
R/W2	Defines the type of access to the address specified in DR2 that the processor will look for a match on. Table 11-7 defines the interpretation of the value in this field.
LEN2	Defines the size of the access to the address specified in DR2 that the debug logic will monitor for. The interpretation of the value in this field is defined in table 11-8.
L2	**Enable local breakpoint 2**. When set to one, a debug exception will be generated if the debug logic detects a match on an access of the type and length specified in the R/W2 and LEN2 fields to the address specified in DR2 while in the current task. This bit is automatically cleared when a task switch occurs. This prevents the generation of a debug exception on an access match while in another task.
G2	**Enable global breakpoint 2**. When set to one, a debug exception will be generated if the debug logic detects a match on an access of the type and length specified in the R/W2 and LEN2 fields to the address specified in DR2 while in any task.
R/W3	Defines the type of access to the address specified in DR3 that the processor will look for a match on. Table 11-7 defines the interpretation of the value in this field.
LEN3	Defines the size of the access to the address specified in DR3 that the debug logic will monitor for. The interpretation of the value in this field is defined in table 11-8.
L3	**Enable local breakpoint 3**. When set to one, a debug exception will be generated if the debug logic detects a match on an access of the type and length specified in the R/W3 and LEN3 fields to the address specified in DR3 while in the current task. This bit is automatically cleared when a task switch occurs. This prevents the generation of a debug exception on an access match while in another task.
G3	**Enable global breakpoint 3**. When set to one, a debug exception will be generated if the debug logic detects a match on an access of the type and length specified in the R/W3 and LEN3 fields to the address specified in DR3 while in any task.

Field	Definition
LE and GE	Both the Pentium and 486 processors ignore the setting of the LE and GE bits. They are provided for backward compatibility with the 386 processor. The 386 processor uses these bits as a master enable for the local and global enable bits associated with each breakpoint (see the explanation of L0-L3 and G0-G3).
GD	When set to a one, the debug logic will generate a debug exception if the next instruction to be executed will attempt to access one of the debug registers while they are in use by a debug tool. In addition, the BD bit in the debug status register, DR6 will be set to one to indicate to the debug exception handler routine the reason for the exception. This bit is automatically cleared when a debug exception does occur so that the processor can freely access the debug registers in the exception handler.

Table 11 - 7. Interpretation of the R/W Field In DR7

R/W Value	Recognized by Pentium or 486?	Access Type To Monitor For
00b	both	Break on memory instruction read.
01b	both	Break on memory data write.
10b	Pentium-only	Break on I/O read or write. Note that the Pentium processor only recognizes this selection if the debug extension bit, DE, in CR4 is set to one.
11b	both	Break on memory data read or write, but not on memory instruction read.

Table 11-8. Interpretation of the LEN Field In DR7

LEN Value	Interpretation
00b	Break on a one byte access of the type specified in the R/W field from the address specified in the respective DR register (DR0-DR3).
01b	Break on a two byte access of the type specified in the R/W field from the address specified in the respective DR register (DR0-DR3).
10b	Undefined.
11b	Break on a four byte access of the type specified in the R/W field from the address specified in the respective DR register (DR0-DR3).

Table 11-9. Debug Status Register Bits

Bit	Description
B0	This bit is set if the processor had a **match on breakpoint zero**. The match is on the access type specified in R/W0, with the access length specified in LEN0 on the address specified in DR0.
B1	This bit is set if the processor had a **match on breakpoint one**. The match is on the access type specified in R/W1, with the access length specified in LEN1 on the address specified in DR1.
B2	This bit is set if the processor had a **match on breakpoint two**. The match is on the access type specified in R/W2, with the access length specified in LEN2 on the address specified in DR2.
D3	This bit is set if the processor had a **match on breakpoint three**. The match is on the access type specified in R/W3, with the access length specified in LEN3 on the address specified in DR3.
BD	This bit is set to one when the GD bit in DR7 is set to one and the processor detects an **attempt to access one of the debug registers**. This protects the debug registers from being altered by the program while they are in use by an ICE or a debug tool.

Bit	Description
BS	This status bit is set to one and the processor generates a debug exception if the trap flag bit, TF, in the EFLAGS register is set to one and an instruction has completed execution. This permits the processor to **single-step** through a program and allows the programmer to examine the state of the processor's registers after each instruction is executed.
BT	This status bit is set to one if a debug exception occurred because the **processor switched to a task with the trap bit set to one in its TSS**. This permits the programmer to detect when a task is about to begin execution.

Part II:

The Pentium 90 and 100MHz Processors

Chapter 12

The Previous Chapter

The previous chapter discussed the Pentium's test and debug features.

This Chapter

This chapter introduces the features of the new Pentium microprocessors, widely known as the P54C processors.

The Next Chapter

The next chapter details the signals that have been removed from and added to the P54C when compared to the original Pentium processors.

Introduction to the P54C Processors

The new Pentium microprocessors, commonly referred to as the P54C processors, currently exist in three versions: the Pentium 90MHz and Pentium 100MHz versions. The actual product names are the 735/90 and the 815/100, respectively. The first three digits refer to the iCOMP index (a measure of performance), while the digits following the slash indicate the internal clock speed. In this document for the sake of brevity, Pentium 735/90 and Pentium 815/100 processors are jointly referred to as the P54C processors.

The P54C processors have the same basic functionality of the original Pentium processors with the additional enhancements listed below:

- Faster processor core (90 or 100MHz) yielding higher performance.
- Fractional bus speed.
- Dual processing support.
- Local Advanced Programmable Interrupt Controller (APIC).
- Enhanced power management features.

- 3.3vdc logic levels.
- Future upgrade socket definition.

Faster Processor Core/Slower Bus Clock

The P54C processors operate at an internal frequency that is a multiple of the processors clock input. This permits the processor to operate at internal clock frequencies that are significantly higher that the input clock frequency. Bus cycles run at the lower input clock frequency making system implementations less costly and much easier to design.

Dual Processing Support

Perhaps the most important enhancement is the dual processor support. The P54C processors may be directly connected to each other, thereby providing dual processing capability without the need for external "glue logic". This dual processor configuration permits two Pentium 90 or 100 processors to communicate directly with one another over a private bus to provide arbitration and cache coherency.

The P54C processors operate as standalone processors or as dual processors when two P54C processors are implemented. In a single-processor system, the processor is designated as the primary (and only) processor. In a dual-processor system, one of the processors must be identified as the primary processor, while the other is identified as the secondary, or dual, processor. The identification process occurs automatically at power-up time. Each processor samples its CPUTYP input at the trailing edge of RESET. A low on CPUTYP indicates that the processor is the primary processor, while a high identifies it as the dual processor.

Advanced Programmable Interrupt Controller (APIC)

An advanced programmable interrupt controller (APIC) is also integrated into each Pentium 90 and 100 processor. This adds to the dual processor support by providing a mechanism to deliver interrupts to either of the dual processors, thus providing symmetrical processing support.

Chapter 12: P54C Processor Overview

Each P54C processor incorporates a local APIC module designed to process interrupts in a multiprocessing environment. An external APIC I/O module monitors system interrupts and directs them to the appropriate target processor's local APIC module. Note that the APIC system implemented in the P54C processors is based on the Intel 82489DX APIC system, however numerous differences exist.

3.3 vdc Logic Levels

The P54C processors use 3.3 vdc logic levels. This renders them incompatible with 5 vdc chip sets designed for use with 5 vdc Pentium processors.

Enhanced Power Management

The P54C processors incorporate the SL power management features. These features include:

- 3.3 vdc operating voltage - this results in considerably lower power dissipation in the P54Cs when compared to the original Pentium processors operating at 5 vdc.

- system management mode (SMM) - this mode provides the system designer with the ability to implement power management features independent of the operation system.

- stop clock capability - a signal called Stop Clock (STPCLK#) causes the processor to stop its internal clock, thereby reducing power dissipation to almost nothing.

These features combine to make the P54C processors extremely energy-efficient when compared to their predecessors.

Future Upgrade Socket

System designers may implement a system with a single P54C processor, but also include a ZIF socket to permit system upgrade with a second processor at a later date. This socket is referred to as socket five, or the *Future Pentium Overdrive* Processor socket.

Chapter 13

The Previous Chapter

The previous chapter introduced the new feature incorporated into the P54C processors.

This Chapter

This chapter details the signals that have been removed and added to the P54C processors when compared to the original Pentium 60/66 processors.

The Next Chapter

The next chapter discusses the dual-processing capabilities of the P54C processors.

P54C Signal Interface

The P54C signal interface is illustrated in figure 13-1. Most of the signals implemented on the P54C processors are the same as the original Pentium 60 and 66 MHz. Many of these signals however, are treated as input and output signals whenever operating in dual-processing mode

The P54C processors add new signals not used with the earlier Pentium processor and are shown shaded in black in figure 13-1. Conversely, the P54C processors do not implement some signals that are used with earlier Pentium processors. (See table 13-1.)

Some of the pins are shared by two signals (e.g., [APICEN] and PICD1). The signal in brackets represents the pin assignment at power-up time when RESET is deasserted. The non-bracketed signal represents the pin's assignment during regular operation.

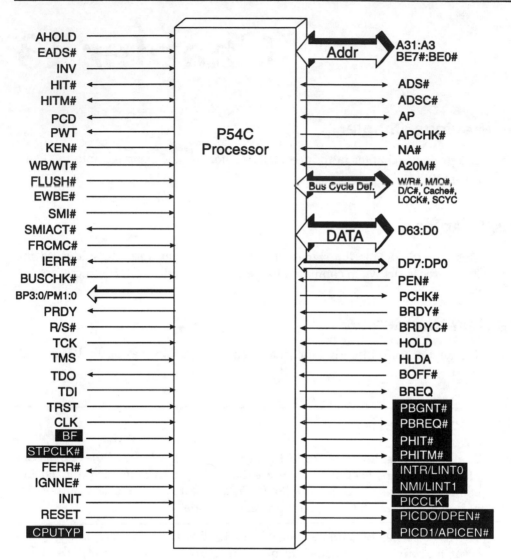

Figure 13-1. The P54C Pinout

Signals Deleted

Table 13-1 lists the signals on the 60/66MHz Pentium processor that have been deleted on the P54C processors. These signals are used for instruction execution tracing inside the Pentium processors. The P54C processors provide execution tracing without the specific pins listed in table 13-1. Refer to the section entitled "Execution Tracing" later in this chapter.

Table 13-1. Signals Deleted On the P90/100 Processor

Signal	Description
IBT	Instruction branch taken.
IU	Instruction completed execution in U pipeline.
IV	Instruction completed in V pipeline.
BT[3:0]	Branch Trace bus.

Dual Processor Signals

Two P54C processors that are operating in dual processor mode share the same external buses and typically access the same Level 2 Cache. Clearly, only one processor at a time can own this bus. For reference purposes, Intel refers to the processor that currently owns the bus (or the one that owned the bus when last used) as the Most Recent Master (MRM), while the processor that does not currently own the bus is called the Least Recent Master (LRM). To support dual processor functionality new signals have been defined and some existing signals definitions have been modified. These signals can be categorized as:

- those signals used during initialization to determine if a dual processor is installed.

- those signals used by the LRM to recognize memory accesses made by the MRM and to snoop the address in order to maintain cache coherency.

- those signals used to manage bus arbitration and report the results of cache snoops. These signals are jointly called the **private bus**.

Dual Processor Present Signals

Table 13-2 lists the signals used to determine whether a dual processor configuration is present in the system.

Table 13-2. Primary/Dual Processor Present Signals

Signal	Description
CPUTYP	CPU Type pin. Sampled by the processor at the trailing-edge of RESET to determine whether it is the primary or the dual (secondary) processor. CPUTYP should be strapped low in a single processor environment or when the processor is the primary of processor pair. CPUTYP should be strapped high if the processor is the dual, or secondary, processor of a dual processor system.
[DPEN#]/PICD0	If present, the dual processor asserts DPEN# (Dual Processing Enable) during RESET. When RESET is deasserted, DPEN# is sampled by the primary processor to determine if a dual processor is present. If DPEN# is sampled asserted, the primary processor enables dual processor operation. During normal operation, this is the PICD0 (Programmable Interrupt Controller Data line 0) I/O pin.

Dual Processor Arbitration Signals

The signals listed in table 13-3 provide a way for the primary and dual processors to arbitrate for control of the bus and indicate which processor is the current owner of the bus.

Table 13-3. Signals used for P54C Bus Arbitration

Signal	Description
PBREQ#	Private Bus Request. Only used in a dual processor system (otherwise, no connect). Asserted by the LRM to request ownership of the private local bus shared by the two processors. PBREQ# is an output from the requesting processor (the LRM) and an input to the MRM.

Signal	Description
PBGNT#	Private Bus Grant. Only used in a dual processor system (otherwise, no connect). Asserted by the MRM to grant ownership of the private local bus (shared by the two processors) to the LRM. PBGNT# is an output from the MRM and an input to the LRM.
D/P#	Dual/Primary. This signal is an output of the primary processor and is not used by the dual processor. It is asserted (low) by the primary processor when it has acquired private bus ownership and has initiated a bus cycle. It is de asserted (high) by the primary processor when it is not the private bus master.

Dual Processor Cache Coherency Signals

Table 13-4 lists the signals used by the primary and dual processors to report the results of internal cache snoop operations causes by the other processor accessing memory.

Table 13-4. P54C Cache Coherency Signals

Signal	Description
PHIT#	Private Bus Hit. PHIT# is an output from the LRM and an input to the MRM. It is not used in a single processor system (no connect). PHIT# is used in conjunction with PHITM# to indicate the results of snoop in the LRM's L1 cache. If neither PHIT# nor PHITM# is asserted by the LRM, a cache miss is indicated. When just PHIT# is asserted by the LRM, a hit on a clean line (E or S) is indicated. If both PHIT# and PHITM# are asserted, this indicates a hit on a modified cache line.
PHITM#	Private Bus Hit on Modified line. See PHIT#.

Other Signals Supporting Dual Processor Operation

Some signals change from output only pins to input/output pins in dual processor mode. Refer to table 13-5. These pins become inputs to the LRM so that it can monitor memory read and write bus cycles run by the MRM so that cache consistency can be maintained.

Table 13-5. Signals Converted from Output Only to Input/Output Signals

Signal Name				
ADS#	W/R#	CACHE#	SCYC	HITM#
D/C#	M/IO#	LOCK#	HIT#	HLDA

APIC Signals

The P54C processors integrate a local APIC module in the CPU. This local APIC communicates with other devices that reside on the APIC bus. In addition to the APIC bus, new local interrupt inputs have also been defined.

The APIC Bus

The APIC bus consists of the signals listed in table 13-6. Note that the local APIC is enabled or disabled during system reset based on the state of the APIC enable signal [APICEN] that is shared with PICD1.

Table 13-6. Signals that Comprise the APIC Bus

Signal	Description
PICCLK	Programmable Interrupt Controller Clock. It is used to clock serial data into or out of the processor's internal, local APIC over the PICD[1:0] bus.
PICD0/[DPEN#]	During normal operation, this is the PICD0 (Programmable Interrupt Controller Data line 0) I/O pin. If present, the dual processor asserts DPEN# (Dual Processing Enable) during RESET. When RESET is deasserted,

Signal	Description
	DPEN# is sampled by the primary processor to determine if a dual processor is present. If DPEN# is sampled asserted, the primary processor enables dual processor operation.
PICD1/[APICEN]	During ordinary operation, this is the PICD1 (Programmable Interrupt Controller Data line 1) I/O pin. When RESET is deasserted, processor samples APICEN to determine if the internal APIC is enabled (1 = APIC enabled).

The Local APIC Interrupt Inputs

The P54C processors have local interrupt input signals that become active when the local APIC is enabled as described in table 13-7.

Table 13-7. The Local Interrupt Signals

Signal	Description
LINT0/ INTR	If the processor's local APIC is enabled (APICEN sampled asserted on training-edge of RESET), this is the LINT0 (Local Interrupt 0) input. If the APIC is disabled, this is the processor's maskable interrupt request input, INTR.
LINT1/NMI	If the processor's local APIC is enabled (APICEN sampled asserted on training-edge of RESET), this is the LINT1 (Local Interrupt 1) input. If the APIC is disabled, this is the processor's non-maskable interrupt request input, NMI.

The Stop Clock Signal

The stop clock signal (STPCLK#) directs the processor to stop its internal clock, resulting in far less power consumption. After the processor has granted the stop clock request, it still has the ability to monitor bus cycles being run by a dual processor and to respond to external snoop requests. This permits the processor to maintain cache coherency even though its internal clock has been stopped.

The Bus Frequency Signal

The bus frequency signal (BF) determines the I/O bus to processor core frequency ratio. When BF is strapped to Vcc the processor operates at a 2/3 (I/O bus to processor core) frequency ratio. When strapped to Vss, the processor operates at a 1/2 frequency ratio. The possible frequency ratios are listed in table 13-8.

Table 13-8. Clock Speed Possibilities

CPU Type	BF State	CLK Speed	Bus Speed	Internal Clock Speed
735/90	1	60 MHz	60 MHz	90 MHz
815/100	0	50 MHz	50 MHz	100 MHz
815/100	1	66.6 MHz	66.6 MHz	100 MHz

Execution Tracing Signals

The original Pentium processors provide execution tracing that includes the assertion of the IBT, IU and IV along with the branch trace special messages. The P54C processors do not have the IBT, IU, and IV signals but still support the branch trace special message cycle.

If branch trace cycles are enabled, the processor outputs the linear address of the branch target location when a branch instruction is taken. The original

Pentium processors use the address bus proper (A31:A3) to deliver the upper 29 bits of the linear address, while the lower three bits of the address are delivered via dedicated pins BT 2:0. BT3 specifies the default operand size (16 or 32 bits). Since the dedicated BT3:BT0 signals have been removed from the P54C pinout, data lines are used to deliver part of the linear address during branch trace special cycles as shown in table 13-9.

The P54C can perform an additional branch trace cycle by following the first special cycle (the branch target linear address) with a second special cycle that broadcast the linear address of the branch instruction that caused the branch to be taken.

Table 13-9. Signals that Deliver the Linear Address During Branch Trace Special Cycles

Signal Name	Definition During Branch Trace Special Cycle
A31:A4	Carries bits 31:4 of the linear address
D63:D60	Carries bits 3:0 of the linear address
A3	Indicates the default operand size: 0 = 16-bit default operand 1 = 32-bit default operand
D59	Defines the linear address: 0 = the branch target linear address 1 = the linear address of the instruction causing the branch to be taken

Chapter 14

The Previous Chapter

The previous chapter detailed the new signals defined by the P54C processors along with signals that are not new, but have some functional differences when compared to the original Pentium processors.

This Chapter

This chapter introduces the uni- and dual-processing capabilities that have been incorporated into the P54C processors. In a uni-processor environment, the P54C processors operate like the Pentium 60 and 66MHz processors in most respects. This chapter focuses primarily on the dual-processing issues.

The Next Chapter

The next chapter discusses the P54C implementation of the Advanced Programmable Interrupt Controller (APIC).

The P54C Processor's Dual Processing Capabilities

The P54C processor is designed to operate either as a standalone processor in a single-processor system or as one of a pair of P54C processors in a dual-processing environment. In a single-processor system, the processor is designated as the primary (and only) processor. In a dual-processor system, one of the processors must be identified as the primary processor, while the other is identified as the secondary, or dual, processor.

In a system with both a primary and a dual processor, the primary processor enables dual processor operation when it samples DPEN# (Dual Processor Enable) asserted at the trailing-edge of RESET. Figure 14-1 illustrates two P54C processors in a dual processor configuration. Since the local buses are shared between the processors, the a bus arbitration mechanism must be employed to determine bus ownership. Additionally, each P54C processor contains internal memory caches, and therefore cache consistency between these caches must be maintained via some cache coherency protocol.

The P54C dual-processor implementation incorporates a private bus that allows the processors to communicate directly. The private bus supports P54C bus arbitration and cache coherency without the additional "glue logic" that is needed when implementing dual-processing capability with other processors.

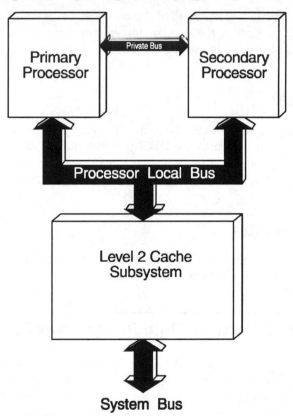

Figure 14-1. Dual P54C Processors Connect to the Same Local and Private Buses

Chapter 14: Dual Processors

Determining Presence of a Dual Processor

At power-up time, each P54C processor samples the state of its CPUTYP input pin to determine if it is the primary or dual processor. The primary processor has its CPUTYP input strapped low, while the dual processor is strapped high. If present, the dual processor asserts its DPEN# output (dual processing enable) during RESET assertion. At the trailing-edge of RESET, the primary processor samples its DPEN# input to determine if the dual processor is present. If DPEN# is sampled asserted, the dual processor is present and the primary processor configures itself for dual processor operation. If DPEN# is sampled deasserted, the dual processor is not present and the primary processor configures itself for single processor operation. Note that when configured for single-processor operation, the private bus is not used.

Multiprocessor Initialization and Configuration

The primary processor automatically initiates program execution at the power-on restart address (FFFFFFF0h). The dual processor initiates program execution when it receives a startup inter-processor interrupt (IPI) from the primary processor. It then initiates program execution beginning at the real mode start address specified by the IPI message. The IPI message specifies the start address of a 4KB page within the first 1MB of memory address space. Refer to the chapter entitled, "The APIC" for details regarding the startup IPI.

An SMP (symmetric multiprocessing) operating system is loaded and initialized by the primary processor. During initialization the operating system programmer places the startup code for the dual processor in the first megabyte of memory starting at a 4KB address boundary. The primary processor's local APIC is then instructed to send a startup IPI to the dual processor. This causes the dual processor to begin program execution at the start address indicated by the IPI startup message. Note that some systems have SMP aware ROM code may use it to initialize the dual processor rather than the operating system.

Pentium Processor System Architecture

Bus Arbitration in a Single-Processor System

When configured as a single-processor system, the P54C processor handles bus arbitration just as a P5 processor does. If its HOLD input is deasserted by external logic, the processor's local bus is parked on the processor. It has exclusive use of the local bus to run transactions. When another entity in the system requires use of the local bus (e.g., to access system DRAM memory), HOLD is asserted to the processor. If the processor has a bus transaction in progress, it is permitted to complete the transaction. It must then yield bus ownership (even if it has additional transactions queued up internally). If it does not have a transaction in progress when HOLD is asserted, it surrenders bus ownership immediately. The bus is surrendered by first floating all bus outputs and then asserting HLDA. Assertion of HLDA indicates to external logic that the processor has honored the HOLD request and has surrendered bus ownership. A new bus master may then initiate a bus transaction.

Bus Arbitration in a Dual-Processor System

In a dual processor implementation, it is obvious that both processors cannot be using the bus simultaneously. Therefore, there must be a method defined for the two processors to arbitrate for ownership of the bus. This could be accomplished in one of two ways:

- An external local bus arbiter could receive bus requests from the two processors, decide which processor to grant ownership to, and then issue a bus grant to that processor. The processor receiving the grant could then initiate a bus transaction, while the loser would have to wait for the arbiter to grant it ownership of the bus.
- The two processors could communicate directly with each other to decide which processor wins bus ownership (assuming both processors require the bus at the same time).

The first approach requires an external local bus arbiter be implemented on the system board. This would increase the cost and complexity of the system. Intel chose to implement the second approach: the two processors negotiate directly with each other to decide which gets to use the bus next. This approach simplifies dual processor system design.

MRM and LRM Defined

Since the primary processor and the dual processor can each own the shared bus, Intel uses new terminology to specify bus ownership. The last processor that used the bus is referred to as the Most-Recent Master, or MRM, while the other processor is referred to as the Least-Recent Master, or LRM. The primary processor automatically comes out of reset as the MRM, while the dual processor comes out of reset as the LRM.

MRM and LRM Arbitration

The private bus used to determine P54C bus ownership consists of two arbitration signals:

- **PBREQ# (Private Bus Request** -- this signal is an output from the LRM and an input to the MRM.

- **PBGNT# (Private Bus Grant** -- this signal is an output from the MRM and an input to the LRM.

The MRM always monitors its PBREQ# input during periods when it owns the local bus. If the LRM issues a request for bus ownership when the MRM is not using the bus (e.g., the bus is idle), the MRM issues PBGNT# to the LRM, granting it ownership of the bus. When the LRM detects its PBGNT# input asserted, it assumes ownership of the bus and initiates a transaction. The LRM now becomes the MRM and the MRM becomes the LRM. The direction of the PBREQ# and PBGNT# signals is then reversed. Figure 14-2 illustrates the relationships of the Private bus handshake between the MRM and LRM. Intel has not disclosed the precise timing of PBREQ# and PBGNT# and as such figure 14-2 is used to shown relationships only, not exact timing.

If the MRM has no more transactions to perform and its PBREQ# input is currently deasserted (the LRM does not need the bus), the bus remains parked on the MRM until either:

- it needs the bus, in which case it starts the transaction immediately; or
- it receives a PBREQ# from the LRM, in which case it cedes bus ownership to the LRM by asserting its PBGNT#. The MRM then becomes the LRM and the LRM becomes the MRM.

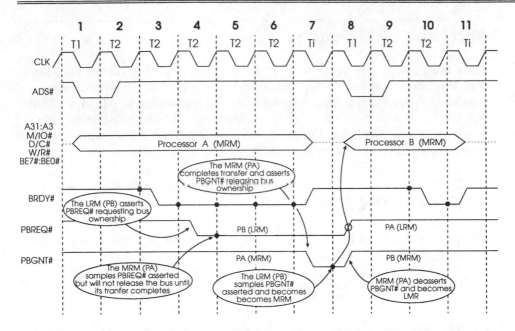

Figure 14-2. Example Arbitration Between Two P54C Processors

Arbitration During Pipelined Transfers

Dual-processor implementations with the P54C processors support inter-processor pipelining. When the MRM samples the NA# pin asserted it recognizes that the target device support pipelined transfers. In the next clock cycle, the MRM can pipeline another transfer just a single Pentium 60/66MHz would do. If however, the LRM has asserted the PBREQ# signal, the MRM will assert PBGNT#, rather than Pipelining another bus cycle. As an example, consider two cache line fills being pipelined between two processors as illustrated in figure 14-3. Since Intel does not disclose private bus timing, figure 14-3 is intended to illustrate the sequence of events and relationships between signals and not precise timing. The example sequence of events is as follows:

1. The current MRM, Processor A (PA), initiates a cache line fill sequence by asserting ADS# and outputting the address and bus cycle definition.

2. The current LRM, Processor B (PB) encounters in internal cache miss during a read operation, and asserts PBREQ# to request use of the buses.

3. The MRM samples PBREQ# asserted, but will not release bus ownership until either a) the current transfer completes or b) the target device requests that the next bus cycle be pipelined (i.e. asserts NA#).

4. The MRM samples BRDY#, KEN# and NA# asserted, and the first quadword is latched into the MRM's cache line-fill buffer. KEN# being sampled asserted confirms that the address is cacheable and the cache line fill continues. NA# sampled asserted indicates that the target device is ready for the next address. The MRM having previously sampled PBREQ# asserted, is now free to grant bus ownership to the LRM.

The LRM samples also monitors the MRM bus cycle and recognizes that a cache line-fill is going to be performed by the MRM and that the target device supports bus cycle pipelining. The LRM knowing that it will pipeline the next bus cycle, monitors BRDY# to track the progress of the cache line fill in progress. Once Processor A completes it cache line fill, Processor B will begin to latch data into its cache line-fill buffer.

5. The MRM grants bus ownership to the LRM by asserting PBGNT#.

6. The LRM samples PBGNT# asserted and in response deasserts PBREQ#, becomes the new MRM and pipelines the next cycle.. The current MRM deasserts PBGNT# and becomes the LRM.

7. The new LRM continues the first cache line fill, while the new MRM starts the second cache line fill. The MRM continues to monitor BRDY# to determine when the LRM's cache line fill completes.

8. After the LRM's cache line-fill completes, the MRM begins latching data from the data bus and completes its cache line fill.

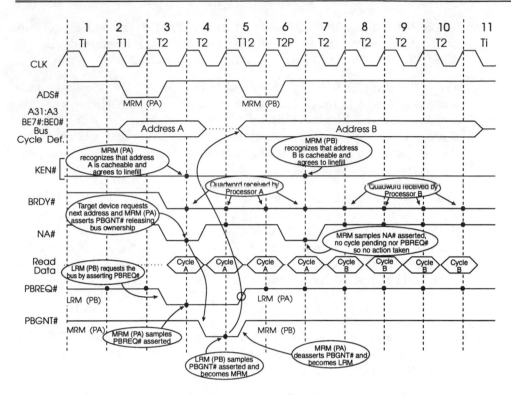

Figure 14-3. Example of Inter-Processor Pipelining

Note that inter-processor pipelining will not occur if the MRM detects that the current transfer is not eligible as a pipelined cycle. In this case, the MRM waits for the transfer to complete before asserting PBGNT#. Table 14-1 summarizes the possible combinations of back-to-back bus cycle types and lists whether or not they can be pipelined.

Table 14-1. Cycles That Can Be Pipelined by Same CPU or Between CPUs

First Cycle Type	Pipelined Cycle Type	Inter-CPU Pipelining?	Intra-CPU Pipelining?
Mem read	Mem read or write	Yes	Yes
Mem read	I/O read or write	No	No
Mem write	Mem read	Yes	Yes
Mem write	Mem write	No	Yes
Mem write	I/O read or write	No	No

First Cycle Type	Pipelined Cycle Type	Inter-CPU Pipelining?	Intra-CPU Pipelining?
Locked Cycle	All Cycle Types	No	No
All Cycle Types	Locked Cycle	No	No
Write Back	All Cycle Types	No	No
All Cycle Types	Write Back	No	No
I/O read/write string	I/O read/write string	Yes	Yes
I/O string	I/O read or write	Yes	No
I/O read or write	I/O string	Yes	No
I/O read or write	I/O read or write	Yes	No

Note that inter-processor pipelining is not permitted when performing back-to-back write operations, but is permitted when performed by a single processor. Conversely, inter-processor pipelining is permitted when performing back-to-back writes but, but not possible when performed by a single processor. Intra-processor pipelining of I/O transactions is supported only when the OUTS and INS strings instructions are executed.

Address Snooping in a Single-Processor System

When a bus master other than the processor is accessing cacheable memory there is the danger that the master is accessing information that the processor has in its internal, L1 cache. External logic must instruct the processor to snoop the memory address about to be accessed by the master, and to report the snoop results back to external logic. The snoop command signals are AHOLD, EADS# and INV. The snoop results are reported by the HIT# and HITM# signals. Note that in a single-processor system, the PHIT# and PHITM# signals are not used. The events that comprise the snoop occur in the following sequence:

1. External logic instructs the processor to disconnect from the address bus by asserting AHOLD.
2. The memory address about to be accessed by the other master is then presented to the processor on the address bus.

3. EADS# is asserted to the processor to tell it the address is valid and should be snooped. In addition, the processor's INV input is deasserted if a read attempt is being snooped, or asserted if a write attempt is being snooped.
4. When EADS# is sampled asserted, the processor latches the address and performs a lookup in its cache.
5. The snoop result is presented on the processor's HIT# and HITM# outputs.
6. If the snoop resulted in a hit on the L1 cache and INV was deasserted, the processor's copy of the line is placed in the shared state.
7. If the snoop resulted in a hit on the L1 cache and INV was asserted, the processor will invalidate its copy of the line.

If the snoop results in a snoop hit on a modified line, HITM# is asserted. This should cause the external logic to issue a back off to the current bus master. The processor then initiates a snoop write-back operation to write the modified line into memory. Upon completion of the write-back, the processor takes one of two actions:

- If the write-back occurred due to a snoop of a read attempt by another master (INV was deasserted during the snoop), the processor transitions the state of its line from modified to shared (because the other master will then read the line, or a portion of it, from memory).
- If the write-back occurred due to a snoop of a write attempt by another master (INV was asserted during the snoop), the processor transitions the state of its line from modified to invalid (because the line just deposited in memory will then be altered when the other master re attempts its write).

Refer to Chapter 4 entitled, "Multiple Processors and the MESI Model" for detailed examples of external snoop transactions.

Address Snooping in a Dual-Processor System

Address snooping a dual-processor environment requires that the two processors maintain coherency between their caches and between their caches and system memory. Specifically, two forms of address snooping are required.

1. **Inter-processor cache snooping.** This is accomplished automatically by the P54C processors, as the LRM always snoops the MRM transactions.

2. **External cache snooping**. This occurs when another bus master reads from or writes to system memory. External logic (typically an L2 cache controller) asserts AHOLD, EADS# and INV, thereby commanding the processors to snoop the external address from a bus master residing on an expansion bus within the system.

Inter-Processor Cache Snooping (The LRM Snoops the MRM)

Whenever the MRM performs a bus transaction, the LRM monitors the bus and snoops the transaction. The following signals act as outputs from the MRM and inputs to the LRM:

- ADS#. Whenever the MRM initiates a bus transaction, it asserts ADS# to indicate the presence of a new address and transaction type on the bus. The LRM monitors its ADS# input to detect a new transaction.
- A[31:5]. The MRM drives the address onto the address bus at the start of each bus transaction. The LRM latches the address when it detects ADS# asserted.
- CACHE#. The MRM asserts CACHE# when it initiates a cache line read or a write back of a modified line to memory. CACHE# is latched by the LRM# whenever ADS# is asserted.
- HIT#. Asserted by a processor whenever it experiences a snoop hit while snooping a memory transaction initiated by a bus master other than the other processor in the pair.
- HITM#. Asserted by a processor whenever it experiences a snoop hit on a modified line while snooping a memory transaction initiated by a bus master other than the other processor in the pair.
- HLDA. Asserted by a processor whenever it detects HOLD asserted by a bus master other than the other processor in the pair.
- M/IO#, D/C#, W/R#, LOCK# and SCYC. These are the bus transaction definition outputs of the MRM. They are inputs to the LRM so that it can determine when the MRM is accessing memory.

When the LRM detects a bus cycle being performed by the MRM it snoops the address to determine if it has a copy of the location being accessed. The specific action taken by the LRM depends on the type of transfer the MRM is performing and the result of the snoop. This following sections detail the various possibilities.

MRM Performs Memory Read

When the MRM initiates a memory read transaction from a cacheable area of memory the transaction is snooped by the LRM. The LRM detects that a bus is being performed by the MRM when it asserts ADS#. The LRM then monitors the bus transaction type (M/IO#, D/C#, W/R#, CACHE#, LOCK# and SCYC). If the LRM detects that a memory read transfer is occurring, it latches the memory address (A31:A5) and submits it to the internal code and data caches for snooping. The following sections define the possible results of these snoops.

Snoop Miss

The target memory line is not cached in the LRM's code nor data cache. The LRM indicates a miss to the MRM by keeping PHIT# and PHITM# deasserted. The MRM completes the memory read and stores the line in the E state.

Snoop Hit Clean

The target memory line is cached in the LRM's code cache in the S state and/or in the data cache in the E or S state. The LRM indicates a hit on a clean line by asserting PHIT# but not PHITM# to the MRM. If the snoop hits a line stored in the data cache in the E state, then the line transitions from E to S as a result of the snoop hit, otherwise no state transition occurs. The MRM completes the memory read and stores the line in the S state.

Snoop Hit Dirty

The target memory line is cached in the LRM's data cache in the M state, when the MRM initiates a memory read transfer. This transaction triggers the following events:

1. The LRM samples ADS# asserted and recognizes that the MRM is starting a bus cycle. Along with ADS#, the LRM samples the bus cycle definition lines and detects that a memory read transfer is being performed. Since a memory transfer is being performed, the LRM also latches the cache line address (A31:A5) and submits it to the code and data caches for a lookup.
2. The LRM indicates the hit on a modified line by asserting PHIT# and PHITM# to the MRM. The LRM also asserts PBREQ# to request ownership of the bus, knowing that it must write the modified line to memory and the modified line is copied to a snoop write-back buffer. Since the cache snoop was triggered by a memory read bus cycle, the cache line is

retained in the data cache, but its MESI state transitions from M to S. The LRM now waits for the MRM to grant it bus ownership.

3. The MRM completes the memory read and discards the data (because the data just read from memory is stale). Then the MRM asserts its PBGNT# output and the MRM and LRM exchange bus ownership.

4. The new MRM performs the snoop write-back of the modified line to memory. The new LRM asserts PBREQ# to request the use of the bus at the conclusion of the snoop write-back to attempt the memory read again.

5. At the conclusion of the write back, the MRM issues PBGNT# to the LRM (the original MRM) and it becomes the MRM again. The memory read is reinitiated and snooped again by the LRM, resulting this time in a snoop hit on a clean line (S state). The memory read completes and the line is stored in the MRM's cache in the S state (because the LRM indicated (by asserting PHIT#) that it also has a copy of the line in the clean state).

MRM Performs a Memory Write

In this scenario, the sequence of events is basically the same as that for a memory read initiated by the MRM. The LRM snoops the memory write initiated by the MRM, resulting in one of the following:

Snoop Miss

The target memory line is cached in neither the LRM's code nor data cache. The LRM indicates a miss to the MRM by deasserting PHIT# and PHITM#. The MRM completes the memory write.

Snoop Hit Clean

The target memory line is cached in the LRM's code cache in the S state and/or in the data cache in the E or S state. The LRM indicates a hit on a clean line by asserting PHIT# but not PHITM# to the MRM. The MRM completes the memory write. The LRM invalidates its copy (or copies) of the line by transitioning the MESI state to I.

Snoop Hit Dirty

The target memory line is cached in the LRM's data cache in the M state, when the MRM initiates a memory write transfer. This transaction triggers the following events:

1. The LRM samples ADS# asserted and recognizes that the MRM is starting a bus cycle. Along with ADS#, the LRM samples the bus cycle definition lines and detects that a memory write transfer is being performed. Since a memory transfer is being performed, the LRM also latches the cache line address (A31:A5) and submits it to the code and data caches for a lookup.

2. The LRM indicates the hit on a modified line by asserting PHIT# and PHITM# to the MRM. The LRM also asserts PBREQ# to request owner-ship of the bus, knowing that it must write the modified line to memory and the modified line is copied to a snoop write-back buffer. Since the cache snoop was triggered by a memory write bus cycle, the cache line is invalidated (its MESI state transitions from M to I). The LRM now waits for the MRM to grant it bus ownership.

3. The MRM completes the memory write and asserts its PBGNT# output, causing MRM and LRM exchange bus ownership.

4. The new MRM performs the snoop write-back of the modified line to memory. The new LRM asserts PBREQ# to request the use of the bus at the conclusion of the snoop write-back to perform the memory read again. This is necessary because the data written by the original MRM will be overwritten when the write-back occurs.

5. At the conclusion of the write back, the MRM issues PBGNT# to the LRM (the original MRM) and it becomes the MRM again. The memory write is reinitiated and snooped again by the LRM, resulting this time in a snoop miss (the line is now stored in the I state). The memory write completes and neither processor has a copy of the target cache line.

External Cache Snooping (Both Processors Must Snoop Transfers by Other Masters)

It has already been established that the two processors, which comprise a processor pair, must each watch memory accesses performed by the other processor in the pair. In addition, bus masters other than the two processors (e.g., a PCI bus master) may access cacheable memory (main DRAM memory). To the system, the processor pair appears to be one processor. When an external bus master performs an access to cacheable memory, the two processors must be forced to snoop the transaction and report back the snoop results. This is accomplished via the AHOLD, EADS#, INV, HIT# and HITM# signals (as described earlier in the section entitled, "Address Snooping in a Single Processor System").

Chapter 14: Dual Processors

Both Processors Snoop Memory Reads by Other Masters

The P54C processors must snoop read transactions performed by other bus masters, if they are operating with write-back caching enabled. When a bus master reads from a system memory location, one of the processors may have a copy of the location in the shared, exclusive or modified state. The following sections describe the possible results of an external snoop triggered by a memory read bus cycle.

MRM Snoop Miss /LRM Snoop Miss

The target memory line is not cached in either processors' code nor data cache. Both processors report a cache snoop miss by keeping their HIT# and HITM# signals deasserted. The bus master completes the memory read normally.

MRM Snoop Hit Clean /LRM Snoop Miss

The target memory line is cached in the MRM's code or data cache. The MRM reports the clean snoop hit (line stored in S state in code cache or in S or E state in data cache) by asserting HIT# and keeping HITM# deasserted. If the snoop hits a data cache line stored in the E state, then the MRM transitions the MESI state from E to S. Otherwise, no state change takes place.

MRM Snoop Miss /LRM Snoop Hit Clean

The target memory line is cached in the LRM's code or data cache. The LRM reports the clean snoop hit (line stored in S state in code cache or in S or E state in data cache) over the private bus by asserting PHIT# and keeping PHITM# deasserted. The MRM in response asserts its HIT# signal to notify external logic the result of the snoop. If the snoop hits a data cache line stored in the E state, then the LRM transitions the MESI state from E to S. Otherwise, no state change takes place.

MRM Snoop Hit Clean /LRM Snoop Hit Clean

The target memory line is cached in both the LRM's and MRM's code or data cache. Both processors report the clean snoop hit (line stored in S state in code cache or in S state in data cache). The MRM asserts the HIT# signal and keeps HITM# deasserted and the LRM asserts PHIT# and keeps PHITM# deasserted. No MESI state change takes place in either processor.

MRM Snoop Hit Modified /LRM Snoop Miss

The MRM has a copy of the target line in its data cache, which is stored in the M state. This causes the following sequence of events:

1. The MRM reports the external snoop hit to a modified line by asserting both the HIT# and HITM# signals. This causes the bus master to be backed-off, if it has not already been backed off by the L2 cache. The MRM also copies the cache line to its external snoop write-back buffer, and transitions the MESI state from M to S.
2. The MRM initiates an external snoop write-back cycle to write the modified line to memory. Note that if the LRM requests bus ownership by asserting PBREQ#, the MRM will wait until the write-back completes before granting the bus to the LRM.
3. When the write-back transfer completes, the MRM deasserts HIT# and HITM#. This releases back-off and the bus master completes the memory read.

MRM Snoop Miss /LRM Snoop Hit Modified

The LRM has a copy of the target line in its data cache, which is stored in the M state. This causes the following sequence of events:

1. The LRM reports the external snoop hit to a modified line by asserting both the PHIT# and PHITM# signals. The MRM in turn asserts the HIT# and HITM# signal. This causes the bus master to be backed-off, if it has not already been backed off by the L2 cache. The LRM also asserts the PBREQ# signal to request bus ownership so it can perform the write-back cycle to memory. The modified line is copied to the external snoop write-back buffer, and the MESI state transitions from M to S.
2. The MRM samples PBREQ# asserted and grants use of the busses to the LRM by asserting PBGNT#. The MRM and LRM swap roles, allowing the original LRM (now the MRM) to write the modified line to memory.
3. The new MRM initiates an external snoop write-back cycle to write the modified line to memory. Note that if the LRM (the original MRM) requests bus ownership again by asserting PBREQ#, the MRM will wait until the write-back completes before granting the bus back to the LRM.
4. When the write-back transfer completes, the MRM (the original LRM) deasserts PHIT# and PHITM# (causing the LRM to deassert HIT# and HITM#). This releases back-off and the bus master completes the memory read.

Both Processors Snoop Memory Writes by Other Masters

It has already been established that the two processors, which comprise a processor pair, must each watch memory accesses performed by the other processor in the pair. In addition, bus masters other than the two processors (e.g., a PCI bus master) may access cacheable memory (main DRAM memory). To the system, the processor pair appears to be one processor. When an external bus master performs an access to cacheable memory, the two processors must be forced to snoop the transaction and report back the snoop results. This is accomplished via the AHOLD, EADS#, INV, HIT# and HITM# signals (as described earlier in the section entitled "Address Snooping in a Single Processor System").

MRM Snoop Miss /LRM Snoop Miss

The target memory line is not cached in either processors' code nor data cache. Both processors report a cache snoop miss by keeping their HIT# and HITM# signals deasserted. The bus master completes the memory write normally.

MRM Snoop Hit Clean /LRM Snoop Miss

The target memory line is cached in the MRM's code or data cache. The MRM reports the clean snoop hit (line stored in S state in code cache or in S or E state in data cache) by asserting HIT# and keeping HITM# deasserted. The MRM transitions the MESI state to I.

MRM Snoop Miss /LRM Snoop Hit Clean

The target memory line is cached in the LRM's code or data cache. The LRM reports the clean snoop hit (line stored in S state in code cache or in S or E state in data cache) over the private bus by asserting PHIT# and keeping PHITM# deasserted. The MRM in response asserts its HIT# signal to notify external logic the result of the snoop. The LRM transitions the MESI state to I.

MRM Snoop Hit Clean /LRM Snoop Hit Clean

The target memory line is cached in both the LRM's and MRM's code or data cache. Both processors report the clean snoop hit (line stored in S state in code cache or in S state in data cache). The MRM asserts the HIT# signal and keeps HITM# deasserted and the LRM asserts PHIT# and keeps PHITM# deasserted. The MESI state changes to I in both processor.

MRM Snoop Hit Modified /LRM Snoop Miss

The MRM has a copy of the target line in its data cache, which is stored in the M state. This causes the following sequence of events:

1. The MRM reports the external snoop hit to a modified line by asserting both the HIT# and HITM# signals. This causes the bus master to be backed-off, if it has not already been backed off by the L2 cache. The MRM also copies the cache line to its external snoop write-back buffer, and transitions the MESI state from M to I.
2. The MRM initiates an external snoop write-back cycle to write the modified line to memory. Note that if the LRM requests bus ownership by asserting PBREQ#, the MRM will wait until the write-back completes before granting the bus to the LRM.
3. When the write-back transfer completes, the MRM deasserts HIT# and HITM#. This releases back-off and the bus master completes the memory write.

MRM Snoop Miss /LRM Snoop Hit Modified

The LRM has a copy of the target line in its data cache, which is stored in the M state. This causes the following sequence of events:

1. The LRM reports the external snoop hit to a modified line by asserting both the PHIT# and PHITM# signals. The MRM in turn asserts the HIT# and HITM# signal. This causes the bus master to be backed-off, if it has not already been backed off by the L2 cache. The LRM also asserts the PBREQ# signal to request bus ownership so it can perform the write-back cycle to memory. The modified line is copied to the external snoop write-back buffer, and the MESI state transitions from M to I.
2. The MRM samples PBREQ# asserted and grants use of the busses to the LRM by asserting PBGNT#. The MRM and LRM swap roles, allowing the original LRM (now the MRM) to write the modified line to memory.
3. The new MRM initiates an external snoop write-back cycle to write the modified line to memory. Note that if the LRM (the original MRM) requests bus ownership again by asserting PBREQ#, the MRM will wait until the write-back completes before granting the bus back to the LRM.
4. When the write-back transfer completes, the MRM (the original LRM) deasserts PHIT# and PHITM# (causing the LRM to deassert HIT# and HITM#). This releases back-off and the bus master completes the memory write.

External Cache Snooping During MRM Transfer

In system that employ a look-through L2 cache design, the processor's local bus and the system bus are isolated by the L2 cache permitting concurrent operations to take place. In these systems, the processor may be performing a bus cycle to its L2 cache while a bus master on an expansion bus is accessing system memory. The following scenarios are included to illustrate how a dual-processor system manages cache coherency when inter-processor snooping and external snooping are combined in worst case scenarios

Scenario One: MRM Performs L2 Read and Bus Master Performs System Memory Read

MRM is performing a cache line fill from its L2 cache when another bus master begins a memory read cycle from system memory. In this example assume that the following conditions exist:

- The MRM is performing a cache line fill from it L2 cache.
- The LRM has a copy of the target line that the MRM is reading from the L2 cache. The target line is stored in LRM's data cache in the M state.
- A bus master starts a read from system memory.
- The MRM has a copy of the target line that the bus master is reading from system memory. The line is stored in the MRM's data cache in the M state.

The sequence of events that take place are:

1. The MRM asserts ADS# at the beginning of the memory read transfer and the LRM detects the cycle type, latches the line portion of the address (A31:A5) and performs the lookup.
2. The LRM's cache lookup results in a snoop hit to a modified line, and the LRM asserts the PHIT# and PHITM# signals to inform the MRM that it is reading stale data. The modified line is copied to a snoop write-back buffer, and the line within the data cache transitions from the M to S state. The LRM also asserts PBREQ# to request bus ownership so that it can perform the snoop write-back.
3. The bus master starts a memory read bus cycle to system memory and the L2 cache snoops the address. The L2 snoop hits a line in the M state. It then backs-off the bus master and performs an inquire cycle (by asserting AHOLD, EADS# and INV=0) to processors' local bus.

4. The MRM floats the address bus when AHOLD is asserted and both the MRM and LRM snoop the bus master's address when EADS# is asserted. The MRM detects a snoop hit to a modified line, asserts both HIT# and HITM# and copies the modified line to the external snoop write-back buffer. The modified line in the data cache transitions from M to S (because INV=0).
5. The MRM completes the cache line fill from memory but discards the data (because it's stale). The MRM retains ownership of the bus and performs the write-back to memory, rather than granting the buses to the LRM as it would normally do. External snoop write-backs take priority over write-backs resulting from inter-processor snoops.
6. When the external snoop write-back cycle completes, the MRM grants the bus to the LRM by asserting PBGNT# and the processors switch bus ownership. The new MRM starts its write-back transfer.
7. The new LRM, still needing to complete the original cache line fill, asserts PBREQ# to request use of the bus again.
8. When the write-back completes, the MRM asserts PBGNT#, thereby granting the bus back to the original MRM.
9. The MRM restarts the cache line fill operation.

Scenario Two: MRM Performs L2 Write and Bus Master Performs System Memory Write

MRM is performing a cache line fill from its L2 cache when another bus master begins a memory write cycle from system memory. In this example assume that the following conditions exist:

- The MRM is performing a memory read that hits the L2 cache.
- The LRM has a copy of the target line that the MRM is reading from the L2 cache. The target line is stored in LRM's data cache in the M state.
- A bus master starts a write to system memory.
- The LRM also has a copy of the target line (different from the line just hit due to the private bus snoop) that the bus master is reading from system memory. The line is stored in the LRM's data cache in the M state.

1. The MRM asserts ADS# at the beginning of the memory read transfer and the LRM detects the memory write, latches the line portion of the address (A31:A5) and performs the lookup.
2. The LRM's cache lookup results in a snoop hit to a modified line, and the LRM asserts the PHIT# and PHITM# signals to inform the MRM that it is reading stale data. The modified line is copied to a snoop write-back

buffer, and the line within the data cache transitions from the M to S state. The LRM also asserts PBREQ# to request bus ownership so that it can perform the snoop write-back.

3. The bus master starts a memory write bus cycle to system memory and the L2 cache snoops the address. The L2 snoop hits a line in the M state. It then backs-off the bus master and performs an inquire cycle (by asserting AHOLD, EADS# and INV=1 and passing the bus master's address) to the processors' local bus.

4. When AHOLD is asserted, the MRM floats the address bus, and when EADS# is asserted, both the MRM and LRM snoop the bus master's address. The LRM detects a snoop hit to a modified line, asserts both PHIT# and PHITM# and copies the modified line to the external snoop write-back buffer. The modified line in the data cache transitions from M to I (because INV=1). Now the LRM has two write-back cycles pending.

5. The MRM completes the cache line fill from memory but discards the data (because it's stale), and grants the buses to the LRM. The MRM and the LRM now change roles.

6. The new MRM starts the external snoop write-back cycle first (Because external snoop write-backs take priority over write-backs resulting from inter-processor snoops). The new LRM, still needing to perform the original cache line fill, asserts PBREQ# to request bus ownership.

7. When the external snoop write-back cycle completes, the MRM performs the inter-processor snoop write-back cycle.

8. When the write-back completes, the MRM grants the bus to the LRM (the original MRM) by asserting PBGNT# and the processors switch bus ownership back to the original MRM.

9. The MRM restarts the cache line fill operation.

Chapter 15

The Previous Chapter

The previous chapter discussed the P54C dual-processing capabilities.

This Chapter

This chapter covers the local Advanced Programmable Interrupt Controller (local APIC) that is integrated into the P54C processors.

The Next Chapter

The next chapter details the system management mode capabilities incorporated into the P54C processors, also known as the Intel SL enhanced features.

Introduction

The P54C processors incorporate a local APIC module designed to process interrupts in a multiprocessing environment. An external APIC I/O module monitors system interrupts and directs them to the appropriate target processor's local APIC module.

Note that the APIC system implemented in the P54C processors is based on the Intel 82489DX APIC system. There are numerous differences between the 82489DX implementation and the P54C version. Refer to the Volume Three of the *Pentium Family User's Manual* for a discussion of the differences.

The P54C processor can either operate with the local APIC module disabled, allowing interrupts to be processed using a standard Intel 8259 interrupt controller for compatible interrupt handling, or in the APIC mode. The local APIC is enabled when the processor samples the APICEN pin asserted (APICEN=1) on the falling edge of reset.

Interrupt Handling with Multiple Processors

The earliest PCs implementing multiple processors relied on the Intel 8259 Programmable Interrupt Controller (PIC). The 8259 was designed for single processor implementations and has no inherent ability to direct interrupts to different processors. The Intel APIC subsystem provides a more flexible and easy to implement solution for handling interrupts in multiprocessing (MP) environments when compared to the 8259 mechanism. To appreciate the capabilities of the APIC implementation the following section highlights how MP solutions based on the 8259 were typically handled, followed by a detailed description of the APIC solution.

The 8259 Solution

Since the 8259 has no mechanism to direct interrupts to different processors, MP implementations based on asymmetrical multiprocessing are easier to implement with the 8259 than symmetrical implementations. Systems built around asymmetric processors are designed to split the overall program workload among multiple processors based on specific functions. The primary CPU typically handles the operating system software, applications programs and interrupt servicing, while I/O tasks such as LAN and file management are handled by one or more specialized satellite processors. In these systems, only the primary processor can handle system interrupts.

The processors found in symmetric multi-processing (SMP) systems are functionally identical. Any processor is capable of executing any task, including servicing interrupts. Operating systems designed to operate with symmetric processors divide the workload into tasks and assign the next task to the next available processor. Symmetrical multiprocessing (SMP) systems based on the 8259 must incorporate additional logic that has the ability to direct an interrupt to any of the processors in the system. This redirection logic routes interrupts to a particular processor based on algorithms specified by the SMP Operating System(s) that the system must be designed to support.

The symmetrical operating system uses two methods to complement the hardware: load balancing and a multithreaded kernel. Load balancing allows the operating system to divide tasks evenly among the processors. The multithreaded kernel distributes the operating system functions and interrupt handlers among the processors so each of them can service interrupt requests and operating system function calls.

The APIC Solution

The Advanced Programmable Interrupt Controller, or APIC, provides interrupt support for both symmetrical and asymmetrical multiple processing environments via its numerous operational modes. The APIC system can also be programmed for several different destination and delivery modes. For example, it can direct an interrupt to a specified processor or to all processors whose local APIC modules then arbitrate to see which one is performing the lowest priority task currently running within the system. The processor running the lowest priority task at any given time is the one that handles the interrupt request.

The APIC Concept

Refer to figure 15-1. The APIC system typically consists of an APIC I/O module that receives system interrupt requests from I/O devices and routes them to the local APIC modules that are integrated into each P54C processor. A three wire bus connects all of these devices, or agents, together. The APIC bus carries messages between the APIC I/O module and the local APIC modules embedded within the processors.

Each processor also has two local interrupt inputs (LINT0 and LINT1) for devices residing on the processor's local bus. These local interrupt pins are shared with the INTR and NMI inputs. Only when a local APIC module is programmed for "bypass" mode will the processor use the INTR and NMI pin definition. In this case, the 8259 should be connected to the INTR pin and the NMI pin connected to the system's NMI logic. All other local APIC modes treat these input pins as local interrupts, rather than INTR and NMI.

The APIC subsystem can also transfer Non-Maskable Interrupts (NMI) and a variety of interrupt messages (that can be passed between processors). These messages include processor startup (STARTUP), initialization (INIT), and system management interrupt (SMI). Each message is transferred via an APIC transfer called an inter-processor interrupt. An APIC bus transfer protocol defines the type of interrupt or message being sent, along with information that identifies which processor or processors should accept and handle the interrupt request or act upon the message.

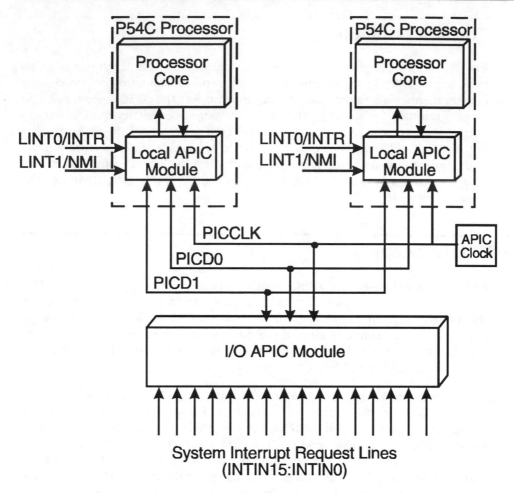

Figure 15-1. The APIC System

In summary, the APIC subsystem handles four basic categories of interrupts:

- System Interrupts — The I/O APIC module directs system interrupt requests from I/O devices to a target processor's local APIC module for handling.
- NMI — The I/O APIC module also directs Non-Maskable Interrupts to a target processor's local APIC module.
- Local Interrupts (LINT0, LINT1, Timer and Error) — Devices connected to the local interrupt lines (LINT) can generate interrupts. Additionally, the local APIC includes an integrated timer interrupt and a local error interrupt.

- Inter-Processor Interrupts (IPI) — Messages in the form of interrupts can be broadcast to other processors under software control by writing to an internal local APIC register. IPI interrupts are also generated during processor startup and when a processor's INIT or SMI signals are asserted.

The following sections detail each category of interrupt handled by the APIC subsystem.

System Interrupts Requests

This sections focuses on interrupts generated by I/O devices within the system. In handling I/O interrupt requests, the I/O APIC periodically takes a "snapshot" of the interrupt inputs (consisting of INTIN15:INTIN0). The interrupts that are pending are sent over the APIC bus to target processors, one at a time. The lowest number interrupt input pin (INTIN0) that has been sensed is sent over the APIC bus first, followed by the next lowest input in sequential order. This order is followed regardless of the programmed priority level of the interrupt.

Note that the interrupt input pins on the I/O module do not have sequentially assigned interrupt vectors as is the case with the 8259. Each interrupt input can be assigned to any interrupt table vector or slot number. This assignment occurs via a redirection register associated with each interrupt input to the APIC I/O module as illustrated in figure 15-2. Each of the sixteen redirection registers are loaded with a vector number, identifying the slot in the interrupt table containing the entry point of the interrupt service routine for each interrupt. The interrupt table located in main system memory consists of 256 entries numbered from 00h to FFh (0 to 255d). Entries 00h to 0F (0-15d) are reserved for internal processor interrupts, allowing 240 entries from 10h to FFh (16 to 255d) to be implemented by the APIC subsystem.

Additional bits within the redirection registers specify other attributes associated with the interrupt including: destination mode, delivery mode, and trigger (edge or level) mode. Each register also contains a destination field that identifies the target processor(s) which should handle this interrupt. In physical destination mode, the destination field contains the APIC ID that identifies the target processor. In logical destination mode, the destination field contains a logical destination that can identify a group of processors that are being targeted. Each mode is discussed in the following sections.

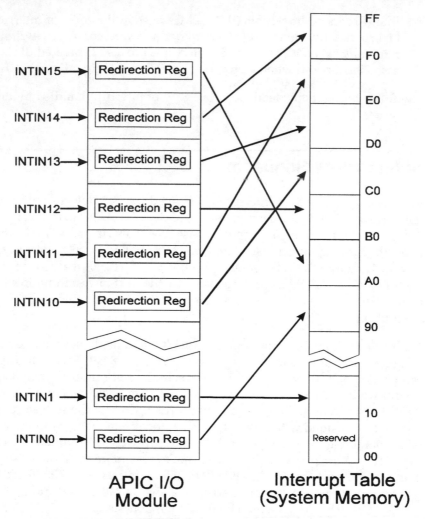

Figure 15-2. The I/O APIC Redirection Registers Contain the Target Interrupt Table Entry Assigned to Each Interrupt.

Determining the Target Processor

The APIC subsystem defines two transfer parameters, called the destination and delivery modes, that characterize every APIC transfer. During initialization, system software must program the I/O APIC module's redirection registers to specify the destination and delivery modes to be used for each in-

Chapter 15: The APIC

terrupt input. The destination and delivery modes are introduced in table 15-1.

Table 15-1. APIC Destination and Delivery Modes Used for System Interrupts

Modes Used for System Interrupt Processing	
Destination Modes	Description
Physical	Target processors are selected based on a unique APIC ID. In this way, each interrupt can be directed to a given processor based on its unique APIC ID value.
Logical	Target processors are selected based on a logical APIC ID value programmed into each APIC. Since a logical ID is programmed, and therefore not necessarily unique to a given processor, they can identify a group of processors to be targeted.
Delivery Modes	Description
Static	The interrupt request is accepted by the processor specified in the destination.
Lowest Priority	The interrupt request is delivered to all processors specified in the destination and the local APICs resolve which processor will accept and handle the interrupt based on the lowest execution priority of the target processors. If two or more target processors have the same lowest execution priority, then the APIC ID is used to break the tie.
External Interrupt	The interrupt request is delivered from an 8259 interrupt controller via the I/O APIC. The target Local APIC accepts the interrupt and directs the processor to perform two back-to-back interrupt acknowledge bus cycles to get the interrupt vector from the 8259 subsystem.

When the APIC I/O module sends an interrupt request over the APIC bus, all local APIC modules evaluate the information transferred over the APIC bus. Each local APIC checks the destination ID along with the destination and delivery modes to determine if they are being targeted to handle the interrupt. The local APIC module that being targeted recognizes accepts and services the interrupt request. Refer to the section entitled "Summary of Interrupt Distribution and Handling" for a detailed discussion of the various interrupt distribution methods.

The I/O APIC Interrupt Transfer

The APIC's interrupt transfer mechanism consists of a serial stream of data sent over the three-wire APIC bus. Each of the three wires has the following function:

PICCLK (Programmable Interrupt Controller Clock) This clock synchronizes all information sent over the bus. During each clock cycle two bits of data can be sent over the APIC bus. An external clock generator produces the APIC bus clock (PICCLK) which has a maximum frequency of 16.67 MHz.

PICD0 (Programmable Interrupt Controller Data Zero) — This signal carries serial data over the APIC bus and is the least significant bit during each clock cycle.

PICD1 (Programmable Interrupt Controller Data One) — This signal carries serial data over the APIC bus and is the most significant bit during each clock cycle.

An APIC bus transfer consists of as few as 14 clock cycles or as many as 39 clock cycles depending on the type of transfer that is taking place. Each of these types is detailed later in this chapter. As an example, consider the simple case of the I/O APIC module sending an interrupt request to a target processor specified by the local APIC ID (called physical destination mode). Assume that the interrupt request is accepted and processed solely by the target processor specified in the destination (referred to as static delivery mode).

Refer to figure 15-3. Notice that this serial transfer requires 21 clock cycles to complete. Each bit shown in figure 15-3 is defined in table 15-2 that follows. Some of these bits pertain to transfer modes described later in this chapter and are not detailed here. The values shown for PICD0 and PICD1 are logical values; however, the electrical values actually placed on the APIC bus are the inverse state of the logical values. That is, the level driven onto the APIC bus state for a logical zero is V_H (Vcc) and V_L (Vss) represents a logical one.

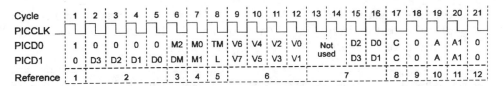

Figure 15-3. APIC Bus Communications
(Physical Destination Mode and Static Delivery Mode)

Table 15-2. Bit Definitions for APIC Bus Communications

Reference	Description
1	Cycle 1 defines this interrupt transfer as a "normal" type. The only other type defined is for EOI (End of Interrupt).
2	Cycles 2 - 5 are used to arbitrate use of the APIC bus in case more than one agent starts a transfer over the APIC bus at the same time. All agents that have started a transfer drive their arbitration ID value one bit at a time starting with the most significant bit, Data 3. Data 3 (D3) contains the highest priority bit of the arbitration ID and Data 0 (D0) contains the lowest priority bit. See the section in this chapter entitled "APIC Bus Arbitration" for details.
3	Cycle 6 defines the Destination Mode (DM). DM=0 (physical) DM=1 (logical). Cycle 6 also contains the most significant bit of the Delivery Mode value (M2).
4	Cycle 7 defines the least two significant bits of the delivery mode (M1-M0). The Delivery mode bits M2:M0 (Mx) are defined as follows: Mx 000b=fixed; Mx 001b=lowest priority; Mx 111b–External 8259 interrupt.
5	Cycle 8 defines the level (used only during IPI INIT transfer) and trigger mode. The trigger mode bit defines the interrupt input type to the I/O APIC. TM=0 (edge-sensitive) TM=1 (level-sensitive).
6	Cycles 9-12 define the 8-bit interrupt vector (V7:V0) being sent to the processor.
7	Cycles 13-16 define the destination ID. Logical mode destination uses 8 destination bits D7:D0; whereas, physical destination uses only bits D3:D0.
8	Cycle 17 is used to transfer a checksum value for cycles 6-16.
9	Cycle 18 always contains zeros. This time period is used by receiving agents to perform the checksum.
10	Cycle 19 is used to report status "A", providing checksum result. Status A = 00b indicates checksum OK.
11	Cycle 20 is used to report status "A1", providing the result of the transmission (i.e. success, failure, retry).
12	Cycle 21 contains data values of 00b for fixed delivery mode and signifies the end of the transfer.

Figure 15-4 illustrates an interrupt being sent from the APIC I/O module to a single processor using the physical destination mode (DM=0) and static delivery mode (Mx=000b). In this mode, all local APIC modules compare the value of the destination ID bits D3:D0 (cycles 15 and 16) to their unique APIC ID. Only the local APIC module whose ID matches the destination code will accept the interrupt request. Note that the destination and delivery mode values along with the destination ID are supplied by the I/O module's redirection register corresponding to the interrupt request pin asserted.

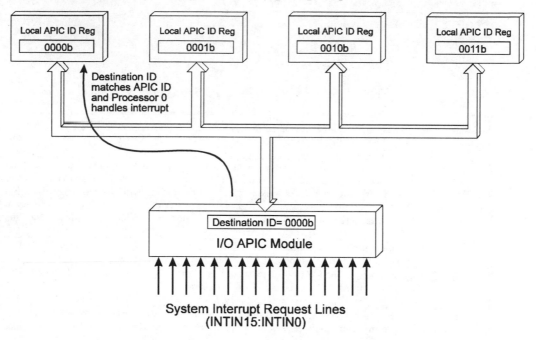

Figure 15-4. Interrupts Delivered Via Physical Destination Mode

The vector number of the interrupt that requires servicing (from the respective redirection register in the APIC I/O module) is passed to the local APIC via the eight vector bits (V7:V0) during cycles nine through twelve. The trigger mode bit in cycle eight specifies whether the interrupt input is defined as edge or level triggered.

The Target Processor Accepts the Interrupt Request

Once the target local APIC module recognizes that it is the target of the interrupt request, it must determine if it should accept, and therefore service, the interrupt request. Whether a target processor should accept the interrupt depends on the delivery mode defined. In this example, the delivery mode is static (Mx=000b), directing the target processor to accept the interrupt.

Chapter 15: The APIC

An interrupt is accepted by setting the respective bit in the appropriate interrupt acceptance registers — IRR, ISR and TMR. Each of these 256-bit registers contains a bit map of all slots in the interrupt table as illustrated in figure 15-5.

IRR (Interrupt Request Register) - When a new interrupt request is accepted from the I/O module, the IRR bit corresponding to the interrupt vector is set. The bits set in this register contains all interrupt requests that have been accepted by this processor and that are currently pending execution.

ISR (In-Service Register) - This register contains a bit map of all interrupt requests that have been delivered to the processor core but have not yet been serviced. The ISR bit for the highest priority interrupt pending in the IRR is set when the processor runs an internal interrupt acknowledge cycle (INTA). Note that no bus cycle is run by the processor since the local APIC registers are within the CPU. ISR bits are cleared when the local APIC receives an EOI command from the processor. EOI clears the highest priority interrupt in the ISR (vector 16 is highest; 255 is lowest).

TMR (Trigger Mode Register) - When the interrupt is accepted, the TMR bit corresponding to the interrupt vector number is reset for edge triggered interrupts and set for level triggered interrupts. The trigger mode bit dictates the action taken by the local APIC upon receipt of the EOI command from the processor core. See the sections entitled, "End of Interrupt (EOI)" and "Trigger Modes" later in this chapter for details.

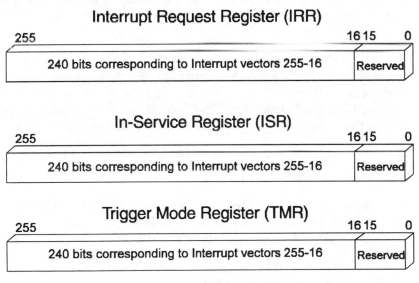

Figure 15-5. IRR, ISR and TMR Registers within the Local APIC

Hardware Interrupt Execution Priority

The APIC subsystem permits the operating system programmer to determine which hardware interrupts can be serviced based on the execution priority of the task currently running. This allows the processor core to accept high priority interrupts, while deferring lower priority interrupts until the current task priority is lowered by the programmer. This mechanism is based on interrupt and execution priority discussed below.

Hardware Interrupt Priority

Interrupt priority within the APIC system is related to the interrupt vector assigned to a device's interrupt pin. An aligned group of 16 interrupt vectors has the same interrupt priority. In other words, the priority of an interrupt is:

priority = interrupt vector/16

Interrupt vectors 00h-0Fh (0-15d) are reserved by the processor and cannot be assigned to the I/O APIC interrupt pins. This leaves the remaining 240 vectors, 10h-FFh (16-255d), for the APIC system. As a result, hardware interrupt priorities range from one to fifteen, with one the lowest and fifteen the highest priority. See figure 15-6. Note that two hardware interrupts assigned to different vectors but belonging to the same block of 16 vectors share the same interrupt priority.

The I/O APIC contains a two-deep FIFO buffer for each priority level. This permits software to assign two interrupt pins to the same interrupt priority. For example, if two interrupt pins are programmed to use vectors 60h and 63h respectively, both would have an interrupt priority of six. The first interrupt request to be asserted would be serviced first, followed by the second.

Execution Priority

Two registers named the task priority register (TPR) and processor priority register (PPR) are used by the APIC to establish the priority threshold that determines which interrupt requests will be sent to the processor for servicing.

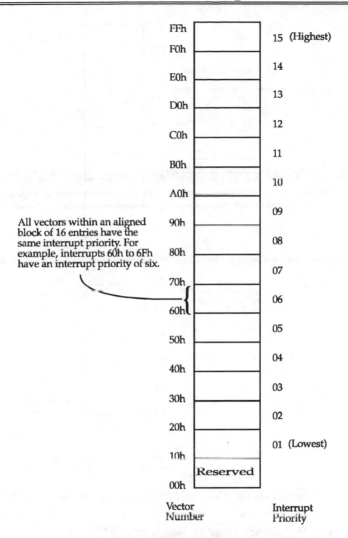

All vectors within an aligned block of 16 entries have the same interrupt priority. For example, interrupts 60h to 6Fh have an interrupt priority of six.

Figure 15-6. Hardware Interrupt Priorities

The Task Priority Register (TPR)

Current execution priority is based on the value programmed into the Task Priority Register (TPR). This register is updated by the operating system to indicate the priority of the task currently executing, relative to the 16 interrupt priorities. The TPR contains an interrupt vector number that is used as a priority threshold for determining which interrupts the operating system will allow to interrupt the processor core.

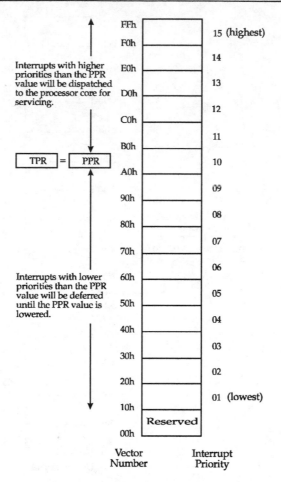

Figure 15-7. The Value of PPR When No Interrupts are being Serviced

The Processor Priority Register (PPR)

The Processor Priority Register (PPR) determines whether a pending interrupt can be sent to the processor core. Its value reflects the execution priority of the code currently running. If a pending interrupt has an interrupt priority that is higher than the PPR value, then the interrupt is dispatched to the processor core for servicing. If its interrupt priority is lower than the PPR value, interrupt servicing is deferred until the current execution priority (reflected by PPR) is lowered to a value less than the pending interrupt's priority.

The PPR contains the same value as the TPR when there are no interrupts currently being serviced. Refer to figure 15-7. In this case, the task currently being executed by the processor is represented by the value of the TPR register. Only pending interrupts having a priority higher than that represented by the PPR value are passed to the processor core for servicing. All other interrupt requests remain masked until the execution priority is lowered below the pending interrupt's priority. When the TPR value is 15 the local APIC will not dispatch any pending interrupts to the processor.

Refer to figure 15-8. Assume that an interrupt request having a priority of twelve has been accepted by the local APIC via the APIC bus. Since interrupt priority twelve is higher than the PPR value (same as TPR), the interrupt will be dispatched to the processor core for servicing. The interrupt's execution priority becomes the new current execution priority for the processor, and the APIC updates the PPR register to reflect the new execution priority.

The Local APIC Module Interrupts the Processor Core

The local APIC module, having accepted the interrupt request, then interrupts the processor core (assuming the requesting interrupt's priority is higher than the processor's current execution priority). On the next instruction boundary, the processor recognizes the interrupt and performs an internal interrupt acknowledge cycle to its local APIC. The APIC responds by sending the vector number of the highest priority interrupt that is currently pending in the IRR to the CPU core. The local APIC then clears the highest priority IRR bit and sets the corresponding bit in the ISR, thereby indicating the interrupt being serviced currently.

The Processor Executes the Interrupt Service Routine

Next, the processor uses the vector number as an index into the interrupt table that resides in memory. The processor performs a memory read from the specified location in the interrupt table and obtains the starting address of the interrupt service routine. The processor then pushes current program status (EFLAGS, CS and EIP registers) to the stack and clears the interrupt enable bit in the EFLAGS register. The processor then fetches and executes the interrupt service routine.

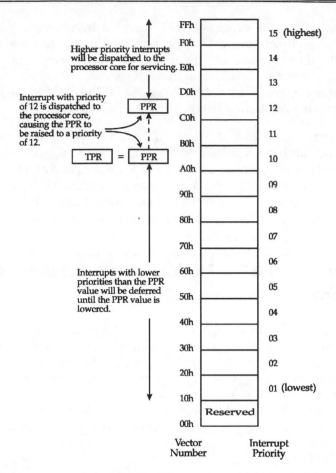

Figure 15-8. Value of PPR When Interrupt is being Serviced

End of Interrupt (EOI)

After servicing the interrupt request, but before the end of the interrupt service routine, the programmer must write an EOI (End-of-Interrupt) command to the local APIC. This forces the local APIC to turn off the highest priority bit in the In-Service Register so that the interrupt won't be double-serviced. Until the ISR bit is reset by the EOI command, the local APIC inhibits recognition of requests from lower priority devices and other requests from devices with the same priority. Only requests from devices with higher priority will be sent to the processor.

The service routine performs an EOI command by writing all zero's to the local APIC's EOI register. This causes the local APIC to clear the highest priority bit in the ISR, indicating completion of the service routine for that interrupt. The local APIC is then free to issue the next highest priority interrupt that is currently pending in the IRR to the processor core for servicing (if permitted by current execution priority). If no additional interrupts are pending, the local APIC takes no further action.

The APIC's EOI register is memory mapped at address location FEE000B0h. A write to the EOI register completes internally without any bus cycle being run externally on the P54C processor's buses.

When the EOI command is issued, the local APIC checks the trigger mode bit in the TMR for the interrupt that is being cleared. The trigger mode of the interrupt determines if additional action must be taken by the local APIC. Edge trigger mode requires no additional action, whereas, level trigger mode requires that an EOI message be broadcast to the I/O APIC module. See the next section for a discussion of the differences between edge and level triggering and the handling of EOI.

Trigger Modes

The I/O APIC's interrupt request inputs can be programmed to recognize either a positive-going edge or a static high level as a valid interrupt request. The programmer may select either of these recognition modes for each interrupt input.

Edge-Triggered Interrupts and EOI

Edge-triggered interrupt inputs support only a single device connected to a given Interrupt input to the I/O APIC. When an interrupt is triggered, the I/O APIC sends an interrupt request over the APIC bus. After the interrupt request is delivered, the I/O APIC automatically clears its interrupt pending bit and is ready to recognize another edge triggered from the same device.

During the interrupt service routine, the programmer clears the interrupt pending bit within the interrupting device. This notifies the device that the current interrupt is being serviced and that another interrupt request can be issued. At the end of the interrupt service routine the programmer must also perform an EOI command by writing all zero's to the local APIC's EOI register. This causes the highest-priority interrupt request in the local ISR register (the one just serviced) to be cleared, preventing it from being serviced again.

Another positive edge trigger at the I/O APIC input is recognized as another interrupt request, and the interrupt servicing sequence repeats.

Level-Triggered Interrupts and EOI Message Cycle

Level-triggered interrupts permit more than one device to share a single interrupt line. When an EOI command is performed by a level triggered interrupt service routine, the local APIC must broadcast an EOI message to the I/O APIC. The EOI message contains the vector of the level-triggered interrupt just serviced. If the interrupt input corresponding to the EOI vector is still asserted, the I/O APIC recognizes that another device that shares the same interrupt line is requesting service and transfers another interrupt request over the APIC bus. The following discussion explains how the sharing mechanism works and why the EOI message must be sent to the I/O APIC when level triggered interrupts are used.

1. **Interrupt table initialization**. When a device is attached to an interrupt input, the device driver or BIOS initialization code associated with the device must read and save the service routine pointer currently residing in the interrupt table entry. It then replaces the current table entry value with the pointer to its devices service routine. If other devices share the same interrupt line that means that they also share the same vector location in the interrupt table. A second device then would also place the starting address of its interrupt service routine into the same vector location, but not until first saving the existing value. In this manner, a linked list of interrupt service routines is maintained as each device hooks the interrupt vector.

2. **Multi-device interrupt triggering**. Existing expansion bus architectures such as Micro Channel, EISA and PCI support interrupt sharing. These architecture all employ low-level interrupt triggering. As a result, hardware devices sharing the same interrupt request line must implement open drain (open collector) drivers. Several devices then can assert a low-level trigger on the same interrupt request line. Since the I/O APIC uses high-level interrupt triggering, the low-level triggers must be inverted before being sent to the I/O APIC input. For this discussion, assume that two devices sharing the same interrupt input both assert interrupt requests at roughly the same time.

3. **I/O APIC transfers the interrupt request and the processor acknowledges**. When the I/O APIC recognized a level-interrupt request, it generates an APIC bus transfer to pass the interrupt to the local APIC that is targeted. Ultimately, the level-interrupt request is dispatched to the processor core and the processor sends an acknowledge back to the local APIC to request the interrupt's vector.

4. **The interrupt request is serviced**. To service the interrupt, the processor accesses the specified vector location within the interrupt table to obtain the starting address of the interrupt service routine. The first service routine executed is the one whose entry point was installed last into the vector location (step 1). Interrupt service routines that are designed to be shared, must check to see if their device has an interrupt pending. If so, they recognize the interrupt request belongs to them and execute their service routine. However, if no interrupt request is pending for their device, then they jump to the location specified by the vector value that was previously saved during initialization. In this way, the device that actually initiated the interrupt request is ultimately located through the interrupt service routine chain. Once the interrupting device is located, the service routine clears the device's interrupt pending bit, allowing the level trigger to be removed from the I/O APIC.

5. In this case, the device just serviced ceases to assert its request to the I/O APIC; however, the I/O APIC continues to detect a valid level trigger from the other device whose interrupt request remains pending.

6. **The EOI command is performed**. The I/O APIC cannot detect whether the interrupt input remains asserted because the device that triggered the initial request has yet to be serviced or because another device is asserting an interrupt request. Consequently, when the EOI command is received by the local APIC it must broadcast an EOI message to the I/O APIC. This notifies the I/O APIC that an interrupt for a device using the specified has just been serviced. Since in this example, the input pin corresponding to the vector remains asserted, the I/O APIC transfers another level-interrupt request to the local APIC. Steps 3 through 5 are repeated until the I/O APIC recognizes that all interrupt requests at this input have been serviced.

The EOI Transfer

The EOI message cycle consists of 14 APIC clock cycles (illustrated in figure 15-9). Each bit within the transfer is detailed in table 15-3. Note that the EOI message cycle is recognized only by the I/O APIC, and is the only transfer it recognizes. As a result, no destination or delivery mode information, nor destination ID is required during an EOI transfer. Instead, EOI transfers are defined by the type field during cycle one of the transfer.

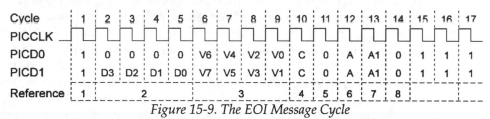

Figure 15-9. The EOI Message Cycle

Table 15-3. Definition of the Bits Transferred During an EOI Message

Reference	Description
1	Cycle 1 defines this interrupt transfer as an "EOI" type. EOI is the highest priority message sent over the APIC bus. All other agents that may be attempting an APIC transfer at the same time, cease to drive the APIC bus when they detect that an EOI transfer has started.
2	Cycles 2 - 5 are used arbitrate use of the APIC bus in case more than one agent starts an EOI transfer over the APIC bus at the same time. All agents that have started a transfer drive their respective arbitration ID value one bit at a time starting with the most significant bit, Data 3. Data 3 (D3) contains the highest priority bit of the arbitration ID and Data 0 (D0) contains the lowest priority bit. See the section in this chapter entitled "APIC Bus Arbitration" for details.
3	Cycles 6 - 9 define the 8-bit interrupt vector (V7:V0) being sent to the processor.
4	Cycle 10 is used to transfer a checksum value for cycles 6-9.
5	Cycle 11 always zeros. This time period is used by receiving agent to perform checksum.
6	Cycle 12 is used to report status "A", which provides the result of the checksum test. Status = 00b (Checksum OK).
7	Cycle 13 is used to report status "A1", which provides the final result of the EOI transmission. (success, failure, retry, etc.)
8	Cycle 14 contains 00b to signify the end of the transfer.

Local Interrupts (LINTs, Timer, & Error)

Each local APIC handles four local interrupts:

- Local Timer Interrupt internal to local APIC)
- Local Interrupt Pin 0 (LINT0)
- Local Interrupt Pin 1 (LINT1)
- Local Error Interrupt (internal to local APIC)

Since these interrupt requests are generated locally, the programmer must be able to specify which interrupt vector each of these local interrupts is assigned to. For example, external interrupt vectors are programmed in the redirection registers of the I/O APIC, and an equivalent mechanism must be defined for the local interrupts. The local APIC includes a four entry vector table used to define the interrupt vector assigned to each of the local interrupts, along with the delivery mode, status information and other interrupt related data. Figure 15-10 illustrates the local interrupt vector table entries. Each local interrupt has its own entry which is memory mapped at the location shown in figure 15-10.

Local Vector Table

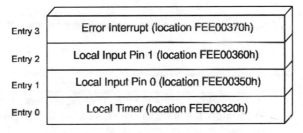

Figure 15-10. Local Vector Table Entry Assignments and Memory Address Locations

Local Timer Interrupt

The local APIC timer is a 32-bit programmable timer designed for use by the processor. The timer can be programmed to generate two types of interrupts:

- periodic interrupts -- these interrupts occur at regular intervals based on a programmed processor clock (PCLK) divisor.

- one-shot interrupt — this interrupt is generated when the programmed timer count reaches zero. No more interrupts are generated until the timer is reprogrammed.

The Timer Local Vector Table Entry

The local vector table entry for the timer permits the timer interrupt to be directed to any entry within the interrupt table from interrupt 0d to 255d. Definition of the local vector entry for the timer is illustrated in figure 15-11. Each of the fields is described in table 15-4.

Local Timer Vector Table Entry

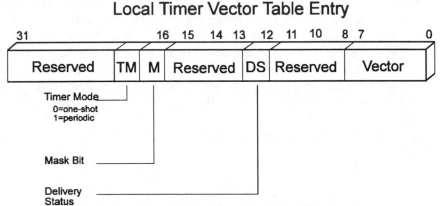

Figure 15-11. Local Timer Vector Table Entry Definition

Table 15-4. Definition of Fields within the Local Timer's Vector Table Entry

Field Name	Description
Vector	This field contains the interrupt table entry in system memory that contains the starting address of the timer's interrupt service routine.
Delivery Status	This read-only field provides the current status of the interrupt's delivery. A state of zero (idle) indicates that there has been no activity on this interrupt. A one (pending) indicates that the interrupt is currently being sent to the APIC. After successful delivery, the respective bit in the APIC's IRR will be set indicating that the interrupt has been accepted, and the delivery status bit returns to the idle state.
Mask Bit	This bit enables (zero) or disables (one) delivery of the interrupt to the APIC's IRR.
Timer Mode	This bit defines the timer for one-shot (0) or periodic (1) interrupt delivery.

Programming the Local Timer

The registers used to program the timer interrupt function include the:

- Initial Count Register (ICR) — This register is loaded with the start count value. The local timer automatically copies the ICR value to the current count register (CCR) to start the timer. The ICR is mapped within the processor's memory address space at location FEE00380h.
- Current Count Register (CCR) — The timer loads this register with the contents of the ICR and begins decrementing the count at the time base rate. When the count reaches zero a timer interrupt is generated. The ICR value is automatically reloaded into the CCR when periodic timer mode is selected. The CCR is mapped within the processor's memory address space at location FEE00390h.
- Divide Configuration Register (DCR) — Three bits (0,1 and 3) within this register define the PCLK divisor yields the time base used to decrement the timer. See figure 15-12. The DCR is mapped within the processor's memory address space at location FEE003E0h.

Divide Configuration Register

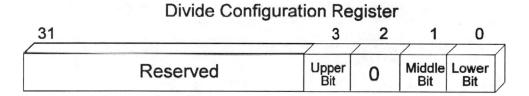

Value	Divisor
000	Divide by 2
001	Divide by 4
010	Divide by 8
011	Divide by 16
100	Divide by 32
101	Divide by 64
110	Divide by 128
111	Divide by 1

Figure 15-12. Timer Divide Register Definition

Local Interrupts (LINT0 and LINT1)

Devices can be connected to the processor's local interrupt pins, thereby generating interrupt requests directly to the local APIC. When an interrupt occurs, the local APIC accesses the local vector table entry that corresponds to the local interrupt pin asserted. The field assignments for entries one and two is illustrated in figure 15-13. Table 15-5 defines the fields within the LINT vector table entries.

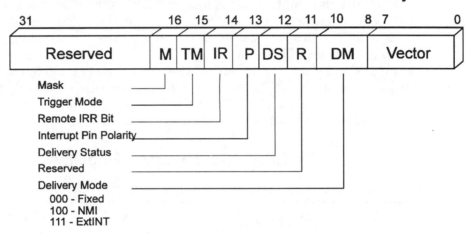

Figure 15-13. LINT0 and LINT1 Local Vector Table Entry Definition

Table 15-5. Definition of Fields within the Local Timer's Vector Table Entry

Field Name	Description
Vector	This field contains the interrupt table entry in system memory that contains the starting address of the timer's interrupt service routine.
Delivery Mode	Three delivery modes can be specified for local interrupts, allowing a local interrupt to be assigned as either: • an 8259 compatible interrupt input (ExtINT) — this means that the input connects to the interrupt request output of the master 8259 interrupt controller. Any interrupt request asserted causes the APIC and processor to handle the request based on the 8259 interrupt handling protocol.

Field Name	Description
	• an APIC compatible interrupt input (fixed) — this means that the interrupt is delivered directly to the APIC when asserted and no lowest priority mechanism is supported. • an NMI interrupt input (NMI) — this means that the interrupt pin connects to the system's NMI logic.
Delivery Status	This read-only field provides the current status of the interrupt's delivery. A state of zero (idle) indicates that there has been no activity on this interrupt. A one (pending) indicates that the interrupt is currently being sent to the APIC. After successful delivery, the respective bit in the APIC's IRR will be set indicating that the interrupt has been accepted, and the delivery status bit returns to the idle state.
Interrupt Pin Polarity	Indicates the polarity of the interrupt pin. (0 = active high and 1 = active low)
Remote IRR bit	If a level interrupt input is defined, this bit is set when the local interrupt request is accepted by the local APIC. When set, no additional interrupt requests are sent to the local APIC, even though an active low trigger is asserted, until an EOI command is received from the processor. When the EOI command is received, the APIC clears the remote IRR bit, allowing another interrupt request to be sent to the APIC.
Trigger Mode Bit	This bit indicates whether is interrupt input is defined as edge sensitive (0) or level sensitive (1).
Mask Bit	This bit enables (0) or disables (1) delivery of the interrupt to the APIC.

Local Error Interrupts

The local error status register records errors detected by the local APIC. The local APIC generates a local error interrupt when any bit within the error status register is set. The register is reset when read by the CPU or by another processor (via an IPI remote read message). Figure 15-14 illustrates the error register bit assignments and table 15-6 defines each bit.

Error Status Register

Figure 15-14. Error Status Register Definition

Table 15-6. Definition of Bits within the Error Status Register

Status Bit	Description
Send CS Error	The local APIC sets this bit when it detects a checksum error when sending a message.
Receive CS Error	This bit is set when the APIC detects a checksum while receiving a message.
Send Accept Error	This bit is set when the local APIC detects that its message was not accepted by any agent on the bus.
Receive Accept Error	The local APIC sets this bit when it detects that the message it received was not accepted by any agent on the bus, including itself.
Send Illegal Vector	This bit is set when the local APIC detects an illegal vector in a message that it is sending over the bus.
Receive Illegal Vector	This bit is set when the local APIC detects an illegal vector in a message that it receives.
Illegal Register Address	This bit indicates that the processor is attempting to access a register not implemented in the Pentium processor 90/100 local APIC register address space.

Non-Maskable Interrupts (NMI)

Non-maskable interrupts can be sent to the processor via one of the I/O APIC inputs (INTIN15:INTIN0) or the one of the local interrupt inputs (LINT0 or LINT1). Additionally, NMIs can be passed from one processor to another via an IPI. The system's NMI logic connects to a single input, therefore all sources of NMI in a system are reported to a single input pin of the I/O APIC.

NMI via LINT0 or LINT1

Either of the local inputs can be defined by software as an NMI input by programming the respective Local Vector Table (LVT) Entry for a delivery mode of 100b (NMI). See figure 15-13. When the LINT pin is asserted the local vector table delivers the NMI request to the processor via the APIC. The vector information is ignored since the NMI always uses vector two in the interrupt table. Also NMI is always treated as an edge triggered input even if programmed otherwise in the LVT. Unlike other processors, the NMI input to the P54Cs can be masked. The LVT entry contains a mask bit that can inhibit the delivery of the NMI to the processor.

NMI via the I/O APIC

Any interrupt input to the I/O APIC can be defined by software as an NMI input by programming the respective redirection register's delivery mode field for NMI (100b). Non-maskable interrupt requests from the I/O APIC are delivered to the target processor via the APIC bus. NMI message cycles consist of a standard 21 clock transfer as shown in figure 15-15. Note that an IPI transfer of an NMI interrupt uses the same transfer mechanism defined in figure 15-15.

Inter- Processor Interrupts (IPI)

A processor generates inter-processor interrupts (IPIs) to pass messages or to forward interrupts to other processors. The message type is encoded in the delivery mode bits transferred during an APIC bus transaction. To initiate an IPI, the processor writes to the interrupt command register (ICR) within its APIC. The types of interrupts and messages supported via the ICR include:

- **Standard Interrupt Request** - This permits a processor to forward interrupts to other processors for handling.
- **Remote Read** - This message allows a processor to read a register within another processor's local APIC.
- **Initialization Message** (INIT) - This forces all target processors to be reset to their initialization state and await a startup message before continuing.

- **INIT with Level De-Assert** - This message commands all local APICs to set their bus arbitration IDs to the values of their APIC IDs. See the section entitled "APIC Bus Arbitration" for related information.
- **StartUp Message** (StartUp) - The startup message passes the power-on restart vector to other processors so they can each perform their initialization sequence.
- **System Management Interrupt** (SMI) - This message broadcasts an SMI to the target processors (specified by the destination code).
- **NMI** - The IPI mechanism can also deliver an NMI interrupt to the target processor (specified by the destination code).
- **Self Interrupts** - Under software control the Interrupt Command Register (ICR) can be loaded with a destination code that specifies this processor as the target processor.

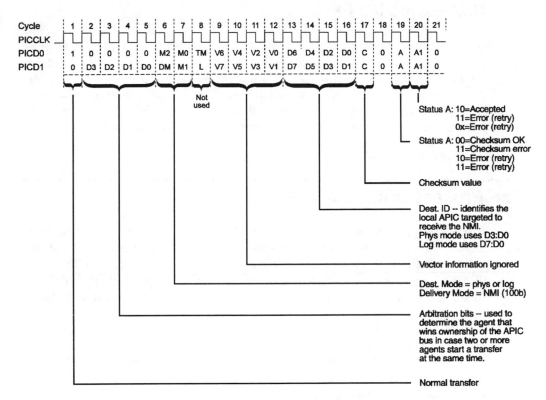

Figure 15-15. NMI Transfer Over the APIC Bus

An inter-processor interrupt (IPI) is initiated when the interrupt command register, or ICR, is written to. The format of the 64-bit ICR is shown in figure 15-16. Refer to the table 15-7 for definition of the fields within the ICR.

Interrupt Command Register Format

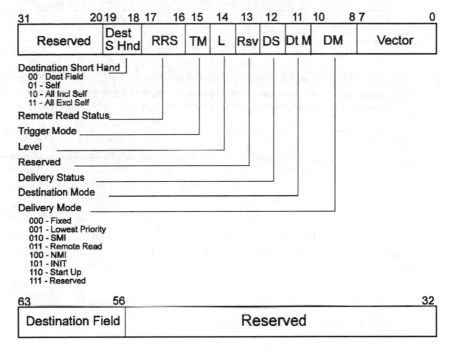

Figure 15-16. The Interrupt Command Register (ICR) Format

Table 15-7. Definition of Bit Fields within the ICR

Field Name	Description
Vector	The value contained in the vector field depends on the delivery mode specified.
Delivery Mode	Seven delivery modes can be specified for IPI transfers. Delivery modes 000b and 001b are used to forward interrupt requests to other processors. NMIs can also be forwarded using a delivery mode of 100b. All other delivery modes identify messages being sent to other processors.
Destination Mode	Specifies the type of destination model used to determine which local APICs are being targeted for delivery of the interrupt request or message. (physical or logical)
Delivery Status	This read-only field provides the current status of the interrupt's

Field Name	Description
	delivery. A state of zero (idle) indicates that there is no activity for this interrupt. A one (pending) indicates that the transfer is delayed, due to the APIC bus being busy, or the receiving local APIC is currently unable to accept the interrupt. After successful delivery, the delivery status bit returns to the idle state.
Level	This bit distinguishes an INIT Level De-Assert message (0) from all others (1).
Trigger Mode Bit	All IPI interrupts default to edge triggered even if programmed as level triggered. This bit is only defined for the INIT Level De-Assert message, and should be set to 1.
Remote Read Status	These two bits define the status of a remote register read from another local APIC. This read-only bit is updated to report the progress and final result of the register read.
Destination Short Hand	This field specifies a shorthand notation to identify the target APICs, without using the Destination ID. The shorthand destination can identify the processor itself and/or all other processor on the APIC bus. Note that using the shorthand destination requires writing only to the lower 32-bit of the ICR.
Destination ID	Specifies which local APICs are being targeted for delivery of the interrupt request or message.

Each of the message types supported by the IPI mechanism are described below.

Initialization Message

This message is defined by a delivery mode of 101b and is delivered to all processors listed in the destination field. All processors will assume their INIT state upon accepting the message. The processor remains in the INIT state until receiving a Start-up message via the APIC bus or until its INIT or RESET pins are asserted. This interrupt is treated as edge-triggered and the vector information is ignored. The INIT message requires 21 APIC clock cycles to complete. Refer to figure 15-17.

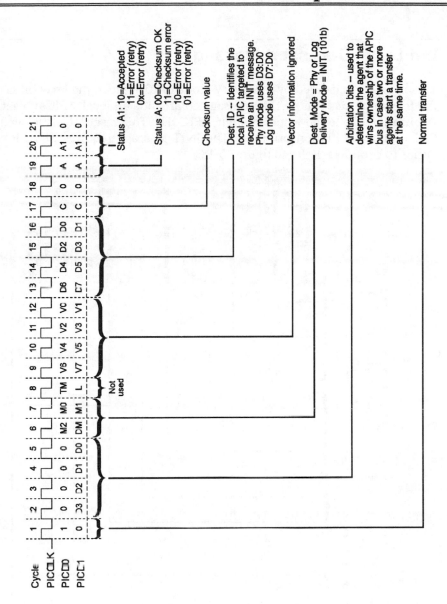

Figure 15-17. The Initialization Message Transfer

Init Level De-Assert Message

This message is defined by a delivery mode of 101b when the level bit is 0 and the trigger mode bit is 1. This message commands all local APICs to set their Arbitration IDs to the values of their APIC IDs. This resets all APIC agents to their initial Arbitration priorities. The INIT message requires 21 APIC clock cycles to complete. Refer to figure 15-18.

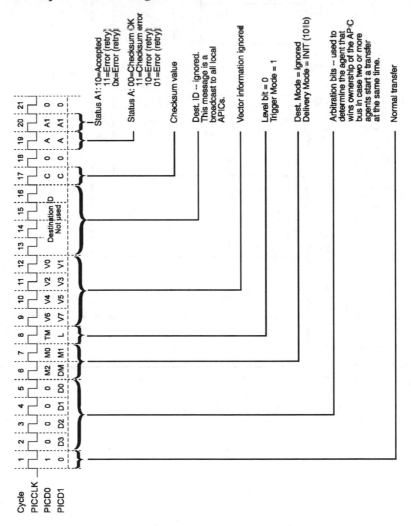

Figure 15-18. The Init Level De-Assert Message Transfer

StartUp Message

This message is defined only for multi-processor implementations. Dual processors must receive a startup message that directs them to perform their initial boot sequence. The startup message also passes the start-up execution address to the dual processor. This start-up address is defined in part by the vector field that is passed to the target processor during the start-up message. The location that the processor begins to fetch and execute instructions from is defined as: 000VV000h, where the vector defines address bits A19:A12 and the 12 upper and lower address lines are zeros. This specifies an address starting at a 4KB boundary within the first 1 MB of address space.

Note that the local APIC sending the startup message will not automatically attempt a retry as is done with most other IPI transfers. It's left up to the programmer to check transfer status and initiate the transfer again. The start up message requires 21 APIC clock cycles to complete. Refer to figure 15-19.

SMI Message

The SMI allows the local APIC to send a system management interrupt to other processes via the APIC message passing facilities. The SMI message is treated as edge triggered and the vector must be set to all zeros. The SMI message requires 21 APIC clock cycles to complete. Refer to figure 15-20.

Remote Read Message

This message is a request to read the contents of a register residing within another processor's local APIC. The vector field contains the partial address (A11:A4) of the target register. When the message is transmitted, the address of the target register to be read from is transferred to the target processor, and the contents of the register are read and transferred back to the requesting processor. A remote read message requires 39 APIC clock cycles to complete. Refer to figure 15-21.

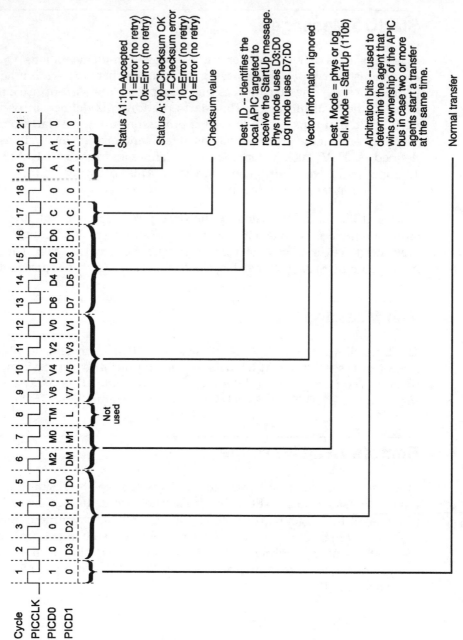

Figure 15-19. The StartUp Message Transfer

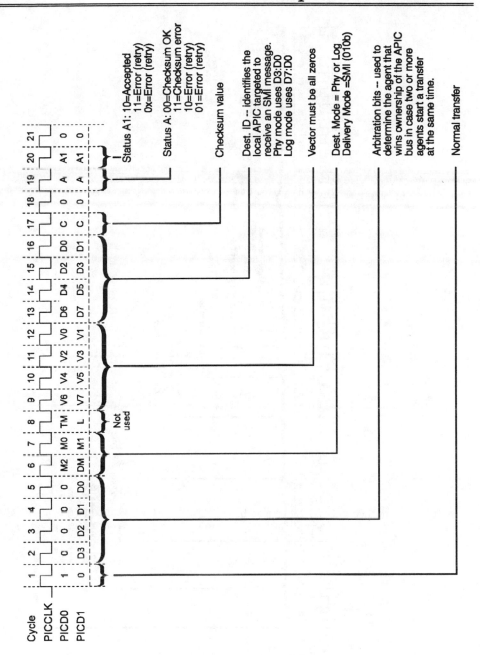

Figure 15-20. SMI Message Transfer

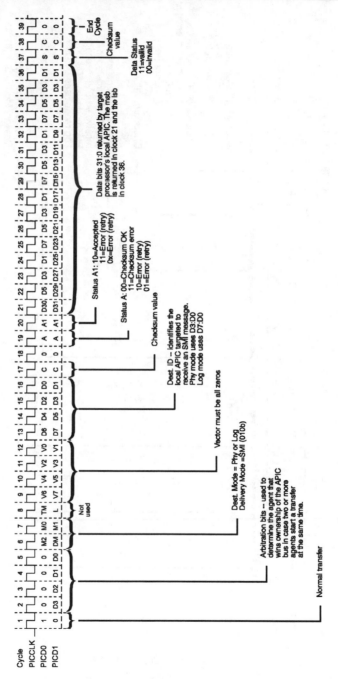

Figure 15-21. Remote Read Transfer

APIC Bus Arbitration

Since multiple agents capable of sending interrupts and messages reside on the APIC bus, more than one agent may start a transaction at the same time. Two mechanisms are defined to determine which agent will retain ownership of the APIC bus and conclude their transfer:

- transfer type
- arbitration cycles

Transfer Type

When agents start a transfer they indicate the transaction type they wish to perform during the first clock cycle of the transfer. Only two types of transfers are defined: the standard transfer and the EOI transfer. The standard transfer is used for every type of transfer except the EOI. If two agents start a transaction at the same time and one is performing a standard transfer, while the other is performing an EOI, then the agent performing the EOI transfer has priority over the other. An agent that performs a standard transfer must monitor the type bits at the end of clock one. If it observes data values indicating an EOI type, it recognizes that another agent has started an EOI transfer in the same clock and therefore, it must release the APIC bus, allowing the EOI to complete.

Bus Arbitration Cycles

If two or more agents start transfers of the same type, then neither will have any idea that another agent is also starting a transfer simultaneously. Therefore, the first cycle of every APIC transfers is immediately followed by four arbitration clock cycles that are used to determine continued ownership of the APIC bus. Only the winner of the arbitration process continues the transfer following the arbitration cycles. All others will have recognized another APIC agent also attempting to use the bus has a higher arbitration priority and therefore discontinue their transfer.

Each Potential owner of the bus has a unique 4-bit arbitration ID that is used during the arbitration process. Each bit of the ID is driven onto the APIC bus one clock cycle at a time over PICD1. The most significant bit of the arbitration ID is transferred first, followed by each successive bit during the remaining cycles. After each arbitration clock cycle, only potential winners of the arbitration processor continue participating in the arbitration process, while losers drop out. By the end of the arbitration cycles only one agent (the winner) will be left driving the bus. This process is detailed below.

Note that APIC arbitration ID (4 bits) permits a maximum of 16 agents, thereby imposing a limit of 16 agents on a single APIC bus implementation.

The Arbitration Process Defined

The highest priority arbitration value is FFh and the lowest is 00h. Since all values are driven onto the bus in the inverted state, a value of 00h on the bus is the highest priority, while FFh is the lowest. The data lines PICD0 and PICD1 are implemented as open-drain outputs from all agents; therefore, the PICD1 line will reflect the composite value of each arbitration bit output by the competing agents.

Figure 15-22 illustrates three agents attempting to use the APIC bus at the same time, and all have indicated they are attempting to perform a *normal* type transfer. The arbitration process begins during clock two and is enumerated below.

1. All three participating agents simultaneously output the MSB (bit 3) of their Arbitration ID at the beginning of the first arbitration clock cycle. Each agent then compares the value that it is outputting against the composite value. If the composite value matches the value that the respective agent is outputting, it continues the arbitration process. In this example, all three agents recognize that the composite value of 1b matches the value that they are outputting and therefore continue with the next arbitration cycle.

2. All three participating agents output the next arbitration ID bit (bit 2) at the beginning of the second arbitration clock cycle. Each agent compares the value (1b) that it is outputting against the composite value (1b), and again recognizes it is still "in the running."

3. All three participating agents output the next arbitration ID bit (bit 1) at the beginning of the third arbitration clock cycle. Once again, each agent compares the value that it is outputting against the composite value. This time both the primary and dual P54C processors detect a composite value of 0b (from the I/O APIC) but each is outputting a value of 1b. The pro-

cessors now recognize that a higher priority APIC agent is attempting to use the bus, and therefore, they cease driving the bus.

4. The I/O APIC outputs the LSB (bit 0) of its arbitration ID at the beginning of the fourth clock arbitration clock cycle. Since it is the only device driving the bus, the composite value and the value that it is driving match. The I/O APIC recognizes that it has won the APIC bus arbitration and continues with its transfer.

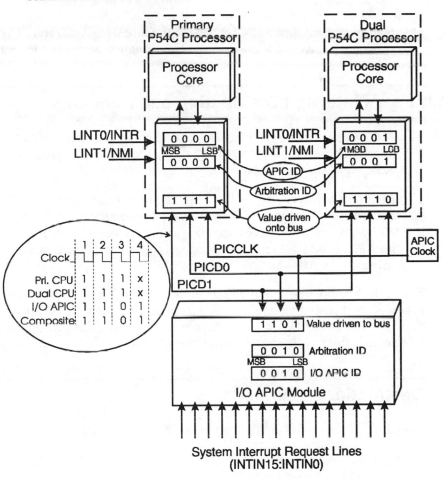

Figure 15-22. Example APIC Bus Arbitration

Maintaining Fairness

The initial arbitration values used by each agent is the same as its APIC ID as illustrated in figure 15-22. Since the APIC ID is fixed, all agents on the APIC bus (including those not participating in the last arbitration) increment their arbitration IDs after each arbitration, thereby creating a rotational priority mechanism. The winning agent of the last bus arbitration resets its arbitration ID to 0000b, thus assuming the lowest priority. As an example, the APIC agents illustrated in figure 15-22 will have the following arbitration IDs for the next transfer: Primary P54C=0001b, Dual P54C=0010b and I/O APIC=0000b.

Summary of Interrupt Distribution and Handling

The APIC subsystem delivers interrupts and messages over the APIC bus using a serial transmission protocol. In short, the APIC subsystem distributes two basic types of information:

- **Interrupt requests** - these interrupt requests originate at the I/O APIC and are sent over the APIC bus to a target processor for servicing.
- **Messages** - these messages originate at a processor and are broadcast over the APIC bus to either a specific agent, a group of agents or all agents residing on the APIC bus.

The APIC provides several methods of distributing these interrupts and messages. The distribution method is a function of both the destination and delivery modes selected under software control. Two destination modes can be selected, along with a variety of delivery modes.

Destination Mode

Two destination modes are defined by the APIC subsystem:

- Physical Destination Mode
- Logical Destination Mode

Chapter 15: The APIC

Physical Destination Mode

A sender that uses the physical destination mode defines the target processor by placing a four bit destination ID onto the bus when transmitting the interrupt request or message. This four-bit code is used by all agents on the bus identify the target agent or agents that should receive the interrupt.

Physical Destination (Single Target Processor)

When a single processor on the APIC bus is targeted, each processor compares the destination ID to its respective four-bit APIC ID. Refer to figure 15-23 . Any of 15 different processors can be identified using mechanism. The 15 destination codes used to identify a single processor are zero (0000b) through fourteen (1110b).

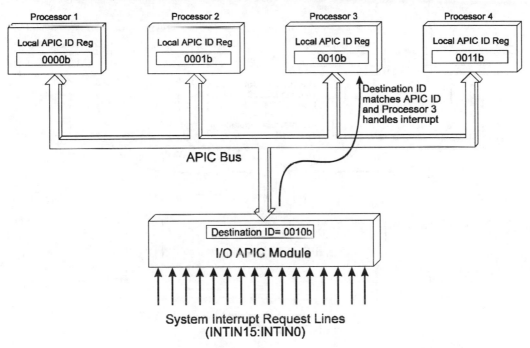

Figure 15-23. Physical Destination Mode with Single Target Specified

Pentium Processor System Architecture

Physical Destination (All Processors Targeted)

The programmer can choose to identify all processors in the destination by using a destination ID of fifteen (1111b), causing all processors to receive the interrupt request regardless of their APIC ID. Refer to figure 15-24.

This method of selecting target processors permits the programmer to include all processors in the interrupt handling process. The processors can then be directed to jointly determine which processor is currently running the lowest-priority task (via the lowest-priority delivery mode). The processor running the lowest priority task then accepts and services the interrupt request, while the other processors simply ignore the request. (See the section entitled, "Lowest Priority Interrupt Distribution" later in this chapter for details regarding the lowest-priority delivery mode.)

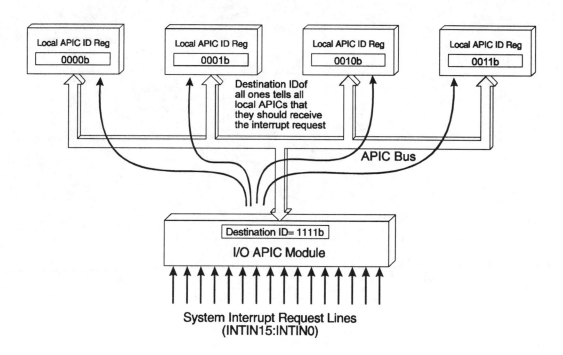

Figure 15-24. Physical Destination with All Targets Specified.

Selecting the APIC ID

Each local APIC obtains its APIC ID by sampling BE3#:BE0# on the trailing edge of RESET, with BE0# as the LSB of the APIC ID. These signals should be set to zero for a dual processor implementation. The primary processor latches the state of the byte enables and places them directly into its APIC ID register, resulting in a APIC ID of 0000b. Likewise, the dual processor latches the byte enables on the trailing edge of RESET, but inverts BE0#, yielding an APIC ID of 0001b for the dual processor.

In a multiple processor implementation, the system designer must ensure that each processor pair sees a unique value on BE3#:BE0# when RESET is deasserted. In the dual-processor implementation if BE3#:BE0# are not driven nor pulled to either Vcc or Vss, then the APIC ID value defaults to 0000b for the primary processor and 0001b for the dual processor.

Logical Destination Mode

Logical destination mode uses an 8-bit logical APIC ID to specify the target processor. Each local APIC has its own logical destination register (LDR) containing an 8-bit field that can be programmed with its logical APIC ID. This 8-bit field can be programmed with any value from zero to 255d. When an interrupt request or message is broadcast over the APIC bus, all local APICs compare the 8-bit destination code sent by the I/O APIC with their local APIC ID to determine if they are being selected.

Logical destination mode permits the programmer to target a group of processors by programming the same logical APIC ID for all processors within the group.

When logical mode is selected, two interrupt delivery models can be implemented: the *flat* model and the *cluster* model. The destination format register (DFR) selects whether a flat or cluster destination is being used. The DFR specifies the interpretation of the logical APIC ID that is contained in the logical destination register (LDR) as illustrated in figure 15-25.

LDR and DFR Definition

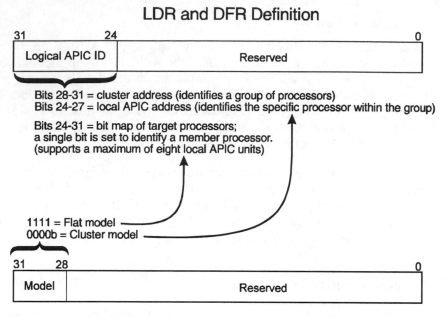

Figure 15-25. The Logical Destination and Destination Format Registers

Flat Model

When the DFR is programmed for the flat model, an arbitrary group of processors can be specified under software control. The programmer sets a single bit in each processor's Logical Destination Register (LDR). This allows a maximum of eight member processors in a flat model implementation. The destination code sent by the I/O APIC selects a target processor by setting the bit in the destination code that corresponds to the member processor. For example, if the programmer wants to select processors one and three the destination code would be programmed with a value of 00000101b as illustrated in figure 15-26. This technique permits the programmer to select any single processor, any combination of processors or all processors (up to the maximum of eight) as the destination.

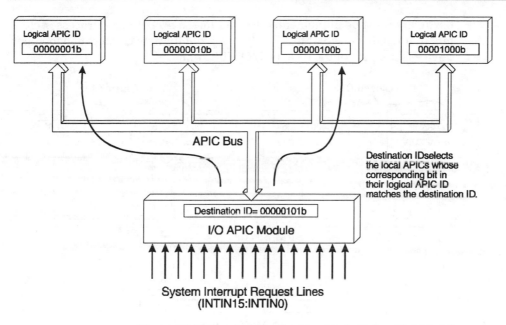

Figure 15-26. Logical Destination Mode Using Flat Model

Cluster Model

The cluster model permits a larger number of processors to be implemented into the logical destination environment. The hardware views the 8-bit logical APIC ID as two separate nibbles: the upper nibble identifies the cluster and the lower nibble identifies target processors within the cluster. Figure 15-27 illustrates the cluster model concept. The APIC subsystem supports two methods of connecting a cluster destination environment:

- **Flat Cluster Model** - This model permits a maximum of 15 clusters to be identified by defining values of zero (0000b) to fourteen (1110b) for the cluster field within the logical APIC ID (LDR, bits 31:28). The lower nibble is bit mapped, allowing a maximum of four processors to be identified within each cluster. Logically, this cluster model can identify up to 60 processors; however, the APIC bus arbitration mechanism supports only 15 agents. APIC bus arbitration is necessary since multiple agents residing on a single APIC bus can start bus transfers concurrently. Refer to the section entitled, "APIC Bus Arbitration" in this chapter.
- **Hierarchical Cluster Model** - This model permits a network of processor clusters that support the logical maximum of 60 processors. To circumvent the limitation imposed by APIC bus arbitration, cluster management

hardware must be implemented to pass messages between processor clusters that reside on separate APIC buses. Note that the cluster management device is not part of the local or I/O APIC units.

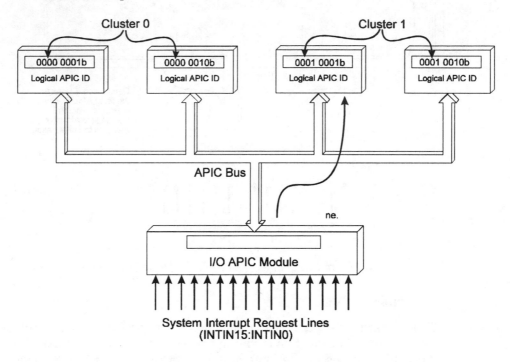

Figure 15-27. Destination Mode Using the Flat Cluster Model

Destination Shorthand (IPIs only)

The local APIC's interrupt command register has a two bit field called the destination shorthand (refer to figure 15-16). This destination shorthand field provide a quick method for the programmer to identify either the processor itself as the target and/or all other processors connected to the APIC bus. When not using the shorthand destinations the programmer must write to both the lower and upper 32-bits of the 64-bit ICR register. When using the destination shorthand the programmer writes only to the lower 32-bits of the ICR, since the destination ID is not used during the transfer. The four possible shorthand destinations include:

- **Destination field** (00b) - this setting indicates that the value specified in the destination field (ICR, bits 63:56) should be used to determine the target processor(s).
- **Self** (01b) - this setting causes the processor to interrupt itself.
- **All including self** (10b) - this setting specifies all processors as targets including itself.
- **All excluding self** (11b) — this setting specifies all processors except itself.

Delivery Mode

The delivery mode can specify a variety of information depending on the originator and type of interrupt or message to be transferred. All APIC transfers originate from either the I/O APIC or a local APIC. Definition of the delivery mode depends on whether a interrupt request is being sent or a message is being broadcast.

Delivery Mode for Interrupt Requests (from the I/O APIC or local APIC)

- **APIC Compliant External Interrupts** (Static and Lowest Priority) - These delivery modes (static and lowest priority) are defined for interrupts that support the APIC protocol. The delivery mode identifies the mechanism used to identify the target processor that should service the interrupt. Static deliver mode is intended primarily to send an interrupt request to a specific processor. In this mode, all processors listed in the destination (typically one processor) should process the interrupt. Lowest priority delivery mode directs all local APICs listed in the destination (typically a group of processors) to determine which processor is currently running the lowest priority code and for that processor to service the interrupt request. Refer to the section entitled, "Interrupt Delivery" for details on these delivery modes.
- **8259 Compliant External Interrupt** (ExtINT) - this interrupt request comes from an 8259 interrupt controller. The processor listed in the destination should service the interrupt request by running two interrupt acknowledge bus cycles to get the vector number from the external 8259 interrupt controller. External Interrupt delivery requires 21 APIC clock cycles to complete, followed by two interrupt acknowledge bus cycles (needed to obtain the vector).

- **NMI** - the processor listed in the destination should service the NMI request. NMI delivery requires 21 APIC clock cycles to complete.

Delivery Mode for Messages (from the local APIC)

- **EOI** - the local APIC forwards the EOI command on to the I/O APIC for all level-triggered interrupts, notifying the I/O APIC that the respective level-triggered interrupt request has been serviced. The EOI message takes 14 APIC clock cycles to complete.
- **SMI** (system management interrupt) - this allows the local APIC to send a system management interrupt to other processes via the APIC message passing facilities. The SMI message is treated as edge triggered and the vector must be set to all zeros. The SMI message requires 21 APIC clock cycles to complete.
- **Remote Read** - this message is a request to read the contents of a register residing within another processor's local APIC. The vector field contains the partial address (A11:A4) of the target register. When the message is transmitted, the address of the target register to be read from is transferred to the target processor, and the contents of the register are read and transferred back to the requesting processor. A remote read message takes 39 APIC clock cycles to complete.
- **Initialization message** (INIT) - this message is delivered to all processors listed in the destination field. All processors will assume their INIT state upon accepting the message. The processor remains in the INIT state until receiving a receiving a Start-up message via the APIC bus or until its INIT or RESET pins are asserted. This interrupt is treated as edge-triggered and the vector information is ignored. The INIT message requires 21 APIC clock cycles to complete.
- **StartUp Message** - this message is defined only for a multi-processor implementation. This message passes the start-up execution address to the target processor. The start-up address is defined in part by the vector field that is passed to the target processor during the start-up message. The location that the processor begins to fetch and execute instructions from is defined as: 000VV000h, where the vector defines address bits A19:A12 and the 12 upper and lower address lines are zeros. This specifies an address starting at a 4KB boundary within the first 1MB of address space. The start up message requires 21 APIC clock cycles to complete.

Chapter 15: The APIC

Interrupt Delivery

A local APIC targeted during an APIC transfer must be able to determine if it should officially accept and service the interrupt request. The delivery mode specifies which processor listed in the destination should process the interrupt. Two delivery modes are defined for interrupt request delivery:

- **Static (Fixed) delivery** - all processors listed in the destination should service the interrupt request. Fixed interrupt delivery requires 21 APIC clock cycles to complete.
- **Lowest priority (dynamic) delivery** - the processor within the group listed in the destination that is currently running the lowest priority code should service the interrupt. Lowest priority interrupt delivery requires 34 APIC clock cycles to complete (21 cycles if a focus processor is discovered). See the section entitled "The Focus Processor" later in this chapter for details.

Static Distribution

The simplest delivery mode is static, or fixed, delivery. In this mode, all local APICs that are specified in the destination field are directed to accept and process the interrupt request. Since all processors listed in the destination are directed to handle the interrupt request, the static delivery mechanism is used when a single processor is specified by the destination mode selected. Static distribution can be used with either physical or any of the logical destination modes.

Lowest-Priority Interrupt Distribution

This delivery mode is typically used when a group of processors are specified in the destination. The processor within this group that is currently executing the lowest-priority code is the processor that should accept and service the interrupt request. An arbitration process, similar to the APIC bus arbitration mechanism, determines which processor is currently executing the lowest priority code.

A group of processors is selected depending on destination mode used. For example, when using physical destination mode a destination ID of all ones directs all local APICs to be selected. Logical destination mode allows for software defined groups of local APICs to be selected. In either case, the local APICs that are selected must jointly participate in the lowest-priority arbitration during the transfer to determine which is currently executing the lowest priority code.

Since the lowest-priority arbitration is specified by the delivery mode, all other forms of interrupts specified by the delivery mode (i.e. NMI, ExtInt, SMI and messages) cannot use the lowest-priority interrupt mechanism.

Determining the Arbitration Priority

The lowest priority method of interrupt distribution employs the interrupt priority mechanism described earlier in this chapter (see the section entitled, "Hardware Interrupt priority"). Each local APIC uses this mechanism to derive its arbitration priority value, which is used during lowest-priority arbitration. This value is maintained within the arbitration priority register, or APR.

The value placed into the APR by the local APIC reflects the highest priority code currently executing or pending execution by the processor. The APR value is the same as TPR when the following conditions are met:

1. An interrupt is currently being serviced but has a lower priority than the TPR. This condition is true when TPR > ISRV (ISRV = the highest priority interrupt vector in the ISR register). If the interrupt currently being serviced (ISRV) has a lower priority than TPR, this indicates that the operating system has raised the TPR value to indicate that higher priority code is pending execution. TPR > ISRV is also true when no interrupts are currently being serviced.

2. The highest priority interrupt currently pending has the same or lower priority than the TPR. This condition is true when TPR ≥ IRRV (IRRV = the highest priority interrupt vector pending in the IRR register). In this case, the value of the TPR (established by the operating system) indicates that the processor is currently executing code that has a priority equal to or higher than any interrupt pending in the IRR register.

If the following conditions are not both met, then the APR value will be the highest priority of either the ISRV or IRRV.

The Lowest-Priority Arbitration Process

When the lowest-priority delivery mode is selected, the decision to either accept or reject an interrupt request from the I/O APIC is based on the current arbitration priority value stored in the arbitration priority register (APR). All local APICs specified in the destination must arbitrate to determine which is currently executing the lowest priority code). This arbitration process is accomplished during an interrupt transfer and requires 34 APIC clock cycles to complete. Figure 15-29 illustrates the timing and bit definition during a lowest priority interrupt transfer.

Arbitration is accomplished over the APIC bus during APIC clock cycles 21 through 28 of the interrupt transfer. Each local APIC inverts the contents of its arbitration priority register. The inverted arbitration values yield the highest priority for the device whose arbitration value is the lowest. This is necessary to ensure that the winner of the arbitration is the processor executing the lowest priority code. The arbitration process then proceeds in exactly the same fashion as the APIC bus arbitration, with the exception that 8-bit arbitration values are used, rather than 4 bits. (Refer to the section entitled, "Bus Arbitration Cycles" for details.) Figure 15-28 illustrates the I/O APIC performing a lowest-priority transfer to a pair of processors.

It is possible that more than one local APIC has the same winning arbitration priority. As a result, the lowest priority transfer implements a final arbitration stage that resolves the tie and determines the winner. This arbitration process begins immediately following the lowest-priority arbitration and uses the APIC IDs to resolve the tie. The local APIC with the highest APIC ID will win the final arbitration, and therefore, accept and service the interrupt request.

The Focus Processor

Prior to beginning the lowest-arbitration, status information is returned by all local APICs specified in the destination over PICD0 and PICD1. The I/O APIC and all local APICs listed in the destination check this status information. If the status information seen on the bus by the APIC agents is pulled low then the I/O APIC and local APICs recognize that one of the local APICs has indicated that it is the focus processor and that lowest-priority arbitration will not occur.

This mechanism is included in case the interrupt vector is already set in either a local APICs IRR or ISR register, meaning that this processor is the focus of

this interrupt. This ensures that another processor does not service an interrupt request that is already pending in another processor. The focus processor
accepts the interrupt without regard to task priority.

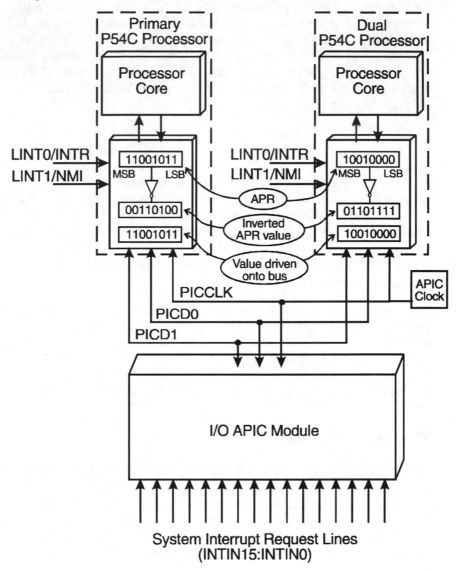

Figure 15-28. Two Local APICs Performing Lowest-Priority Arbitration

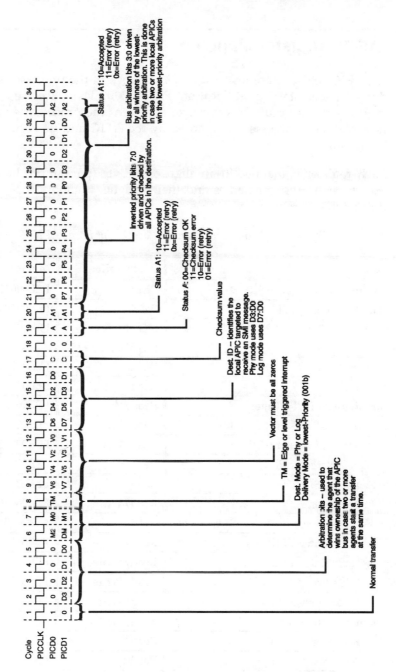

Figure 15-29. The Lowest-Priority Interrupt Transfer

Pentium Processor System Architecture

Local APIC Register Mapping

All APIC registers are mapped in a 4KB block of the processor's memory address space, starting at location FEE00000h. Data accesses to the APIC registers do not cause bus cycles to appear at the processor's external buses; however, code accesses are ignored by the APIC and do result in bus cycles being run.

Each register is mapped at an aligned 16 byte (paragraph) boundary. Table 15-8 lists the register names and their assigned memory location. Locations not specified are reserved.

Table 15-8. Name and Memory Location of Local APIC Registers

Register Name	Read/Write	Memory Address (h)
Arbitration Priority Register (APR)	Read	FEE00090
Current Count Register (CCR) Timer	Read	FEE00390
Destination Format Register (DFR)	bits 27:0 Read bits 31:28 R/W	FEE000E0
End of Interrupt Register (EOI)	Write	FEE000A0
Error Status Register	Read	FEE00280
Initial Count Register (ICR) Timer	Read/Write	FEE00380
Interrupt Command Register (ICR) 31:0	Read/Write	FEE00300
Interrupt Command Register (ICR) 63:32	Read/Write	FEE00310
Interrupt Request Register (IRR) 255:0	Read	FEE00200-FEE00270
In-Service Register (ISR) 255:0	Read	FEE00100-FEE00170
Local APIC ID Register	Read/Write	FEE00020
Local APIC Version Register	Read	FEE00030
Local Vector Table Entry 0 (Timer)	Read/Write	FEE00320
Local Vector Table Entry 1 (LINT0)	Read/Write	FEE00350
Local Vector Table Entry 2 (LINT1)	Read/Write	FEE00360
Local Vector Table Entry 3 (Error)	Read/Write	FEE00370
Logical Destination Register (LDR)	Read/Write	FEE000D0
Processor Priority Register (PPR)	Read	FEE000A0
Remote Read Register	Read	FEE000C0
Spurious Interrupt Vector Register	bits 3:0 Read	FEE000F0

Register Name	Read/Write	Memory Address (h)
Spurious Interrupt Vector Register	bits 9:4 R/W	
Task Priority Register (TPR)	Read/Write	FEE00080
Timer Divide Configuration Register (TDC)	Read/Write	FEE003E0
Trigger Mode Register (TMR)	Read	FEE00180-FEE001F0

Local APIC Modes of Operation

The APIC subsystem is designed to support 8259 compatible operation. This support exists in all local APIC modes of operation. The local APIC supports four operational modes:

- **Masked Mode** — When the local APIC is enabled during Reset (APICEN asserted), the local APIC begins operation in masked mode. In mask mode, all interrupts from I/O devices are masked. This includes all interrupt requests from the I/O APIC, as well as those from LINT0 and LINT1. The interrupts and messages that remain active are NMI, SMI, INIT, remote read, and StartUp.

  The local APIC remains in masked mode until initializing software enables interrupts.

- **Normal Mode** — Previous discussions in this chapter are based on normal mode operation. In this mode all APIC features are available.

- **Through Local Mode** — This mode allows an external 8259 interrupt controller and the system's NMI logic to be connected to the local input pins (LINT0 and LINT1). The APIC's IPI message passing facilities remain active to support multi-processing environments, but interrupt requests from the I/O APIC are masked.

- **Bypass Mode** — The APIC is hardware disabled in bypass mode as a result of APICEN being sampled deasserted during Reset. In this state the LINT0 pin is defined as INTR and the LINT1 pin as NMI. None of the local APIC functionality is active in bypass mode.

Pentium Processor System Architecture

8259 Compatible Operation

The APIC subsystem is designed to support 8259 compatible operation. This support exists in all local APIC modes of operation. In bypass mode, the APIC is hardware disabled, therefore the P54C processors function exactly like the Pentium 60 and 66Mhz processors.

The APIC subsystem interrupt inputs that an 8259 interrupt controller can be connected to depends on the local APIC's mode of operation. The 8259 can be connected to either a local APIC input or any of the I/O APIC inputs as follow:

- LINT0 or LINT1 (Normal and Through Local Modes)
- I/O APIC inputs (Normal Mode only)

The input used to connect the 8259 must be programmed for IntExt delivery mode. Normally, the local APIC intercepts the two interrupt acknowledge cycles run by the processor core when it recognizes an APIC compatible interrupt. The local APIC simply returns the vector to the processor, thereby eliminating the need for the interrupt acknowledge bus cycles to run externally. However, when the local APIC sends an 8259 interrupt request to the processor core, it allows the processor's interrupt acknowledge cycles to run normally. This results in two external interrupt acknowledge bus cycles that are used to obtain the interrupt vector from the external 8259 interrupt controller. Once the processor receives the vector, it then proceeds to service the interrupt.

Chapter 16

The Previous Chapter

The previous chapter provided an overview of the APIC subsystem and details the operation of the local APIC.

This Chapter

This chapter discusses the enhancements to System Management Mode (SMM) implemented with the P54C processors.

The Next Chapter

The next chapter discusses the key features included the Pentium 610\75MHz processor.

System Management Mode (SMM) Enhancements

Several changes has been implemented in the P54C's system management mode (SMM) capabilities when compared to the Pentium 60 and 66MHz processors. These changes include:

- A System Management Interrupt (SMI) can be delivered via the local APIC, in addition to the SMI# pin.
- An I/O instruction restart extension has been added. The SMM revision identifier has also changed to indicate support for the I/O instruction restart feature and to permit the feature to be enabled and disabled.
- Clock control features have been added, allowing the processor to run at speeds that are either 2x or 1.5x the speed of the input clock and bus frequency. Stop clock control has also been implemented through a STPCLK# interrupt pin.
- Dual processor support requires that the LRM (least recent master) wait until it becomes the MRM before accessing SMRAM.

• The SMI# pin is not recognized when a P54C processor is in the shutdown state.

I/O Instruction Restart

In many instances, the SMI# pins is asserted by external hardware when an access occurs to an I/O device that is powered down. When the SMI handler is called, it re-applies power to the target device and returns to the interrupt program. Since the I/O instruction that caused the SMI has not actually written to the target device, it must be executed again. The P54C processors support an I/O instruction restart feature, that instructs the processor to restart the I/O instruction that caused the SMI.

The state-save map implemented by the P54C processors defines an additional entry, called the I/O instruction restart slot. Figure 16-1 illustrates the state-save map with the new entry shaded. This slot permits the SMI handler to inform the processor to restart the I/O instruction that completed when the SMI# is recognized. Thus, when the RSM instruction is executed, the processor re-executes the I/O instruction again. This time the instruction has its intended effect since the SMI handler re-applied power to the target device.

When the processor saves it state, the value of the I/O restart slot is always 0000h. The SMI handler, recognizing that the SMI was triggered by an access to a device that is powered down, re-applies power and writes 00FFh to the I/O instruction restart slot. When the processor restores the state-save map the new I/O instruction restart slot value of 00FFh causes the processor to execute the I/O instruction again.

In order for I/O instruction restart to work correctly, the SMI# signal must be recognized on the instruction boundary of the I/O instruction causing the SMI. To meet the setup time for recognizing SMI# on an instruction boundary, SMI# must be asserted at least 3 PCLKs prior to BRDY# being sampled asserted.

Offset		
7FFC	CR0	
7FF8	CR3	
7FF4	EFLAGS*	
7FF0	EIP*	
7FEC	EDI*	
7FE8	ESI*	
7FE4	EBP*	
7FE0	ESP*	
7FDC	EBX*	
7FD8	EDX*	
7FD4	ECX*	
7FD0	EAX*	
7FCC	DR6	
7FC8	DR7	
7FC4	Reserved	TR
7FC0	Reserved	LDT Base
7FBC	Reserved	GS
7FB8	Reserved	FS
7FB4	Reserved	DS
7FB0	Reserved	SS
7FAC	Reserved	CS
7FA8	Reserved	ES
7FA7-7F98		
7F94	IDT Base	
7F93-7F8C	Reserved	
7F88	GDT Base	
7F87-7F04	Reserved	
7F02	Reserved	Auto HALT Restart Slot*
7F00	Reserved	I/O Instr. Restart Slot*
7EFC	SMM Revision Identifier	
7EF8	SMBASE Slot*	
7EF7-7E00	Reserved	

31 · · · · · · · · · · Bits · · · · · · · · · · 0

Offset from
SMRAM Base

* Locations are writable

Figure 16-1. State-Save Map for P54C Processors

When an SMI that is currently executing sets the I/O instruction restart slot and a second SMI is asserted, the processor services the second SMI before restarting the I/O instruction. Note that two back-to-back SMI sequences that both specify I/O instruction restart will be handled incorrectly. Therefore, the SMI handler must not set the I/O instruction restart slot during the second of two consecutive SMIs. A second consecutive I/O instruction restart causes the EIP to be decremented a second time, and therefore, no longer points to the I/O instruction.

SMI Delivery via APIC Bus

In dual processor environments, the APIC bus can be used to transfer SMIs. The local APIC integrated into a P54C processor can pass messages to local APICs residing in other P54C processors. These messages, called interprocessor interrupts (IPIs), can cause a target processor to receive an SMI, even though its SMI# pins remains deasserted. (See the chapter entitled, "The APIC" for details on the IPI transfers.)

Note that I/O instruction restart is not supported when using the APIC bus for SMI delivery. The I/O instruction restart capability requires synchronization between the I/O instruction that caused the SMI and the recognition of the SMI# pin. This synchronization can be accomplished when the SMI# pin delivers the SMI, by ensuring that the appropriate setup times are met. This means that the SMI is recognized at the I/O instruction boundary. However, the APIC transfer mechanism is asynchronous, and the I/O instruction cannot be synchronized with SMI delivery. In other words, SMI# recognition cannot be guaranteed at the I/O instruction boundary.

Clock Control Features

Core/Bus Frequency Control

The P54C processors are designed to operate with an input clock frequency of 60 or 66MHz and is used as the bus clock frequency. The processor core operating frequency is determined by the state of the BF pin during reset. When BF is strapped to Vcc the processor operates at a 2/3 (I/O bus to processor core) frequency ratio. When strapped to Vss, the processor operates at a 1/2 frequency ratio. The possible frequency ratios are listed in table 16-1.

Table 16-1. Clock Speed Possibilities

CPU Type	BF State	CLK Speed	Bus Speed	Internal Clock Speed
735/90	1	60 MHz	60 MHz	90 MHz
815/100	0	50 MHz	50 MHz	100 MHz
815/100	1	66.6 MHz	66.6 MHz	100 MHz

Chapter 16: P54C SMM Enhancements

Stop Clock

The P54C processors provide a STPCLK# pin that allows system hardware to reduce power consumption by stopping the CPU's internal clock. STPCLK# is implemented as the lowest priority interrupt input to the processor. This ensures that all other forms of interrupt request are handled prior to stopping the processor's internal clock.

When the Stop clock request is the highest priority interrupt pending execution, the processor stops execution on the instruction boundary that STPCLK# is recognized. STPCLK# must remain asserted for the processor to retain the stop clock condition. Once STPCLK# is recognized the processor takes the following actions:

- stops the prefetch unit
- flushes the instruction pipeline
- completes all pending (buffered) writes
- waits for EWBE# to be asserted
- performs a "stop grant" special cycle
- stops the internal clock (enters the "stop grant" state)

Note that the processor cannot enter the stop grant state while HLDA is asserted (because the stop grant special cycle cannot be performed).

The stop grant special cycle is performed when the processor outputs the signals shown in table 16-2. Following the stop grant special cycle, the processor stops its internal clock and enters the stop grant state.

Table 16-2. Stop Grant Special Cycle Definition

Signal(s)	Signal State(s)
M/IO#	0b
D/C#	0b
W/R#	1b
A31:A3	00000010h
BE7#:BE0#	11111011b

The processor restarts it internal clock and returns to the interrupted application when STPCLK# is deasserted (driven high, not floated).

Part III:

Other Pentium Processors

Chapter 17

The Previous Chapter

The previous chapter discussed the system management mode enhancements that have been added to the P54C processors.

In This Chapter

This chapter discusses the key features employed by the Pentium 610/75MHz processor

The Next Chapter

The next chapter discusses the Pentium OverDrive processors and related ZIF sockets.

Primary Feature of the Pentium 610/75MHz Processor

The Pentium 610/75MHz processor is intended for use in the mobile computing environment. This processor contains a Pentium processor core and a full 64-bit data bus. The key features that are different from the Pentium 60/66MHz products are:

- Two physical packages:
    320 lead TCP (Tape Carrier Package)
    - 296 pin SPGA (Staggered Pin Grid Array)
- 50 MHz input clock frequency
- Faster processor core (75MHz) yielding higher performance.
- Fractional bus speed.
- Local Advanced Programmable Interrupt Controller (APIC).
- Enhanced power management features.
- 3.3vdc logic levels.

Faster Processor Core/Slower Bus Clock

The Pentium 610/75MHz processor operates at an internal frequency that is one and one-half times the clock input. This permits the processor to operate at internal clock frequency of 75MHz, while bus cycles can be run at the lower input clock frequency of 50MHz. This makes system implementations less costly and much easier to design.

Advanced Programmable Interrupt Controller (APIC)

The Pentium 610/75MHz processors incorporate a local APIC module. The local APIC provides flexibility in implementing interrupts in mobile computing designs.

Enhanced Power Management

The Pentium 610/75MHz processors incorporate the SL power management features. These features include:

- 3.3 vdc operating voltage — this results in considerably lower power dissipation in the Pentium 610/75MHz when compared to the original Pentium processors operating at 5 vdc.
- System Management Mode (SMM) — this mode provides the system designer with the ability to implement power management features independent of the operation system.
- Stop Clock capability — a signal called Stop Clock (STPCLK) causes the processor to stop its internal clock, thereby reducing power dissipation to almost nothing.
- Auto Halt Power Down — the processor automatically enters a lower power state when a HALT instruction is executed.
- I/O Instruction Restart — when the processor enters SMM as a result of an I/O access to a device that is powered down, the SMM handler can cause the processor to automatically re-execture the I/O instruction upon return from SMM.

These features combine to make the Pentium 610/75MHz processors extremely energy-efficient when compared to the original Penitum processors.

Chapter 18

The Previous Chapter

The previous chapter introduces the key features of the Pentium 610/75MHz processor.

In This Chapter

This chapter discusses the future Pentium OverDrive processors and upgrade sockets.

Overview of the Pentium OverDrive Processors

Intel provides an upgrade path for all systems based on 486 and Pentium processors. OverDrive processors provide end users with the option of upgrading their existing PCs by adding a faster OverDrive processor. All Pentium upgrade sockets use ZIF (zero insertion force) technology for easy removal and installation of the processors. Currently, Intel has defined four upgrade sockets for various future Pentium OverDrive processors. These Pentium upgrade sockets are designated by number and include:

- Sockets 2 and 3 (486DX2 and 486DX4 systems)
- Socket 4 (Pentium 60/66MHz systems)
- Socket 5 (Pentium P54C systems)
- Socket 6 (486DX4 systems)

Following is a brief review of each socket and the systems for which they are intended.

Pentium Processor System Architecture

Sockets Two and Three

Socket two can be implemented in 486DX2 and 486DX4 systems. These sockets are implemented in 486 systems that are announced as "Pentium Ready" and can be implemented as a single or dual socket solution.

- **Single socket solution** — In single socket solutions, system come with the original 486 microprocessor installed in the upgrade socket (socket 2 or socket 3). The user simply removes the original 486 processor and replaces it with the Pentium OverDrive processor. The OverDrive processors implement active cooling mechanisms to ensure that the parts do not overheat.

- **Dual socket solution** — The 486DX2 and Pentium OverDrive processors include a UP# (upgrade present) pin. This pin is normally pulled up to 5vdc with a pullup resistor internal to the 486DX2. When a Pentium OverDrive processor is installed in the second socket, the UP# signal is asserted by the OverDrive processor, causing the 486DX2 to float its outputs and reduce power consumption.

The Pentium OverDrive processors contain an active heat sink with a fail safe mechansim that can signal the processor to reduce its internal core clock frequency if the fan speed falls below the specified RPM limit.

Note that the 486DX2 is a 5vdc processor, whereas, the 486DX4 is a 3.3vdc processor. (See Socket Six.)

Socket Four

Socket four is designed to provide upgrade capability in systems based on the 5vdc Pentium 60 and 66MHz systems. The socket is pin compatible with the Pentium 60/66MHz processors, however some signals implemented on the Pentium processors are not included in the Pentium OverDrive processor. The pins that have been removed include:

- IU, IV and IBT
- BT3:BT0

The CPUID instruction used to obtain processor-specific information will return the contents of the CPUID register as it does with Pentium 60/66MHz products. However the register definition has been extended to include a type field that defines the "turbo-upgrade" classification. This Pentium OverDrive processor wills also employ a fan/heatsink to dissipate heat.

Socket Five

Socket five is designed for use in the 3.3vdc P54C systems and is pin compatible with the P54C processors. The upgrade socket is a 320 pin SPGA ZIF socket. It can be implemented in a single or dual socket configuration.

- **Single socket implementions** include a single upgrade socket that initially contains a P54C processor. This single processor system can be later upgraded with a P54C OverDrive processor, by simply removing the original P54C and replacing it with the OverDrive processor.

- **Dual socket implementations with one upgrade socket** include a 296 pin socket (does not support upgrade processor) for the primary P54C processor and socket 5. Another P54C processor can be inserted into the upgrade socket, or it can be populated with an OverDrive processor. When populated with another P54C processor (dual processor) the system can support dual processing. When populated with a P54C OverDrive processor the OverDrive processor takes over as the primary CPU and disables the P54C processor.

- **Dual socket implementation with two upgrade sockets** will typically ship with a single P54C processor installed in the first upgrade socket. That processor can be replaced with an OverDrive processor to upgrade the single processor implementation. Alternatively, another P54C processor can be inserted into the second upgrade socket for dual processor support, or it can be populated with an OverDrive processor for a uniprocessing upgrade.

The OverDrive processor also defines a FANFAIL input signal that indicates to the processor that the fan RPM has slowed to the point that it no longer provides sufficient cooling. When asserted, this signal causes the OverDrive processor to reduce power consumption. The signal originates from the processor's fan/heatsink assembly and connects directly to the processor's core. The FANFAIL signal is not accessible and cannot be used by the system designer. FANFAIL conditions can be monitored via the Machine Check Type Register. An additional bit called THERR (thermal error, bit 5) is set when the FANFAIL signal is asserted.

Socket Six

Socket six is an upgrade socket intended to be implemented in the 3.3vdc 486DX4 systems. This socket permits the installation of future Pentium Over-Drive processors that operate at 3.3vdc. Note that socket six is designed for 3.3vdc operation only. Socket three may also used in 486DX4 systems since it can operate in both 3.3vdc and 5vdc systems.

Appendices

Appendix A: Glossary

4MB pages. The Pentium processor permits page sizes of both 4KB and 4MB. The new 4MB page size improves the TLB hit rate.

Address Bus. The address bus used by the Pentium processors consists of A31:A3 and BE7#:BE0#.

Address parity. The Pentium processor generates even address parity based on address lines A31:A5. Address parity is generated on all write transfers and checked during external snoops.

Address Translation. The process of converting linear addresses to physical address when the processor is operating with paging enabled.

Allocate-on-write. A write policy implemented by some cache controllers in which a write miss results in a cache line fill operation. The end result is that the target memory location is updated by the write and a copy of the cache line and the cache controller automatically read from memory and stored in cache. Not supported by the Pentium processor.

APIC. The Advanced Programmable Interrupt Controller, or APIC, provides interrupt support for SMP implementations. The APIC system consists of two distinct elements: the I/O APIC and the Local APIC (integrated into the P54C processors.

APIC bus. The three-wire bus (Pentium based systems) that connects the all APIC agents, allowing transfer of interrupts and messages.

APIC ID. The unique ID used by all APIC agents during APIC bus transfers to identify the target agent.

Auto-halt restart. An SMM feature allowing the processor to re-execute the HALT instruction upon exiting SMM, if the processor was in the halt state when the SMI# pin was asserted, or under software control the processor may be directed to execute the instruction following the halt instruction.

BIST (Built-in Self Test). This automatic self-test is run by the processor when RESET is removed and the INIT signal is asserted.

Boundary scan. This is a test procedure that uses the Pentium processor's test access port (TAP) interface to perform functional tests, typically used in manufacturing test.

Branch prediction. The mechanism used by the Pentium processor to determine whether or not a conditional branch will take the predicted branch.

Branch target buffer. The buffer used employed by the branch prediction mechanism to store branch target addresses of branch instructions that have previously executed.

Branch trace message. A special cycle performed by the Pentium processor to facilitate execution tracing. This special cycle is performed when the TR bit in TR12 is set and a branch instruction is taken by the processor. This message cycle broadcasts the linear address of the branch target's location.

Buffered write-through. A write policy employed by cache controllers that latches (buffers) write operations, returns ready to the processor (permitting it to continue executing instructions), and writes the data on through to external memory when it has time.

Built-in self test. See BIST

Burst bus cycles. A bus cycle performed by the Pentium processor that can transfer four quadwords of data in consecutive processor bus clock ticks. In the Pentium processor, burst transfers are supported only for transfers to (cache line fill cycles) and from (cache write-back cycles) the cache

Burst linefill sequence. The sequence of quadword address locations that the processor expects to be returned during a burst cache line fill. Also called toggle addressing.

Bus concurrency. A single computer system having the ability to perform simultaneous operations over isolated buses.

Bus cycle control signals. The signals used by the processor to define and control transactions that take place over the processor's local bus.

Bus frequency selection. This refers to the ability of some Pentium processors to select the bus to core frequency ratio to be used by the processor.

Bus snooping. A process used by cache controllers to monitor memory address locations being accessed by other bus masters in a system, which will potentially result in cache incoherency between it contents and other copies of the same location.

Bus unit. The processor unit that interfaces the processor core to external devices.

Cache coherency. This term refers to the state of a memory cache and system memory which ensures that the latest contents of a memory location is always supplied to a requester.

Cache consistency. See cache coherency.

Cache disable (CD). A bit within control register zero (CR0) in the Pentium processor that, in conjunction with the NW bit, controls the operation of the internal caches.

Cache Line. The minimum block of data/code that a cache controller reads and maintains within its memory cache.

Cache line-fill request. A request made by a cache controller to read a cache line from external memory.

Cache controller. Logic that performs the operations necessary to read, store and maintain copies of memory locations that it is requested to supply.

Cache not write-through (NW). A bit within control register zero (CR0) in the Pentium processor that, in conjunction with the CD bit, controls the operation of the internal caches.

Cache read hit. A read operation submitted to a cache subsystem, whose memory location resides in the memory cache, resulting in fast access.

Cache snooping. See snooping

Cache write hit. A write operation submitted to a cache subsystem, whose location resides within the memory cache, resulting in fast access.

Cache write miss. A write operation submitted to a cache subsystem, whose address location is not found within cache memory.

Checker processor. A Pentium processor that monitors all bus activity generated by a second (master) processor. A checker processor converts its outputs to inputs when configured as checkers, and compares the signals that it would have driven if it were the master to the master's outputs. Any variation is reported via the checker's IERR# signal.

Clean data. Data contained within a memory cache that has not been modified. The cache location and system memory location are consistent.

CLI (Clear Interrupt Enable). An x86 instruction that causes the processor to ignore (mask) its interrupt request input (INTR)

CMPXCHG8B (Compare and Exchange Eight Bytes). This Pentium processor instruction reads 8 bytes of data from memory and compares it with 8 bytes of information contained in general registers EAX and EDX. This instruction is not supported on previous x86 processors.

Code cache. A dedicated memory cache inside the Pentium processor, used to store only instructions.

Control registers. Registers inside the Pentium processor that control various aspects of the CPUs operations.

CPUID (CPU Identification). This new instruction permits the programmer to read the contents of the CPUID register to determine the processor class, type and revision.

CR4 (Control Register four). This register enables/disables new features, or extensions, implemented by the Pentium processor.

D1 stage. Stage one decode within the processors instruction pipeline where the opcodes are identified and the instruction pairing test is performed.

D2 stage. Stage two decode within the processors instruction pipeline where addresses are formed when memory operands are accessed.

Data bus steering. The process of transferring bytes of data between data paths to ensure information gets to the intended destination. This is sometimes required when data is transferred between devices of differing sizes. The Pentium processor contains no data bus steering logic, therefore it must be implemented in external logic.

Data cache. An internal cache within the Pentium processor that is dedicated for data storage only.

Cache Directory. Memory array employed by cache subsystems that store the address location of the data stored in each cache line.

Data Parity. The parity bits generated by the Pentium processor for each byte of data written by the processor. Data parity is checked by the processor during read operations.

Debug control register. Register inside the processor that is used to set up the breakpoints that are loaded into the debug registers.

Debug exception. An internal interrupt generated by the processor when a breakpoint match has been detected by one of the breakpoint registers.

Debug Mode Control register. Register inside the Pentium processor that is used to control the use of the breakpoint and performance monitoring output pins.

Debug port. An interface provided by the Pentium processor that permits implementation of a special feature debug tool that can probe the processors internal registers.

Delivery mode. A software selectable mode that specifies the type of interrupt or message being sent by an APIC agent over the APIC bus.

Destination Format Register. See DFR

Destination mode. A software selectable mode that specifies the target APIC agent or agents of a given APIC bus transfer.

DFR (Destination Format Register). A local APIC register that determines the format of the destination field used during an APIC bus transfer.

Dirty line. A cache memory line that has been updated by not written through to memory, leaving old (stale) data in main memory.

Dual processor. The secondary processor in a pair of P54C dual processor implementation is called the dual processor. The primary processor boots first, followed by the secondary, or dual processor. The dual processor waits for the primary processor to command it (via an APIC Startup message) to perform the initialization.

Edge triggered interrupts. Interrupts inputs that are recognized by the I/O APIC on the low to high transition.

End of interrupt. See EOI

EOI command. End of interrupt command. A command performed by the interrupt service routine to cause the interrupt to be cleared, so it won't be serviced again. The interrupt is cleared at either the 8259 interrupt controller, within the local APIC, or at the I/O APIC depending on the source and trigger mode used.

EOI message cycle. An APIC message transfer that directs the I/O APIC to clear a level-triggered interrupt.

Error interrupt. A local APIC interrupt used to report errors resulting from failed APIC bus transfers.

Exclusive state. A MESI state indicating that no other cache controllers possess a copy of this cache line, therefore it is owned exclusively by this cache.

Execution priority. The priority of code being executed by the processor relative to the hardware interrupt request priorities. This execution priority is updated by the operating system to specify an interrupt priority threshold for determining which interrupts should be allowed to interrupt the processor core and which should be masked until execution priority is reduced.

Execution tracing. The process of tracking instructions as they execute inside the Pentium processor.

External cache. A cache external to the processor.

First level cache. A cache integrated into the processor, making it the first cache to be accessed during a memory read or write operation.

FPU. Floating-Point Unit. The FPU is integrated into the Pentium processor.

Flush acknowledge special cycle. This special cycle is run by the Pentium processor in response to the FLUSH# pin having been asserted. This causes the processor to write-back all modified lines to memory, invalidate all cache entries and perform a flush acknowledge special cycle to notify external logic that the operation has completed.

Focus processor. A processor that has an interrupt pending execution when another interrupt request from the same device is transferred over the APIC bus is said to be the focus of the interrupt. The focus processor always accepts interrupt requests from devices they already have interrupt request pending for.

Functional redundancy checking. The process employed by the Pentium processors that permits one processor (a checker) to monitor signals output the another (the master) to detect potential error conditions.

History bits. Attribute bits used in conjunction with the Branch Target Buffer (BTB) to track the history of branch operations, allowing branch instructions to be predicted dynamically.

Hit rate. The ratio of the number of cache hits to total number of memory operations performed.

I/O instruction restart. The SMM feature that permits the processor to re-execute an I/O instruction (the instruction that accessed a device that was powered down, causing entry to SMM) upon returning from SMM.

ICR (Interrupt Command Register). This register is used by the programmer to initiate an inter-processor interrupt (IPI). Values written into this register specify the type of interrupt or message to be transferred, along with the target processor.

Init level de-assert IPI. An APIC message transfer that commands all APIC agents to initialize their APIC IDs to the default values.

Inquire cycles. A snoop transaction performed by the Pentium processor as directed by external logic. The snoop results are reported via the HIT# and HITM# signals.

In-service register. A register contained inside the local APIC that indicates the interrupts currently being serviced. In 8259 interrupts environments, this register is contained inside the 8259 interrupt controller.

Instruction pairing. The process implemented by the Pentium processors to execute two instructions in parallel using the dual instruction pipeline.

Instruction pipeline. The path taken by an instruction after being fetched from memory until its execution completes. The Pentium processor employs a five stage instruction pipeline, allowing five instructions to execute simultaneously, each at different stages.

Internal snooping. the split caches (code and data) inside the Pentium processor snoop each others accesses to memory. Internal snoop hits result in the invalidation of the cache line.

Inter processor cache snooping. Memory snooping that takes place between the primary and dual processor in a dual processor implementation. This insures that the dual processors maintain cache coherency.

Inter-processor cycle pipelining. The ability of both processors in a dual processor implementation to have a bus cycle running on the buses at the same time.

Inter-processor interrupts. See IPI

Interrupt acknowledge bus cycles. The two back-to-back cycles performed by x86 processors, to acknowledge 8259 interrupt requests.

Interrupt command register. See ICR

Interrupt request register. A register inside the 8259 interrupt controller and the Local APIC that keeps track of all interrupt requests currently pending servicing.

Invalid state. A MESI state indication that a cache line currently contain no valid data.

INVD. (Invalidate) An instruction that commands the internal caches inside the processor to invalidate all entries. Modified data is not written back to memory before the cache is invalidated, therefore, modified data contained in the Pentium's data cache will be lost when this instruction is executed.

I/O APIC. An APIC subsystem component that connects to the hardware interrupt request lines and sends interrupts request to the local APICs via the APIC bus.

IPI (Inter-processor Interrupt). Software initiated interrupts or messages sent between processors via the APIC bus.

L1 cache. See first level cache

L2 cache. See second level cache

Level-triggered interrupts. Interrupt requests to the I/O APIC module that are recognized by a high level on the input.

Line fill. The action taken by a memory cache when encountering a cache miss to a cacheable memory location.

Local APIC. The interrupt subsystem logic used to receive interrupt requests from the I/O APIC and transfer them to the processor core when the processor's execution priority permits.

Local interrupts. Interrupts requests handled directly by the local APIC. The local interrupts are comprised of two local interrupt pins (LINT0 and LINT1) along with a timer and an error each generated within the local APIC.

Local timer. A timer inside the local APIC that can be programmed under software control to generate either one-shot or periodic interrupt requests to the processor.

Local vector table (LVT). A vector table included in the local APIC that can be programmed with the vectors for each of the APIC's four local interrupts.

Logical destination register (LDR). Specifies the logical ID to be used during logical destination mode transfers. This register is programmed under software control specifies a destination ID.

Look-aside cache. A cache memory design in which the cache controller sets in parallel with main system memory. When memory is addressed both the cache controller and system memory are addressed. Compare Look-through.

Look-through cache. A cache memory design in which the cache controller is in series between the processor and main system memory. Memory request go first to the cache controller, which looks through its internal cache to determine if the request is a hit or miss. If the access hits the cache, information is returned to the processor and no bus cycle appears on the system buses. If the access misses the cache, the bus transaction is passed on to main system memory. Compare Look-aside.

Lowest-priority arbitration. An APIC delivery mode in which more than one processor (local APIC) is listed in the destination. Lowest-priority arbitration specifies that all processors listed in the destination should perform an arbitration procedure that identifies the processor that is currently executing the lowest priority code, and therefore the processor that should accept and service the interrupt request.

LRM. (Least Recent Master). In a dual processor implementation specifies the processor currently not having ownership of the local bus.

LRU (Least Recently Used) algorithm. Used by the Pentium processor to determine which cache line is to overwritten with newer data.

Machine check registers. Registers within the Pentium processor used to store the address and transaction type of a failed bus cycle when BUSCHK# is asserted or the address and transaction type of a bus cycle that encountered a data parity error when the PEN# signal is asserted.

Machine check enable. See MCE

Machine check exception. A new exception generated by the Pentium processor when the MCE bit is set and one of the condition cause the machine check register to be loaded. (See machine check registers.)

MCAR (Machine Check Address Register) See machine check registers.

Pentium Processor System Architecture

MCE. Machine check enable. This bit in CR4 enables the machine check exception. This exception occurs when data parity errors are detected and PEN# is asserted, and when the BUSCHK# signal is asserted.

MCTR. Machine Check Type Register (See machine check registers.)

MESI Model. A cache coherency model in which a cache line may be stored in any one of four states: Modified, Exclusive, Shared and Invalid. See each state for definitions.

Microcode Control ROM. The ROM inside x86 processors that contains the processor commands necessary to execute complex instructions.

Modified line. A cache line that has been updated due to a write hit in the cache. Also known as a dirty line.

MRM (Most Recent Master). In a dual processor implementation, the MRM is the processor that currently owns the bus or owned the bus last.

NCA logic (Non-cacheable Address logic). Programmable logic that performs a lookup on every memory access to determine if the address is cacheable from the system perspective. System software programs the NCA logic with the address ranges that should not be cached.

Non-Cacheable Address logic. See NCA logic.

OverDrive processor. A processor, designed to replace the original Pentium processor, to obtain higher performance.

OverDrive socket. A socket designed to accept both the original Pentium processor and a future OverDrive processor.

P54C. Intel's code name for the Pentium 90 and 100MHz processors.

Page Cache Disable. (PCD) A bit defined for the Page Table Entries that specify whether a page of memory should be cached or not cached, when the processor has paging enabled. This bit is set by the operating system.

Page Directory. A data structure set up by the operating system that defines the location of Page Tables. The page directory and page tables are needed to translate linear to physical addresses when paging is enabled.

Page size extension. The Pentium extension that allows 4MB pages to be implemented.

Page Table. Data structure set up by the operating system to map the physical location of memory pages, corresponding to each page of linear address space.

Paging unit. A portion of the processor's memory management unit used to support the processor's paging mechanism.

Pairability check. A check performed by the processor in the decode one stage of the instruction pipeline to determine if two instructions can be paired in compliance with the Pentium processor's instruction pairing rules. If pairable both instruction will execute in parallel through the dual instruction pipeline.

Pipelined cycles. Cycles that are driven to the bus before the current bus cycle ends. This results in two cycles being performed at the same time to increase performance. Pipelined cycles are only possible when the target device supports pipelining, by asserting the NA# signal.

PPR (Processor Priority Register). This register contains the highest processor priority and is used to determine whether and interrupt request with a given priority can interrupt the processor. An interrupt request whose interrupt priority is higher than the PPR value is allowed to interrupt the processor core.

Prefetch buffers. Buffers used to store instructions that have been fetched from memory. The Pentium processor employs two 64 byte buffers that alternate operation each time a branch predication is made by the BTB. The prefetch buffers submit consecutive instructions to the dual pipeline.

Prefetcher. Performs speculative in-line memory reads, to obtain the next instructions to be executed. Operates on the assumption that the instruction stream resides in sequentially in memory.

Primary processor. The processor which performs system initialization in a dual processor configuration and is responsible for sending an Startup message to the dual processor.

Private bus. A bus implemented in the P54C processors to support dual processor operation. The private bus support dual processor cache coherency and arbitration.

Probe mode. A debug mode supported by the Pentium processor that allows a debug, which interfaces directly with the processor, to probe internal registers.

Processor execution priority. See execution priority.

Processor priority register. See PPR

RDMSR. Read Model Specific Register instruction. This instruction is used to access a variety of registers within the Pentium processor. These registers, some documented publicly and some under non-closure, involve the following functionality: CPI identification, Performance Monitoring, Testability, Execution Tracing and Machine Check Errors.

Read model-specific register instruction. See RDMSR.

Remote read IPI. A inter-processor interrupt generated by the local APIC that provides the software programmer the ability to read the register contents of a local APIC in another processor.

RSM (Return from System Management Mode) instruction. This instruction is the last instruction executed by the SMM handler. When executed, the processor returns to normal program execution.

Second level cache. An external cache implemented with a processor that contains an internal cache is called a second level cache or L2 cache.

Shutdown special cycle. A special cycle performed by the Pentium processor when it encounters a triple fault condition, or has encountered an internal parity error.

Simple instruction. An instruction that is a candidate for being paired with another instruction. Simple instructions are hardwire decoded and make no access to the micro-control ROM.

SMI handler. The System management interrupt service routine. This routine is responsible for determining the cause of the SMI and performing the requisite tasks. Upon completion, it executes the RSM instruction.

SMI (System management Interrupt). Causes the processor to enter the SMM mode of operation.

SMM (System Management Mode). This operational mode permits tasks such as power management relatively easy to implement, since the address space that is accessed to perform such tasks is transparent to the operating system and application programs.

SMM base address. The base address at which the SMRAM resides within the 1MB of real address space.

Appendix A: Glossary

SMM Revision Identifier. A register value that reflects the SMM extensions supported by a particular processor.

SMM state save map. The processor's current state (context) is mapped to SMRAM before entering SMM, permitting the return to the interrupted program. When the RSM instruction executes the state save map is restored to the processor and it continues program execution at the point of interruption.

SMRAM (System Management RAM). Used to implement the SMI handler and store the processor's state.

Snarf. A cache memory implementation that snoops memory write transfers and automatically updates, rather than invalidating, the cache entries that hit the cache.

Snooping. A technique used by cache memory controllers to monitor the system buses to detect an access to main memory that might cause a cache consistency problem.

Special cycles. Transaction broadcast on the Pentium processor's local bus to indicate one of the following conditions: halt, shutdown, flush (INVD or WBINVD instruction executed), write-back (WBINVD instruction executed), flush acknowledge (FLUSH# pin asserted) branch trace message (branch taken by processor and tracing enabled) or the stop grant message (in response to STPCLK# being asserted, P54C only).

Split-line access. Two address submitted to the code cache simultaneously to fetch the upper half of line N and the lower half of line N+1. This permits the prefetcher to access an instruction that crosses a cache line boundary in a single cache memory access.

StartUp IPI. An APIC transfer used by the primary processor to send a startup address to the dual processor. The dual processor then begins its initialization by fetching and executing code beginning at the startup address.

State save map. See SMM state save map.

Stop grant state. The processor enters the stop grant state to notify external logic that it has stopped its internal clock in response to the STPCLK# signal being asserted.

Strong write ordering. A policy ensuring that memory writes appear externally on the processor's buses in the same order as the instruction causing the writes were executed. The Pentium processor enforces strong ordering.

Strongly not taken. A branch predication history state indicating that the branch has a strong history of correctly predicted being taken. The next prediction will again be that the instruction will be taken.

Strongly not taken. A branch predication history state indicating that the branch has a strong history of correctly predicted being not taken. The next prediction will again be that the instruction will not be taken.

System management mode. See SMM

TAP (Test Access Port). A five signal serial interface that supports boundary scan testing

Task priority register. See TPR.

Test access port. See TAP.

Tightly-Coupled Processors. Multiple processors that share the same memory subsystem.

Time stamp disable. See TSD.

Timer interrupt. See Local timer.

Time-stamp counters. Counters within the Pentium processor that provide statistical information about internal hardware events that impact performance.

TPR (Task Priority Register). A register containing the execution priority of instruction that are currently executing or pending execution by the operating system or application. This value is updated by the operating system to specify the priority of code being executed relative to hardware interrupt priorities. The TPR value provides a priority threshold used by the local APIC to determine which interrupts should be dispatched to the processor core for servicing.

Trigger mode register (TMR). This APIC register contains a bit for each interrupt pending within the Interrupt Request Register to indicate the trigger mode that was used for each respective interrupt request. Level triggered interrupts require that an EOI special cycle be performed over the APIC bus to notify the I/O APIC that the interrupt can be cleared.

TSD (Time Stamp Disable). A enable/disable bit in CR4 used to control access to the time stamp functions.

U and V pipelines. Name given by Intel to the instruction pipelines that comprise the dual instruction pipeline.

VIF (Virtual Interrupt Flag). Bit added to the Eflags register. Use of this bit is not disclosed by Intel.

VIP (Virtual Interrupt Pending). Bit added to the Eflags register. Use of this bit is not disclosed by Intel.

WBINVD (Write-Back and Invalidate) instruction. This instruction causes all modified lines to be written back to memory, followed by all cache lines being invalidated. The Pentium processor performs a write-back special cycle, followed by a flush special cycle upon completing execution of this instruction.

Weakly not taken. A branch predication history state indicating that the branch has a weak history of correct prediction. The next prediction will be that the instruction will not be taken. If the predication is incorrect, the next prediction will switch to the opposite prediction. If the prediction is correct the prediction is reinforced.

Weakly taken. A branch predication history state indicating that the branch has a weak history of correct prediction. The next prediction will be that the instruction will be taken. However, a wrong prediction will cause the branch prediction to change its decision and predict the branch to be weakly not taken. If the prediction is correct the prediction is reinforced.

Write policy. The method employed by a cache controller to maintain cache coherency on memory write operations.

Write-back policy. A cache coherency policy that updates its cache on memory write operations, but does not write the data on through to external memory. Such caches implement modified, or dirty bits to track which locations contain the latest information (and which memory location contain stale data). The write-back policy requires that cache controllers snoop both memory reads and writes, and either back the bus master off to prevent access to a location containing stale data, or employ snarfing to ensure other bus masters always obtain the latest data.

Write-back special cycle. A special cycle performed by the Pentium processor when a WBINVD instruction is executed. The write-back special cycle will be performed after the processor has written all modified cache lines back to memory, followed by a flush special cycle.

Write-once policy. A write policy that forces the first write to a cache line to be written through to external memory. Subsequent writes update the cache but are not written through to external memory, thus the cache line is marked modified.

Write-through cache. A cache write policy that guarantees cache coherency by forcing all write operation to update external memory.

WRMSR (Write Model Specific Register) instruction. This instruction is used to access a variety of registers within the Pentium processor. These registers, some documented publicly and some under non-closure, involve the following functions: CPU identification, Performance Monitoring, Testability, Execution Tracing and Machine Check Errors.

ZIF socket. A zero insertion force socket designed for easy removal and insertion of parts. ZIF sockets are used by the Pentium OverDrive sockets.

Appendix B: Pentium Signal Glossary

Signal Name (s)	Input/Output P5	P54C	
A20M#	I	I	When the **Address Bit 20 Mask** pin is active, the Pentium microprocessor masks physical address bit 20 (A20) before performing a lookup to the internal cache or driving a memory bus cycle onto the buses. A20M# emulates the address wrap-around at the 1MB boundary that occurs on the 8086/8088. This pin should only be asserted by external logic when the microprocessor is in Real Mode.
A31:A5	I/O	I/O	A31:A3 comprise the Pentium microprocessor's address bus. When the Pentium processor wishes to address an external device, the address is driven out onto the address bus. Address bits 0, 1 and 2 do not exist and should always be treated as if zero. This means that the Pentium processor is only capable of placing the address of every eighth location on the address bus (0, 8, 10, 18, etc.). This is known as the quadword address , and identifies a group of eight locations starting at the indicated address. This group of eight locations is known as a quadword. The microprocessor uses the eight Byte Enable outputs, BE7#:BE0#, to indicate which of the four locations in the quadword it wishes to communicate with and to also indicate the data path to be used when communicating with each location in the quadword. A3 and A4 are output-only, while A31:A5 are bidirectional. A31:A5 are used to drive cache line addresses into the microprocessor during cache line invalidations (bus snooping).
A4:A3	O	O	
ADS#	O	I/O	When active, the **Address Status** output indicates that a valid bus cycle definition and address are available on the Bus Cycle Definition and address bus lines.

Pentium Processor System Architecture

Signal Name (s)	Input/Output P5	P54C	
AHOLD	I	I	The **Address Hold Request** input allows another bus master access to the Pentium microprocessor's address bus for a cache invalidation, back invalidation, or inquire cycle. These cycle are necessary ensure that consistency is maintained between the Pentium microprocessor's internal caches, the level 2 cache, other bus master caches and main memory. In response to the assertion of AHOLD, the Pentium processor will stop driving its address bus in the clock following AHOLD going active. Only the address bus will be floated during Address Hold. The remainder of the buses will remain active. See also EADS# below.
AP	I/O	I/O	The Pentium process generates **address parity** during memory write operations and checks address parity during cache invalidation cycles (address bus snooping). Address parity is generated and checked only on address lines A31:A5 since A4 and A3 are not used during address snooping. AP is the Address Parity bit that is output during memory write operations. The state of the AP signal ensures that even parity is being generated by the Pentium processor (A31:A5). The AP signal is sampled during cache invalidation cycles along with the address to ensure that even parity is returned. The AP bit should be asserted along with the address when EADS# is active.
APCHK#	O	O	The Pentium processor asserts the **Address Parity Check** output when an address bus parity error is detected during a cache invalidation cycle. APCHK# is asserted 2 clock cycles after EADS# is sampled active. APCHK# remains active for one clock cycle.
[APICEN] or PICD1	NA	**I/O**	**APIC Enable.** During initialization, when RESET is deasserted, the processor samples this pin to determine if the internal APIC is enabled (1 = APIC enabled). During ordinary operation, this pin carries data to and from the local APIC.
BE0#	O	0	**Byte Enable, Path 0.** Asserted by the microprocessor to indicate that the Pentium processor wishes to perform a transfer between itself and the first location (byte 0) in the currently addressed quadword over the first data path, D7:D0.
BE1#	O	O	**Byte Enable, Path 1.** Asserted by the microprocessor to indicate that the Pentium processor wishes to perform a transfer between itself and the second location (byte 1) in the currently addressed quadword over the second data path, D15:D8.

Signal Name (s)	Input/Output		
	P5	**P54C**	
BE2#	O	O	**Byte Enable, Path 2.** Asserted by the microprocessor to indicate that the Pentium processor wishes to perform a transfer between itself and the third location (byte 2) in the currently addressed quadword over the third data path, D23:D16.
BE3#	O	O	**Byte Enable, Path 3.** Asserted by the microprocessor to indicate that the Pentium processor wishes to perform a transfer between itself and the fourth location (byte 3) in the currently addressed quadword over the fourth data path, D31:D24
BE4#	O	O	**Byte Enable, Path 4.** Asserted by the microprocessor to indicate that the Pentium processor wishes to perform a transfer between itself and the fifth location (byte 4) in the currently addressed quadword over the fifth data path, D39:D32.
BE5#	O	O	**Byte Enable, Path 5.** Asserted by the microprocessor to indicate that the Pentium processor wishes to perform a transfer between itself and the sixth location (byte 5) in the currently addressed quadword over the sixth data path, D47:D40.
BE6#	O	O	**Byte Enable, Path 6.** Asserted by the microprocessor to indicate that the Pentium processor wishes to perform a transfer between itself and the seventh location (byte 6) in the currently addressed quadword over the seventh data path, D55:D48.
BE7#	O	O	**Byte Enable, Path 7.** Asserted by the microprocessor to indicate that the Pentium processor wishes to perform a transfer between itself and the eighth location (byte 7) in the currently addressed quadword over the eighth data path, D63:D56.
BF	NA	I	The **bus frequency** signal (BF) determines the I/O bus to processor core frequency ratio. When BF is strapped to Vcc the processor operates at a 2/3 (I/O bus to processor core) frequency ratio. When strapped to Vss, the processor operates at a 1/2 frequency ratio.
BOFF#	I	I	**Backoff** is used to ensure that the processor doesn't fetch stale data from main memory. The Backoff input forces the Pentium microprocessor to float its buses in the next clock. The microprocessor will disconnect itself from its external buses, but will not assert HLDA. BOFF# has a higher priority than RDY# or BRDY#. If a bus cycle was in progress when BOFF# was asserted, the bus cycle will be restarted when BOFF# is deasserted.
BP3:2	O	O	The **BreakPoint** outputs indicate that a breakpoint match has been detected through the breakpoint registers. The BP3:BP0 signals correspond directly to breakpoint matches associated with registers DR3:DR0.

Signal Name (s)	Input/Output P5	P54C	
BP/PM1:0	O	O	**Breakpoint and Performance Monitoring** pins 1:0 are multiplexed depending on the state of the PB1:0 bits in the Debug Control register.
BRDY#	I	I	The **Burst Ready** input indicates that the currently addressed device has presented valid data on the data bus pins in response to a read or that the currently addressed device has accepted data from the Pentium processor in response to a write.
BRDYC#	I	I	The **Burst Ready Cache** input indicates that the level 2 cache has presented valid data on the data bus pins in response to a read or that the level 2 cache has accepted data from the Pentium processor in response to a write.
BREQ	O	O	The Internal Cycle Pending output indicates that the Pentium microprocessor has a **bus cycle request** pending. BREQ is generated whether or not the Pentium microprocessor is currently the bus master. It is used by a CPU bus arbitrator in a multiple-processor system to determine which processors are currently requesting the host bus.
BT3:BT0	O	NA	The **Branch Trace 3:0** lines are driven during a branch trace special cycle. BT2:BT0 provide address bits A2:A0 of the linear address for the branch target. BT3 specifies the default operand size: either 16-bits (low) or 32-bits (high).
BUSCHK#	I	I	The **Bus Check** signal allows system designers to notify the Pentium microprocessor if a bus cycle has not completed successfully. The microprocessor will automatically latch the address and control signals into the internal machine check registers, and if the "Machine Check Enable (MCE) bit in Control Register 4 (CR4) is set an machine check exception will be generated.
CACHE#	O	I/O	The CACHE# signal is active when information is being transferred between external memory and an internal cache. During memory read bus cycles, an active CACHE# signal indicates that the address is cacheable inside the Pentium processor and that the returned data will be placed in an internal cache unless the KEN# signal is sampled inactive. During a writeback cycle, CACHE# is active indicating a burst writeback cycle will be performed. CACHE# will not be active on a write miss since the Pentium processor does not support "allocate on write" operations (cache line fills resulting from write misses).

Signal Name (s)	Input/Output P5	P54C	
CLK	I	I	**Clock** provides the fundamental timing and the internal operating frequency for the Pentium microprocessor. Unlike the double-frequency clock necessary for proper operation of some Intel microprocessors, this clock is not divided by two by the microprocessor. This was done to simplify system design and minimize the problems inherent in the design of high frequency systems.
CPUTYP	NA	I	**CPU Type** pin. Sampled by the processor at the trailing-edge of RESET to determine whether it is the primary or the dual (secondary) processor. CPUTYP should be strapped low in a single processor environment or when the processor is the primary of processor pair. CPUTYP should be strapped high if the processor is the dual, or secondary, processor of a dual processor system.
D7:D0	I/O	I/O	**Data path zero** is used to transfer data between the Pentium processor and the first location (byte 0) in the currently addressed quadword. See also A31:A3 and BE0#.
D15:D8	I/O	I/O	**Data path one** is used to transfer data between the Pentium processor and the second location (byte 1) in the currently addressed quadword. See also A31:A3 and BE1#.
D23:D16	I/O	I/O	**Data path two** is used to transfer data between the Pentium processor and the third location (byte 2) in the currently addressed quadword. See also A31:A3 and BE2#.
D31:D24	I/O	I/O	**Data path three** is used to transfer data between the Pentium processor and the fourth location (byte 3) in the currently addressed quadword. See also A31:A3 and BE3#.
D39:D32	I/O	I/O	**Data path four** is used to transfer data between the Pentium processor and the fifth location (byte 4) in the currently addressed quadword. See also A31:A3 and BE4#.
D47:D40	I/O	I/O	**Data path five** is used to transfer data between the Pentium processor and the sixth location (byte 5) in the currently addressed quadword. See also A31:A3 and BE5#.
D55:D48	I/O	I/O	**Data path six** is used to transfer data between the Pentium processor and the seventh location (byte 6) in the currently addressed quadword. See also A31:A3 and BE6#.
D63:D56	I/O	I/O	**Data path seven** is used to transfer data between the Pentium processor and the eighth location (byte 7) in the currently addressed quadword. See also A31:A3 and BE7#.

Signal Name (s)	Input/Output P5	P54C	
D/C#	O	I/O	**Data or Control.** At the start of a bus cycle, the Pentium processor sets this line high if data (not code) will be transferred during the current bus cycle. It sets D/C# low if the current bus cycle is not a data transfer bus cycle (Interrupt Acknowledge, Halt/Special or a code read bus cycle).
D/P#	NA	O	**Dual/Primary.** This signal is an output of the primary processor and is not used by the dual processor. It is asserted (low) by the primary processor when it has acquired private bus ownership and has initiated a bus cycle. It is de asserted (high) by the primary processor when it is not the private bus master.
DP0	I/O	I/O	This is the **parity bit for data path 0**, D7:D0. Even data parity is generated on all write bus cycles and is checked on all read bus cycles. If a parity error is detected on a read operation, the Pentium processor will assert its PCHK# output. The action taken by the Pentium processor depends on the state of the Parity Enable input (PEN#). See PEN# below.
DP1	I/O	I/O	**Parity bit for data path 1**, D15:D8. See explanation of DP0.
DP2	I/O	I/O	**Parity bit for data path 2**, D23:D16. See explanation of DP0.
DP3	I/O	I/O	**Parity bit for data path 3**, D31:D24. See explanation of DP0.
DP4	I/O	I/O	**Parity bit for data path 4**, D39:D32. See explanation of DP0.
DP5	I/O	I/O	**Parity bit for data path 5**, D47:D40. See explanation of DP0.
DP6	I/O	I/O	**Parity bit for data path 6**, D55:D48. See explanation of DP0.
DP7	I/O	I/O	**Parity bit for data path 7**, D63:D56. See explanation of DP0.
[DPEN#] or PICD0	NA	I/O	**Dual Processor Enable.** If present, the dual processor asserts this pin during RESET. The primary processor samples the Dual Processor Enable signal when RESET is deasserted, to determine if a dual processor is present. During ordinary operation, this pin carries data to and from the local APIC.
EADS#	I	I	The **External Address Strobe** signal indicates that a valid external address has been driven onto the Pentium's A4:A31 address lines by another bus master. This address will be used to perform an internal cache snooping. As a result, if a cache directory entry indicates that a cache line has a copy of the addressed memory data (snoop hit). The action taken by the microprocessor depends on the type of snoop operation in progress, value of the state bits in the entry and the state of the INV line. Also see the description of AHOLD.

Signal Name (s)	Input/Output P5	P54C	
EWBE#	I	I	The **External Write Buffer Empty** signal is used to ensure that memory operations occur in order of execution (strong memory ordering). Sometimes cache system that employ write buffers, permit read operations to be ordered ahead of buffered writes causing bus cycles to be performed out of sequence from the actual execution sequence. The EWBE# signal provides a way to ensure that all buffered writes in external caches are completed before executing the next instruction, thus preserving the strong memory ordering.
FLUSH#	I	I	The **cache Flush** input forces the Pentium processor to flush the contents of its internal cache.
FERR#	O	O	The **Floating-Point Error** output pin is driven active when a floating-point error occurs. This pin has been included to remain compatible with DOS-oriented systems that use the ERROR output of the Numeric Co-Processor to generate IRQ13 when a Floating-Point error is encountered.
FRCMC#	I	I	The **Function Redundancy Checking Master/Checker#** pin is sampled by the Pentium microprocessor during RESET to determine whether the microprocessor should be configured as a functional redundancy master or checker. When configured as a master (FRCMC# high) the microprocessor operates in normal fashion, but when configured as a checker (FRCMC# low) the microprocessor monitors the output pins that are normally driven during master mode. These pins would be driven by another Pentium microprocessor that is configured in master mode.
HIT#	O	I/O	The Pentium microprocessor drives the HIT# signal active to indicate a snoop hit in either the internal code or data cache.
HITM#	O	I/O	The Pentium microprocessor drives the **Hit Modified** signal active to indicate a snoop hit to a modified line in the data cache. HITM# going active means that a writeback cycle must take place to update main memory; therefore the bus master accessing memory must be backed off the bus when HITM# is asserted.
HLDA	O	I/O	**Bus Hold Acknowledge**. See the description of HOLD above.

Signal Name (s)	Input/Output P5	P54C	
HOLD	I	I	The **Bus Hold Request** input allows another bus master to gain complete control of the Pentium's local buses. In response to HOLD going active, the Pentium processor will disconnect itself from most of its output pins after the current bus cycle completes. HLDA (Hold Acknowledge) is then asserted to inform the requesting bus master that is now the owner of the external bus structure and can run a bus cycle. The Pentium microprocessor will not be able to use the external buses again until the current bus master de-asserts HOLD.
IBT	O	NA	The **Instruction Branch Taken** signal is driven active for one clock cycle when the Pentium microprocessor executes an instruction resulting in an execution branch. When execution tracing is enabled, a branch trace special cycle will be run directly following the IBT signal.
IERR#	O	O	**Internal Error** is asserted when a parity error is encountered inside the Pentium microprocessor. IERR# is also asserted by the Pentium microprocessor when it is operating in "checker" mode and a mismatch is detected between the values sampled on the monitoring pins and the corresponding value computed internally.
IGNNE#	I	I	When the **Ignore Numeric Error** input is asserted by external logic, the Pentium microprocessor will ignore a numeric error and continue executing non-control floating-point instructions. When IGNNE# is inactive, the Pentium processor will freeze on a non-control floating-point instruction if a previous floating-point instruction caused an error. IGNNE# has no effect when the NE (Mask Numeric Error) bit in CR0 is set.
INIT	I	I	The Pentium microprocessor INIT input has the same effect as the RESET signal except that the following retain the values they had prior to INIT going active: • internal caches • model specific registers • floating point registers
INTR	I	I	This is the maskable **Interrupt Request** input. If interrupt recognition is enabled when INTR is asserted, the Pentium processor will service the interrupt request.

Signal Name (s)	Input/Output P5	P54C	
INV	I	I	The **INVALIDATE** input tells the Pentium microprocessor whether the cache line state should be marked invalidated (I) or shared (S) as a result of a snoop hit. In the case of a snoop during a write operation the INV signal will be active indicating that if a snoop hit occurs, the line should be invalidated. Conversely, the INV input is inactive during snoops that occur during read operations and the line should be marked as shared on a snoop hit.
IU	O	NA	The IU signal indicated that an instruction in the "u" pipeline has completed execution. The IBT signal cannot occur unless IU is active.
IV	O	NA	The IV signal indicated that an instruction in the "v" pipeline has completed execution. The IV signal cannot occur unless IU is also active, since and "v" pipeline instructions cannot complete independent of the "u" pipeline.
KEN#	I	I	The **Cache Enable** pin is sampled to determine if the current bus cycle is cacheable (from memory's point of view). When the Pentium processor generates a memory read bus cycle that the processor would like to cache and KEN# is sampled active, the bus cycle will be converted to a cache fill cycle. Returning KEN# active one clock before the last ready during the last read in the cache line fill will cause the line to be placed in the on-chip cache.
LINT0 or INTR	NA	I	If the processor's local APIC is enabled (APICEN is sampled asserted on training-edge of RESET), this is the LINT0 (**Local Interrupt 0**) input to the APIC. If the APIC is disabled, this is the processor's maskable interrupt request input, INTR.
LINT1 or NMI	NA	I	If the processor's local APIC is enabled (APICEN is sampled asserted on training-edge of RESET), this is the LINT1 (**Local Interrupt 1**) input to the APIC. If the APIC is disabled, this is the processor's non-maskable interrupt request input, NMI.
LOCK#	O	I/O	The LOCK# signal is asserted when the Pentium microprocessor wants to run multiple bus cycles without having the buses taken away by another bus master. When LOCK# is asserted the HOLD input will not be honored.

Signal Name (s)	Input/Output P5	P54C	
M/IO#	O	I/O	**Memory or I/O.** At the start of a bus cycle, the Pentium processor sets this line high if addressing a memory location and low if addressing an I/O location. Combined with D/C# and W/R#, comprises the Pentium's Bus Cycle Definition lines. These signals are driven at the start of a bus cycle.
NA#	I	I	The **Next Address** input indicates that the memory subsystem is capable of taking advantage of the Pentium microprocessor's address pipelining. When NA# is sampled active, the microprocessor outputs the address for the next bus cycle before the current bus cycle ends.
NMI	I	I	When sensed active, the **Non-Maskable Interrupt Request** signal causes the Pentium processor to immediately suspend normal program execution and begin to service the NMI. After saving the CS, EIP and EFlag register contents on the stack, the Pentium processor will jump to the NMI Interrupt Service Routine through Interrupt Table slot 2.
PBREQ#	NA	I/O	**Private Bus Request.** Only used in a dual processor system (otherwise, no connect). Asserted by the LRM to request ownership of the private local bus shared by the two processors. PBREQ# is an output from the requesting processor (the LRM) and an input to the MRM.
PBGNT#	NA	I/O	**Private Bus Grant.** Only used in a dual processor system (otherwise, no connect). Asserted by the MRM to grant ownership of the private local bus (shared by the two processors) to the LRM. PBGNT# is an output from the MRM and an input to the LRM.
PCHK#	O	O	See DP0.
PCD	O	O	The **Page Cache Disable** pin reflects the state of the page attribute bit, PCD, in the Page Table or Page Directory entry. If paging is disabled or for bus cycles that are not paged (Interrupt Acknowledge, Halt/Special, etc.), PCD reflects the state of its respective bit in CR3.
PEN#	I	I	The **Parity Enable** (PEN#) input, along with the Machine Check Exception (MCE) bit in Control Register Four (CR4), determine the action the Pentium processor takes when a parity error occurs as the result of a memory read bus cycle. If the MCE bit in CR4 is set and the PEN# input is sampled active, the Pentium processor generates a machine check exception interrupt. If either the MCE bit is reset or the PEN# is sampled inactive, the Pentium processor takes no action. The parity error can then be handled by external logic.

Signal Name (s)	Input/Output P5	P54C	
PHIT#	NA	I/O	**Private Bus Hit**. PHIT# is an output from the LRM and an input to the MRM. It is not used in a single processor system (no connect). PHIT# is used in conjunction with PHITM# to indicate the results of snoop in the LRM's L1 cache. If neither PHIT# nor PHITM# is asserted by the LRM, a cache miss is indicated. When just PHIT# is asserted by the LRM, a hit on a clean line (E or S) is indicated. If both PHIT# and PHITM# are asserted, this indicates a hit on a modified cache line.
PHITM#	NA	I/O	**Private Bus Hit on Modified** line. See PHIT#.
PICCLK	NA	I	Programmable Interrupt Controller Clock. It is used to clock serial data into or out of the processor's internal, local APIC over the PICD[1:0] bus.
PICD0 or [DPEN#]	NA	**I/O**	**Programmable Interrupt Controller Data line 0**. During ordinary operation, this pin carries data to and from the local APIC. If present, the dual processor asserts this pin during RESET. The primary processor samples the Dual Processor Enable signal when RESET is deasserted, to determine if a dual processor is present.
PICD1 or [APICEN]	NA	**I/O**	**Programmable Interrupt Controller Data line 1**. During ordinary operation, this pin carries data to and from the local APIC. During initialization, when RESET is deasserted, the processor samples this pin (APICEN) to determine if the internal APIC is enabled (1 = APIC enabled).
PRDY	O	O	**Probe ready**. Asserted by the processor when it has stopped execution in response to the R/S# signal being asserted low.
PWT	O	O	The **Page Write-Through** pin reflects the state of the page attribute bit, PWT, in the Page Table or Page Directory entry. If paging is disabled or for bus cycles that are not paged (Interrupt Acknowledge, Halt/Special, etc.), PWT reflects the state of its respective bit in CR3.
RESET	I	I	The Reset input has two important effects on the Pentium: 1. Keeps the microprocessor from operating until the power supply voltages have come up and stabilized. 2. Forces known default values into the Pentium processor registers. This ensures that the microprocessor will always begin execution in exactly the same way.
R/S#	I	I	**Run/Stop**. When set high, the processor is permitted to run normally. When set low, the processor ceases to execute instructions and enters probe mode. This permits the debug tool to access the processor's internal registers through the boundary scan interface.

Signal Name (s)	Input/Output P5	P54C	
SCYC	O	I/O	**Split Cycle** is valid for locked bus cycles only. SCYC is asserted when a locked transfer results in a misaligned memory access. In such cases, the misaligned transfer causes more than two bus cycles to be performed during the locked transfer.
SMI#	I	I	The **System Management Interrupt** informs the processor that a system management interrupt service routine, residing in System Management (SM) address space, needs to be performed.
SMIACT#	O	O	**System Management Interrupt Acknowledge** informs external logic that the processor is in System Management mode. The SMIACT# signal is used to specify access to System Management RAM (SMRAM) so the SM address space can be accessed.
TCK	I	I	**Test Clock.** Used to clock state information and data into and out of the device during boundary scan.
TDI	I	I	**Test Input.** Used to shift data and instructions into the Test Access Port in a serial bit stream.
TDO	O	O	**Test Output.** Used to shift data out of the Test Access Port in a serial bit stream.
TMS	I	I	**Test Mode Select.** Used to control the state of the Test Access Port (TAP) controller.
TRST#	I	I	Test Reset. Used to force the Test Access Port controller in to an initialized state.
WB/WT#	I	I	The **Write-Back or Write-Through** input allows external logic to determine whether a cache line is placed in the Write Back (E) or Write Through (S) state.
W/R#	O	I/O	**Write or Read.** At the start of a bus cycle, the Pentium processor sets this line high if the current bus cycle is a write bus cycle. W/R# is set low if the current bus cycle is a read bus cycle.

Appendix C: Pairable Instructions

Integer Instructions

Instruction	Description	Pipeline
ADC	Add with Carry	U only
ADD	Add	U or V
AND	Logical AND	U or V

CALL	Call procedure (same segment)
	   - direct
	   - register indirect
	   - memory indirect
		
		V only
		NA
		NA

CMP	Compare two operands	U or V
DEC	Decrement by 1	U or V
INC	Increment by 1	U or V
Jcc	Jump is condition is met	V only

JMP	Unconditional jump (same segment)
	   - short
	   - direct
	   - register indirect
	   - memory indirect
		
		V only
		V only
		NA
		NA

LEA	Load Effective Address	U or V

MOV	Move data
	   - to/from memory or general register
	   - to/from Control Registers
	   - to/from Debug Registers
	   - to/from Segment Registers
		
		U or V
		NA
		NA
		NA

NOP	No operation	U or V
OR	Logical inclusive OR	U or V

Instruction	Description	Pipeline

POP	Read a word from the stack
	   - reg
	   - memory
		
		U or V
		NA

PUSH	Write operand to the stack
	   - reg
	   - memory
	   - immediate
		
		U or V
		NA
		U or V

RCL	Rotate through carry left
	   - reg by 1
	   - memory by 1
	   - reg by CL
	   - memory by CL
	   - reg by immediate count
	   - memory by immediate count
		
		U only
		U only
		NA
		NA
		U only
		U only

RCR	Rotate through carry right
	   - reg by 1
	   - memory by 1
	   - reg by CL
	   - memory by CL
	   - reg by immediate count
	   - memory by immediate count
		
		U only
		U only
		NA
		NA
		U only
		U only

ROL	Rotate left (not carry through)
	   - reg by 1
	   - memory by 1
	   - reg by CL
	   - memory by CL
	   - reg by immediate count
	   - memory by immediate count
		
		U only
		U only
		NA
		NA
		U only
		U only

ROR	Rotate right (not carry through)
	   - reg by 1
	   - memory by 1
	   - reg by CL
	   - memory by CL
	   - reg by immediate count
	   - memory by immediate count
		
		U only
		U only
		NA
		NA
		U only
		U only

Appendix C: Pairable Instructions

Instruction	Description	Pipeline
SAL	Shift arithmetic left - reg by 1 - memory by 1 - reg by CL - memory by CL - reg by immediate count - memory by immediate count	 U only U only NA NA U only U only
SAR	Shift arithmetic right - reg by 1 - memory by 1 - reg by CL - memory by CL - reg by immediate count - memory by immediate count	 U only U only NA NA U only U only
SBB	Integer subtraction with borrow	U only
SHL	Shift left - reg by 1 - memory by 1 - reg by CL - memory by CL - reg by immediate count - memory by immediate count	 U only U only NA NA U only U only
SHR	Shift right - reg by 1 - memory by 1 - reg by CL - memory by CL - reg by immediate count - memory by immediate count	 U only U only NA NA U only U only
SUB	Integer subtraction	U only

Instruction	Description	Pipeline
TEST	Logical compare	
	- register 1 and register 2	U or V
	- memory and register	U or V
	- immediate and register	NA
	- immediate and accumulator	U or V
	- immediate and memory	NA
XOR	Logical exclusive OR	U or V

Floating-Point Instructions

The Floating-Point Exchange (FX) instruction can be compared with the following instructions. These instructions only pair in the U pipeline with an FX instruction in the V pipeline.

U-pipe Instruction	Description
FABS	Absolute value
FADD	Add
FADDDP	Add and pop
FCHS	Change sign
FCOM	Compare real
FCOMP	Compare real and pop
FCOMPP	Compare real and pop twice
FDIV	Divide
FDIVP	Divide and pop
FDIVR	Reverse divide
FDIVRP	Reverse divide and pop
FLD	Load real (except 80-bit)
FMUL	Multiply
FMULP	Multiply

Appendix C: Pairable Instructions

U-pipe Instruction	Description
FSUB	Subtract
FSUBP	Subtract and pop
FSUBR	Reverse subtract
FSUBRP	Reverse subtract and pop
FTST	Test
FUCOM	Unordered compare real
FUCOMP	Unordered compare and pop
FUCOMPP	Unordered compare and pop twice

Appendix D: References

The following Intel publications were used as references:

Intel486™ SL Microprocessor SuperSet Programmer's Reference Manual, November 1992.

Microprocessor: Volume II, Intel486™ Microprocessors, 1994.

Multiprocessor Specification, Version 1.1, April 1994.

Optimizations for Intel's 32-Bit Processors, by Gary Carleton, AP-500, November 1993.

Pentium™ Family User's Manual, Volume 1: Data Book, 1994.

Pentium™ Family User's Manual, Volume 3: Architecture and Programming Manual, 1994.

Pentium™ Processor (610\75) Design Considerations For Mobile Systems, by Masaru Ishigami, Applications Note, Rev. 1.1, October 1994.

Pentium™ Processor (610\75) Power Consumption, by Amy Bloom, Applications Note, Rev. 1.1, October 1994.

The iCOMP™ Index: A new Way to Compare Intel Processor Performance, FaxBack No. 7046, Version 1.1, May 1994.

Index

Index

C

D

E

F

H

I

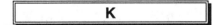

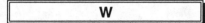

W

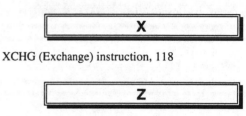

X

Z

MindShare, Inc.
Technical Seminars

MindShare Courses

- PCI System Architecture
- AMD K5 System Architecture
- PCMCIA System Architecture
- 80486 System Architecture
- EISA System Architecture
- CardBus System Architecture*

- Pentium System Architecture
- Plug and Play System Architecture
- ISA System Architecture
- PowerPC Hardware Architecture
- PowerPC Software Architecture
- Cyrix M1 System Architecture*
- PowerPC PReP System Architecture

Public Seminars

MindShare offers public seminars on their most popular courses on a regular basis. Seminar schedules, course content, pricing and registration are available immediately via MindShare's BBS, or you may contact us through email with your request. Periodically, seminars are held on older technologies, (e.g., ISA and EISA) based on customer demand. If you are interested in attending a public seminar currently not scheduled you may register your request via the bulletin board or email.

On-Site Seminars

If you are interested in training at your location, please contact us with your requirements. We will tailor our courses to fit your specific needs and schedules.

Contact MindShare at:

BBS: (214) 705-9604
Internet: mindshar@interserv.com
CompuServe: 72507,1054

Note: New courses are constantly under development. Please contact MindShare for the latest course offerings.

*Available summer '95